The Gold Book

The Complete Investment Guide to Precious Metals

PIERRE LASSONDE

THE GLOBE AND MAIL

Penguin Books

PENGUIN BOOKS
Published by the Penguin Group
Penguin Books Canada Ltd., 10 Alcorn Avenue, Suite 300, Toronto, Canada M4V 3B2
Penguin Books Ltd., 27 Wrights Lane, London W8 5TZ, England
Viking Penguin Inc., 40 West 23rd Street, New York, New York 10010, USA
Penguin Books Australia Ltd., Ringwood, Victoria, Australia
Penguin Books (NZ) Ltd., 182-190 Wairau Road, Auckland 10, New Zealand
Penguin Books Ltd., Registered Offices: Harmondsworth, Middlesex, England

Published in Penguin Books, 1996

10 9 8 7 6 5 4 3 2 1

All queries should be addressed to Globe Information Services, 444 Front Street West, Toronto, Ontario M5V 2S9 (416) 585-5250

Canadian Cataloguing in Publication Data
The National Library of Canada has catalogued this publication as follows:
Lassonde, Pierre, 1947 -
The gold book
(Financial Times personal finance library)
Annual.
Description based on: 1993
At head of title: Financial Times, 199—1995; The Globe and Mail, 1996
Issues for 1996- ... published in the series: The Globe and Mail personal finance library.
ISSN 1196-1600
ISBN 0-14-026250-4 (1996)

1. Metals as an investment – Periodicals. 2. Gold – Periodicals. 3. Precious metals – Periodicals. I. Title II. Title: Financial Times. III. Title: Globe and Mail. IV. Series. V. Series: The Globe and Mail personal finance library.
HG293.L37 332.63'05 C93-031408-5

Cover design: Creative Network
Cover illustration: Peter Yundt
Charts: Ivy Wong

The information contained in this book is intended only as a general guide and may not be suitable for certain individuals. If expert advice is warranted, readers are urged to consult a competent professional. While the legal, tax and accounting information has been obtained from sources believed to be accurate, constant changes in the legal and financial environment make it imperative that readers confirm this information before making financial decisions.

CONTENTS

Tables and Illustrations

CHARTS

TABLES

Dedication

To Claudette who, after 25 years, is still the most important person in my life, and Julie and Chris, my favourite children, for all the time I have been away.

Acknowledgments

The magnitude of the task of writing this book didn't hit me until I was halfway through it. However, it pales in comparison to the amount of work I created for others to publish it.

I would like to acknowledge the invaluable friendship and support of **Donn Morgan, Bob Hoye, Bill Tehan** and the other gold bugs I talk to regularly for their willingness to share their insights on the gold markets with me.

I couldn't have done without the help and input of my colleague and associate **David Harquail**. He updated this revised edition to include the latest information.

A special thanks to **Bob Bishop**, veteran analyst and letter writer, who makes a living sorting the gold from the dross.

I am grateful for the support I have received from my senior partners at Beutel, Goodman & Company Ltd. and I wish to particularly thank my partner in Franco-Nevada and Euro-Nevada, **Seymour Schulich**, for his unfailing support through the years. As for **Donna Yoshimatsu**, my devoted secretary, there are no words to describe my appreciation for her effort in putting this book together and keeping a semblance of normalcy in the office.

To the people at the *Financial Times*, who have put in so much work to help me realize my dreams, many thanks. Finally, a special acknowledgment to **Tom Mohide**, a legend of the Canadian gold scene, who graciously read the manuscript for accuracy and completeness.

Pierre Lassonde
September, 1996

Introduction

THE FIRST TIME I WAS TO tour an underground mine, I was filled with the same excitement as a young child about to climb aboard a roller coaster. As we entered the "dry," the mine's change room where the miners change from wet, dirty work clothes into dry, street clothes, the reality of the situation hit me.

The mine was under a lake in Northern Ontario and we were expecting it to be wet. I donned a pair of coveralls and knee-high boots encircled with steel rings that would protect my feet from loose pieces of rock and the heavy, steel equipment used in the mine. Then came a helmet with a headlight that would let me see in the utter darkness of the mine and a safety belt with steel hooks and straps for a battery and safety respirator. I had just 10 minutes to find my way to an underground shelter if there was a mine fire or an explosion. I was given a pair of earmuffs to protect my ears against the incredible noise of the drills and shatterproof eyeglasses to protect my eyes from flying bits of rock. Finally, I slipped on a pair of rubberized gloves to protect my head-office hands — hands that are too delicate for the harsh reality of underground mining.

Then came the warnings: "Stay close to your guide. Always walk exactly where he walks or you'll fall in an ore pass. If you fall in, we won't be able to get you out alive. [Ore passes are holes drilled through the floors of the tunnels.] Watch the roof and your head and before doing anything dumb, ask permission."

By the time we headed for the cage, the elevator that would take us down into the mine, I had experienced a subtle change of mind. Why did I ever get talked into doing this? How could I get out of it? But just like a kid on a roller coaster inching its way up the first hill, I couldn't turn back. I had to save face, after all I was from head office. So I entered the cage and began a career that has taken me to more than a hundred mines in Canada, the United States, Europe,

Russia, Africa and South America. The tour was actually quite uneventful and, despite my trepidation, I really wasn't in any danger.

This was not true in 1985 when I toured a 100-year-old mine in California that had been abandoned for more than 30 years. Nearly a million ounces of gold had come out of the mine over the years and the deposit had been honeycombed with miles of tunnels excavated in every direction. A hopeful company was trying to reopen the mine and had excavated a new portal and adit to replace those that had caved in after years of neglect.

As soon as I entered the old workings, I was scared at the sight of large excavations without any kind of support. The roof pillars had disappeared! The operator of the mine had been robbing the pillars for the gold in them. As I gingerly walked up a slope I saw some native gold shining through the quartz on the wall of the cavern. When I tapped it with my hammer, it burst out of the wall. With the stone pillars gone, the pressure from the thousands of tons of rocks above us was being distributed throughout the walls. I couldn't wait to get out. Not more than a month later, on a Saturday night, the main shaft pillar in the mine collapsed. Thank God, there was nobody in the mine at the time.

Mining is a harsh business and finding gold isn't easy. It is impossible for geologists to see through rock; just as it is impossible for economists to see into the future. Both professions are dealing in *probabilities* and *possible* courses of actions. Their views of the future are based on what they see and what they have seen in the past. To be successful as an investor in gold, you will have to remember this.

As you look back over mankind's history, you'll find one thread of continuity — man's fascination with gold and its undisputed value as money. Historian Roy Jastrum, in an exhaustive study of gold, called the metal the "golden constant" because it has always retained its ability to buy a basket of goods. Gold has also been a mirror of economic times because of its role as a reserve currency or as the currency of last resort. Gold is the only money that is not someone else's debt: Even a dollar bill is a debt of the government.

Despite gold's undeniable value in times of economic or political dislocation, it is not a dynamic asset. It doesn't grow nor does it pay dividends or interest. In fact, if you hold gold you have to pay to store it. You can regard gold as an insurance policy against chaos but the amount you hold is a function of your need for security and your aversion to risk. By investing in the shares of gold mining companies, you can increase the returns you will enjoy from your gold portfolio.

This book is organized to help you understand gold as an investment. After a brief historical review of gold, it takes a look at world gold production and demand and the impact of the economic environment on gold. I've tried to give you enough information on the most important factors behind the movements in the price of gold to be able to decide for yourself which way the gold price is likely to jump next.

Chapters 5 and 6 provide an overview of the three main components of the world gold market — gold bullion, gold equities and the futures markets — and your investment options within each of these markets. Chapters 7 and 8 deal exclusively with North American gold mining companies, guiding you through the gold equities universe from the penny stocks of the exploration companies to the blue-chip stocks of the multinational giants.

Unfortunately, gold triggers a destructive greed and the gold marketplace is rife with scams and swindles. Chapter 9 covers the common ploys and provides you with enough information to spot a con game. It's difficult enough as it is to make money in the mining business; there's no need for you to lose your money learning the hard way.

Gold is not the only precious metal; silver, platinum and palladium also have an investment appeal from time to time. However, these metals are not money, just expensive commodities. You can invest in these metals and improve the performance of your precious metals portfolio but you should do so with moderation.

Gold investors are most interested in the answer to one question: What will the price of gold be in the future? But as my partner, an astute gold investor himself, likes to say, "If I really knew, I wouldn't have to work for a living!" But you don't really have to know — you only have to be right more often than you're wrong to be a winner in the investment game.

Throughout *The Gold Book* I have explained how you can value gold by using historical benchmarks. By any of these benchmarks, gold at $385 (U.S.) was very good value in late 1996. Could the price of gold climb to $1,000 (U.S.) in the next 10 years? Certainly. Can you count on it? Definitely not. Could gold go to $200 (U.S.) an ounce? Possibly. Is it likely? I don't think so. Simply by knowing how to value gold you are already a step ahead of your fellow investors. By learning how to value gold stocks, you could be two steps ahead. That knowledge could prove to be even more valuable to you than gold at $1,000 (U.S.) an ounce.

CHAPTER 1

The Gold of the Gods

IN THE EGYPTIAN MUSEUM IN Cairo lie the artifacts from the tomb of the Pharaoh Tutankhamen — golden beds and couches of state, chariots and a throne encrusted with gold and silver and sparkling with jewels. The king's mummy lies within a nest of three coffins, the innermost made of solid gold weighing 240 pounds. The two outer coffins are of gold hammered over wooden frames. The funeral mask and numerous pieces of gold jewelry and amulets are richly decorated. The coffins and stone sarcophagus were themselves surrounded by four portable shrines of hammered gold over wood.

Tutankhamen was the boy king of Egypt 3,300 years ago. He was only nine or 10 years old when he ascended to the throne and reigned for a scant nine years before he died when he was less than 20. As Pharaoh, he had sat on a golden throne, covered from head to foot in gold. He would have used utensils and accessories made of beaten gold. The Pharaohs were worshipped as gods and when they died they were buried with their treasure. It was Tutankhamen's tomb that gave us such an incredible legacy.

I stood before Tutankhamen's ancient caskets in the spring of 1980. The world was in turmoil. Inflation was roaring ahead at double-digit speed around the globe, propelled by soaring oil prices — the result of the world's insatiable thirst for oil and the squeeze from the oil cartel. Iranians had taken the American embassy staff hostage, the Soviets had invaded Afghanistan and war had erupted between Iraq and Iran. There were predictions that within a few years oil would be $100 (U.S.) a barrel and the U.S. dollar would collapse against stronger currencies such as the German mark and Japanese yen. The demand for the Swiss franc was so high that Switzerland instituted negative interest rates: You had to pay interest to keep your money in Swiss francs. Confusion reigned everywhere and the world was as close to chaos as it had been for generations.

As a mirror of the times, gold reached the incredible price of $850 (U.S.) an ounce on Jan. 21 that year. Barely 10 years earlier, the price had been fixed at $35 (U.S.) an ounce. Television newscasts began broadcasting the gold price as if it were a barometer of people's anxiety. I was struck by the thread of fascination that weaves its way through thousands of years of history, touching on the mystical essence of wealth and security that transcends time, empires, fashion and monetary theories. Without doubt, gold has been the world's most enduring measure of value.

Gold throughout history

The oldest known gold objects are Egyptian and date back to around 5000 BC. Gold was first used strictly for decoration, mostly for the personal use of the Pharaoh or in religious rituals. In the Old Testament of the Bible there are many references to gold. The Pharaoh gave Joseph two pieces of gold jewelry — a ring and a necklace — as symbols of his power and authority. When the Hebrews escaped from Egypt in the 13th century BC, the people asked Aaron, brother of Moses, to fashion a golden calf which they could adore during the long absence of Moses on Mount Sinai. The ancient Egyptians were also practical people and seem to have been the first to fill their decayed teeth with gold, a tradition that was adopted by the Romans and has not been replaced by modern technology — every year the world uses around 1.6 million ounces of gold to fill teeth.

It was not until 3000 BC that gold was first used as money when the Pharaohs of Egypt introduced a half-ounce gold wafer of fixed weight and value as a medium of payment. The oldest known gold coin was stamped with the name of King Menes who, according to tradition, joined Upper and Lower Egypt in a single, centralized monarchy. Menes reigned for a very long 62 years and was supposedly killed by a hippopotamus!

In ancient Egypt most of the gold came from the rivers of northern Africa, the Middle East and in Eastern Africa, where the Ashanti still mine the gold fields of Ghana. The Greek historian Diodorus, who lived around 200 BC, described the conditions in the Egyptian mines of the time. The inescapable conclusion is that mining was only possible because of cheap slave labour. The slave force was made up of convicts, prisoners of war and captive populations defeated by Egypt. "All are bound with fetters," Diodorus wrote, "working day and night, living in darkness because of the bends and twists in the galleries, contorting their bodies this way and that, working without rest under the lash of their overseer."

Some of the mines at Fatiri on the Red Sea had galleries running for miles under the mountains. The miners excavated the tunnels with iron picks, using fire to crack and break the toughest rocks. Chain gangs of children hand-carried the ore outside where it was pulverized in stone mortars by the older men whose health was failing after years underground. The coarse powder was then passed to a line of hand mills run by women and old men where it was pulverized to the consistency of flour. Finally, the gold-bearing sands were gently washed by expert craftsmen, much like gold is washed by today's placer gold miners. The lives of the miners must have been insufferable, thanks to the stale air in the underground galleries, the choking dust, the searing heat from the fires and the brutal lash if gold quotas were not met.

In Arabia, there were mines west of Bahrain, along the Red Sea coast just below the Gulf of Aquaba and in the Upper Yemen. These mines were probably the source of the fabled wealth of the Queen of Sheba, who reigned in the 10th century BC. The Old Testament recounts her visit to King Solomon, travelling at the head of a caravan bearing gold, jewels and spices. During the sixth century BC, the Persian civilization came to dominate the world, giving them access to the mines of Egypt, Nubia and Ethiopia. For all the hard work, the loss of life and the wars that were fought over gold, it is thought that only 17.5 million to 20.4 million ounces of gold were mined in the two millennia of the Pharaohs' reign — a mere four months of modern production.

Gold as money

Mankind used more primitive forms of monetary coinage for hundreds of years before turning to gold and silver as currencies. China in the eighth century BC used a miniature hose and a sort of pruning implement called a billhook as currencies. Any metals, whether copper, bronze or iron, were popular as exchange mediums because they were durable, easily divided and portable. Of course, the choice of metal depended on the availability at the time. Once gold and silver had gained acceptance as metals of high value that were divisible and portable, the stage was set for the appearance of true coinage. The first gold coins appeared in Asia Minor and were quickly spread around the world by the forces of trade and commerce.

According to the historian Herodotus, it was King Croesus of Lydia in Asia Minor who first established a currency of pure gold and silver coins with a fixed parity between the two in 550 BC. His great wealth is thought to have come from the gold-rich rivers of Asia Minor, especially from the gold in the Pactolus River near his capital.

King Croesus first minted coins of white gold or electrum, a mix of gold and silver, before he introduced the first bimetallic currency system of gold and silver — silver being used for the smaller denominations. The early electrum coinage consisted of small, thick, bean-shaped pieces weighing about seven to eight grams and stamped with a guarantee of authority. As the proportion of gold to silver varied, the value of the coin itself changed.

Although this was the first known currency of gold and silver, small pieces of silver had been used as money. It is believed that silver was related to gold as a standard of value. In biblical times, 13.3 silver shekels equalled one ounce of gold in value. At the time, the coins were not of uniform weight and had to be weighed in commercial transactions. When Judas betrayed Jesus Christ for 30 pieces of silver, these shekels would have been the equivalent of two and a quarter ounces of gold. In today's values, Judas sold Jesus for about $900 (U.S.). It was a significant sum of money and the Bible tells us Judas "bought a field with the reward of his wickedness." It doesn't mention the field's size but any purchase of land was a major transaction. You couldn't buy a field for $900 today, which may mean land is a better hedge against inflation than gold.

At about the same time King Croesus minted coins of white gold, the first Greek silver coins appeared. The oldest are from Aegina, whose maritime ascendancy was growing rapidly. The weight standard of the Aegetina was based on a silver drachma that weighed about six grams. During the 500 years that preceded the Roman Empire, the two most important coinages were minted by Philip II of Macedonia and Alexander the Great. Both men struck coins in vast quantities at mints from Macedonia to Babylonia but all of the coins had a uniform look and weight. Evidence of the influence of this coinage can be found from India to Sweden and Norway, where vast quantities of these coins have been found. The dispersion of the Macedonian coins is proof of the supremacy of the Greeks and the extent of trade and travel as far back as 600 BC. The gold pieces paid for everything from furs in the Nordic countries to spices and silk in the Far East.

Although Philip II minted thousands of gold coins, Alexander rarely used gold in coinage. Silver, which was available from the Laurium mines in Greece, became the metal of coins. The Attic standard adopted by Alexander the Great for his tetradrachmas became the monetary standard of the Western world. At the same time, bronze coins became increasingly popular in everyday use.

Hand in hand with the minting of money came the first episode of devaluation. The cost of the Peloponnesian War mounted but the production of gold and silver could not be increased to pay for the war. The number of coins in circulation was increased by melting down the old coins and minting new coins with the same face value but less gold. In 400 BC, Aristophanes, the great Greek philosopher, described the event in verse:

"For your old and standard pieces valued and approved and tried,
Here among the Grecian nations and in all the world beside,
Recognized in every realm for trusty stamp and pure and assay,
And rejected and abandoned for the trash of yesterday,
For a vile, adulterate issue, drossy, counterfeit and bare
Which the traffic of the City passes current in their place."

Aristophanes was probably the first economic commentator reporting on the devaluation of the currency by the governments. Unfortunately, the practice was picked up by the bankrupt Roman emperors a few centuries later and has been used by kings and governments for over 2,500 years. What makes inflation so insidious is that money, whether it's in gold coin form or a piece of paper, is supposed to be a medium of exchange, a unit of account and a store of value. The minute you tamper with the value of the currency it is no longer a store of value nor can it properly be a unit of account. If the public loses confidence in the currency, it collapses.

As Italy replaced Greece as the dominant civilization, gold mining and the use of gold expanded rapidly. The Romans soon replaced the Egyptians and the Greeks as the leading gold producers by mining gold throughout Europe from Spain, France, northern Italy and Greece, as well as in the Middle East and Africa. Under the Roman Empire, gold coins were issued to ease commerce and travel and to support the vast military empire that dominated most of the known world at the time. In the first century BC, campaigning Roman generals began to issue coins to pay their troops in the field. Julius Caesar issued his first coin in the late 50s and early 40s BC, and in the latter years of his life developed personal control of the coinage and mints of the empire. In effect, Caesar named himself chairman of the central bank, declining to be anointed emperor and god.

The Emperor Augustus issued a gold coin called the aureus that weighed 0.0238 pounds. The aureus was equivalent to 25 denarii, a silver coin that weighed 0.0119 pounds. The aureus, at slightly more than a third of an ounce of gold, would be worth $160 at today's prices. The coin also equalled two weeks' pay for the common soldier. That is far less than a soldier's pay today but Roman soldiers also got a share of any pillage or war booty. A gold aureus was also the only way a slave could buy his freedom. Everyday coins were made of brass and copper.

The story of gold is really the story of trade, economic dominance and power. The first copper coins bore the figures of cattle, sheep or hogs and were called *pecunia* — the Latin word for money derived from the word *pecus*, which means cattle. It's widely known that cattle themselves were the earliest and best-known standard of exchange, but this had serious drawbacks. Cattle are neither portable nor easily divided for smaller transactions. You also have to feed and care for cattle. The advent of metallic currency such as copper, brass, silver and gold allowed commerce and trade to expand and grow.

The impact can be seen at Pompeii, the ancient town near Naples that was destroyed during the volcanic eruption of Mt. Vesuvius in AD 79. Pompeii was buried by a blanket of ashes and the buildings are well preserved. You can walk through the dwellings of the rich and poor and bakeries complete with mills, kneading machines and ovens. Some of the ovens still contain loaves of bread. There are shops, inns and restaurants. Pompeii gives the visitor a glimpse of life in a busy port town — and the necessity of coins in keeping economic activity alive. The people of Pompeii revelled in their fortune and loved everything foreign. More than 100 million coins — 300,000 ounces — left Italy every year to pay for imports from India, China and Arabia.

A great deal of Italy's fortune came from the legendary gold mines of Spain. At the headwaters of the Guadalquivic River, it is said that gold was so plentiful that peasants could scrape up sand with their hoes, put it through sieves and extract gold. When these deposits were depleted, the Romans turned their attention to the underground mines abundant in Spain's northwest. The development and production of these mines required highly trained engineers who were educated at special government schools. These Roman engineers introduced hydraulic mining into Spain, whereby large quantities of water were used to wash down whole mountains for the gold-bearing sands. This technique was revived 18 centuries later in the California gold boom before being outlawed in the 1880s as environmentally destructive. The Romans also sank shafts as deep as 650 feet, installing sophisticated pumping systems powered by men and animals to keep the water out of the galleries. By using tens of thousands of slaves and engineers, the Romans were able to produce 200,000 ounces of gold a year in Spain. This gold was enough to feed and equip an army of more than 200,000 men and leave enough spare change to build temples and arenas for the people.

Some of the Roman mining operations were massive. In one area alone, an open pit mine is estimated to have produced more than one million ounces of gold from the movement of 35 million tons of rock. Even today, with giant trucks and shovels, a 35-million-ton mine would require a great deal of capital and time to bring into production. Not surprisingly, when the Roman Empire fell in the fifth century, gold output was drastically reduced as the technical and organizational capabilities to develop these large mines disappeared with the empire. The Spanish mines were abandoned to water and the mining of the river deposits returned to individuals with pans.

Despite the gold wealth of the Roman Empire, it could not cover the excesses of the emperors. Nero devalued the aureus and denarius in AD 64 and, under the relentless trade and budget deficits, the debasement continued until it reached 40 per cent of its original value. During that time, the emperors controlled all metals and coinage, stamping their portraits as gods and emperors on every coin. The coins circulated throughout the vast Roman Empire and the emperors didn't miss the powerful propaganda value of their pictures on a coin. The debasement of the currencies stopped temporarily around AD 300 and new coins were minted. But as economic conditions worsened, the later emperors gradually removed the gold and silver from the coins until they were almost worthless, hastening the collapse of the empire in AD 476.

As the Roman Empire disappeared, the Byzantine Empire became the world's dominant force. The wealth of the Byzantine emperors was built upon the structure for administering domestic and foreign affairs created by Anastasius I, tax reform and improvements in the monetary system. Upon his death in AD 518, Anastasius I left the phenomenal personal fortune of more than five million ounces of gold. Most of that gold later found its way to Italy during the Crusades.

The Middle Ages were troubled by a shortage and inconsistency of coinage throughout the world, mainly because there was not an effective central government for almost 700 years. Gold and silver all but vanished from the fifth century to the 12th century, when there was more gold circulating in the world than at any other time. After the fall of the Roman Empire, no country was able to emerge as the dominant power. The world was in economic and political turmoil with incessant wars and a collapse of both currencies and authority. People were frightened — having gold hidden beneath a floorboard or buried in the garden could mean the difference between life and death, eating and starving, a future or nothing. It wasn't until the 11th century, when the Roman Catholic Church inspired the Crusades, that some sense of order and authority started to emerge.

The Crusades of the 12th century sparked a global reopening of trade and commerce as the Crusaders not only brought back the booty of war but opened trade with the countries of the Mediterranean and the Middle East. One of the great conquests of the time was the capture of the great city of Constantinople in 1203 by the armies of the Fourth Crusade. As trade and commerce grew around the Mediterranean, the kingdoms of Italy and France began to flex their authority. A new money was needed to represent the changed world. It was during this time that merchants from all over Europe regularly gathered in the town of Troyes in the Champagne area of France and used a specific weight of gold in their transactions — the troy ounce. It wasn't until the 13th century that Florence issued its famous gold florins. The florin weighed approximately 3.5 grams and was of such fineness that it won Florence universal fame and wide imitation. In 1284, Venice introduced its gold ducat as a competing currency. The florin gained wide acceptance abroad and became the most popular gold coin in the world for more than five centuries.

At the same time, Britain established a metallic currency standard with the introduction of a system of pounds, shillings, and pence. In 1280, it was decreed that the penny should weigh 24 grains, which was really the enactment of an old tradition. At that time, the penny was called a sterling from the Latin word *steorra* for the star imprinted on the coin. Because of their consistent silver fineness and their wide distribution on the continent, they came to be known as sterling silver, with 240 coins being called a pound. Ultimately, the designation "pound" moved up to the pound sterling, which was literally a pound of silver. The English pound's reputation was built on the quality of the silver penny and not on the fact that it represented a pound of silver.

In 1257, Henry III minted the first English gold penny with a deemed value first of 20 pence of silver and later 24. It never really caught on for two reasons; its high value in relation to the income of most people denied it the convenience of money and, second, it was worth more than 20 pence of silver. People would rather keep the gold penny and pay in silver. Eventually, it was withdrawn.

In 1485, after having vanquished his rival Richard III, King Henry VII commissioned a gold coin imprinted with a portrait of himself on the throne. This coin became known as a "sovereign." The gold content of the 1489 sovereign was exactly 0.5 ounces. With the advent of the mill and screw machine in 1561, it became possible to produce coins of uniform weight and consistency. Coins were minted with a "mill hedge," the grooved imprint around the edge of a coin, to prevent counterfeiting and to thwart heavily indebted kings from easily tampering with the coins in circulation.

Even in those days, the world was not immune from the greed and foolishness of the kings and emperors. Indeed, when they ran short of money they indulged in "coin clipping" — clipping the edges of the coins. From five coins they could make a sixth, yet both old and new would be ascribed the same value. There would be 20 per cent more coins in circulation but no increase in the amount of gold. That amounted to 20 per cent inflation.

During the 14th century, the mines of central Europe, especially the rich mines of Hungary, had produced close to one million ounces of gold. In Africa, gold from the River Niger as well as from Ghana travelled across the desert by caravans that headed north from Timbuktu, the City of Gold. Timbuktu was the transfer point for commerce between the Arabs of the north and the blacks of the south as well as the main centre for smelting ore destined for Europe.

The arrival of Christopher Columbus in the New World in 1492 was a turning point in mankind's history. Columbus had been searching for a passage to India as part of his quest for its gold, silk and spices, but within 50 years of landing the Spaniards had discovered two of the richest gold and silver mining areas of the world. The discovery couldn't have been more timely. European commerce was severely limited by the sparse supply of gold and silver. While the Crusades had brought back some gold from the east, no new major production of gold had occurred since the Romans. Because the only money available at the time was made of gold and silver, the price of both precious metals increased over time, reflecting not inflation but simply a shortage of the metals.

In 1534, Pizarro returned to Spain with the first treasure from Peru. These early treasures were taken from rich native burial mounds, but as the supply dwindled, the Spaniards moved into Aztec and Inca territory and soon started to operate mines themselves.

In 1545, the rich silver deposit of Potosi in Bolivia went into production, to be augmented 10 years later by the discovery of more silver at Guanajuato in Mexico. News of these giant discoveries spread throughout Europe. In Spain, there was a renewed sense of energy, particularly in literature and the arts which finally enjoyed a renaissance. The genius of men like Lope de Vega, Cervantes, El Greco and Velasquez were to be acclaimed throughout Europe.

However, the great quantities of new gold and silver had a disastrous impact on prices as inflation appeared throughout the continent. The Hapsburgs, the Catholic sovereigns of Spain, were fighting religious wars against the Protestants and the Moors while defending themselves from French and British pirates who constantly preyed upon Spanish shipping. At the same time that the Hapsburgs were desperately trying to hold their impossibly large empire together, they were forced to send gold and silver to the great banking houses of Germany and Italy from which they had borrowed too heavily. Spain's power gradually declined in the face of rising British economic might.

At the height of South American gold and silver production, the bankers and merchants who had financed the expeditions of the

Spanish government waited at the docks along with government tax agents for the arrival of the bullion ships. Of course, much of the gold and silver was diverted by tax collectors and crown agents and never made it to Spain. In one case, a Spanish galleon was shipwrecked and 10 times as much gold and silver was found than was reported in the ship's manifest.

Despite the richness of the discoveries, gold production in the peak years from 1500 to 1520 was less than 300,000 ounces a year. (Today, gold mines around the world produce over 200,000 ounces of gold a day.) It's hard to imagine how a country could rise so rapidly in economic and political power and fall so abruptly. The Spaniards devastated the Aztecs and Incas for gold that in time destroyed them. Spain never recovered from the inflationary spiral that was sparked by the immense wealth of the Americas and to this day remains one of western Europe's poorer countries.

The end of Spain as a political power in Europe came during the reign of King Louis XIV of France. The war that had begun in 1635 between France and Spain was to transfer European hegemony from the Hapsburgs to the French Bourbons. Louis was blessed with incredible health and he was able to reign for over 54 years, building a country that was to be the envy of the world. From the arts to the economy, Louis controlled everything, albeit with an extraordinarily talented entourage of men like Jean Baptiste Colbert, who supervised the creation of an economy designed to make France self-sufficient and a major exporter of goods. Manufacturing, shipbuilding, the merchant marines, the navy, roads, ports and a modern police organization all emerged under Colbert's watchful eye and energetic command.

Of course, the Sun King, as Louis came to be known, is best remembered for his extravagant palace at Versailles near Paris. The palace is universally admired, particularly the gold-gilded Great Hall of Mirrors. But Versailles cost Louis almost as much as a modern airport and was blamed for ruining the nation. Louis also fought many wars during his reign and when he finally died in 1715 at the age of 77, France's national debt reflected the 54 years of *La Gloire*. The crushing burden of debt and taxation was borne with resentment by a population that was growing restless and didn't mourn Louis' passing.

The regency council that took over the government of France upon Louis' death seized upon a revolutionary theory advanced by

John Law, a Scottish financier and son of a wealthy Edinburgh goldsmith. Law had just written *Money and Trade Considered,* in which he had a proposal for supplying the nation with money. He suggested the government issue paper money backed by the credit of the government. In 1716, he was given permission by the French government to found a private bank in imitation of the Bank of England, with the authority to issue paper notes. A year later, he was allowed to start his famous Compagnie d'Occident, better known as the Mississippi Company, which had the exclusive right to develop the vast French territories of the Mississippi Valley.

Law's theory promised to reduce the public debt. However, in practice, nothing of the sort happened. John Law's bank, which had become the state bank, began pouring out paper money that circulated freely instead of gold and silver, scarce because of political turmoil. Along with the issuance of paper money, the value of shares in the Mississippi Company began to climb rapidly in value. After three years of frantic speculation, the whole scheme collapsed in 1720 and Law was forced to leave France.

This was Europe's first taste of inflation caused by paper money. It was also the first taste for governments of the time of a very sweet fruit — money that could be squeezed, expanded, coloured and pressed at one's will. It was just too good to leave alone. Much of the rest of the world's financial history is the tale of abuse by governments of their paper currencies.

CHAPTER 2

Gold and the Monetary System Over Three Centuries

FOR ENGLAND, THE END OF the 17th century was also a traumatic period. The country had been at war with France since 1689. The strain of this war on the British treasury, along with the losses under the Spanish War, the Dutch War, the plague and the Great Fire of London, was intolerable. William III, who had taken the throne the year war broke out with France, managed to spend almost twice as much on the army alone than his revenues allowed.

How was William to pay his debts? First, he and his government raised taxes as far as they dared and borrowed from anyone who would lend to them, even pledging the crown jewels for personal loans. They then created a lottery in which they gave out only 10 per cent of the money in prizes and kept the rest to pay the government debt. Sound familiar? Finally, in desperation they came up with an almost magical concept — in 1694, they founded the Bank of England, the mother of all central banks.

Patriotic or not, few Englishmen were willing to lend the government any money at the time. But the prospect of buying a share of the first joint-stock bank in England was enough to attract the necessary investors to set up the institution. While the bank was not created entirely for the purpose of bailing out the government, its first act was to do exactly that. From a subscription base of 720,000 pounds, the bank issued 1.2 million pounds of notes bearing interest of 8 per cent. Within six months, another million pounds had been issued, giving the government some relief from its financial strain. The 20-year period that followed was one of great economic development, as well as steadily rising prices caused by relentless credit inflation.

It was at this time that engraved and watermarked private bank notes were developed. The banker's promissory note to the client was the most common paper money, while exchequer bills became a mainstay of credit currency. These different forms of paper money were mainly used by merchants, young companies and financiers, while the public used gold and silver coins in their daily lives. Not until 1713 did France and England realize that they were broke and weary of war: They signed the treaties of Utrecht, Rastratt and Baden that restored peace on land as well as on the seas.

With shipping lanes now open to commercial traffic without fear of pirates and credit abundantly available in France and England, there was a rapid increase in commerce and the development of a new form of commercial organization — the joint-stock companies — which caught the imagination of the time. For the first time in history, people could pool their financial resources into one large entity. England was taken by storm by a speculative financial scheme that came to be called the South Sea Bubble. This scheme had been launched in 1711 by Robert Harley when he formed the South Sea Company to take over England's entire national debt in return for commercial concessions, including a monopoly over British trade in South America and the Pacific islands. Harley promised to pay the government a premium in its own stock and the price of South Sea shares soared.

As speculative fever raged among the rich and poor, the stock jumped from £128 to £1,000 in the first six months of 1720. The market collapsed in August, the stock plummeted and the government fell. The South Sea Company survived until 1853 but its share of the government debt was assumed by the Bank of England and the East India Company.

The South Sea episode and events spawned in France by John Law were similar and fed upon each other. Under Law's monetary system, France spun into an inflationary cycle. In Britain, speculation in the stock of the South Sea Company was fuelled by high expectations, increased revenue and credit inflation created by the Bank of England. As the interminable wars ended, the money of both French and English speculators crossed the channel, only to drive stock prices higher. The British were buying shares in the Mississippi Company in Paris while the French were buying South Sea shares in London. One French banker sunk 500 pounds into the South Sea Company with the remark, "When the rest of the world is mad, we must imitate them in some measure."

The peak of the speculating frenzy was reached in December, 1719, the same time that John Law's paper money system reached its zenith in France. Both the French and London markets were united in frenzied speculation and ready for disaster. The bubble burst when the French, weary of Law's monetary system, started selling their South Sea shares for gold, which they imported back into France. As disenchanted investors began to drain the Bank of England reserves, credit tightened and the British began selling their Mississippi shares. Both markets collapsed in 1720.

Just three years earlier, Sir Isaac Newton, Master of the Mint, had issued a proclamation fixing the gold mint price of an ounce at 3 pounds, 17 shillings, 10.5 pence. Along with the strength of Britain's government and its merchant fleet, the universal acceptance of Britain's money as a measure of value in international trade was at least partly responsible for the 200 years of "Pax Britannica" — so called because of the peace brought about by the mighty power of England's navy and economic dominance of the world. Because Britain fixed its gold price higher but its silver price lower than prices on the continent, it was unwittingly shifting its currency from a silver standard to a gold standard. Over the next hundred years, the gold bullion of France, Spain and Germany began to find its way into England, while silver bullion was exported. In 1816, after the Napoleonic Wars, gold was established as the sole standard.

By 1914, when the tremendous economic and inflationary pressures of the First World War forced Britain to abandon the strict gold standard, it had endured for over two centuries. By the time the country returned to a gold standard in 1934, the pound had been replaced as the world reserve currency by the U.S. dollar.

In the period from 1343 to 1544, the price of gold rose 94 per cent. But in the following 200 years, when discoveries of gold and silver in the Americas were made, the price of gold rose only 62 per cent. Throughout the 14th, 15th and 16th centuries there had not been enough gold to keep pace with economic development and demand forced the price up. With the influx of Spanish gold, the price of other goods rose dramatically — but the price of gold itself did not.

From 1717 to 1914, the gold price was flat, except when a burst of inflation during the Napoleonic Wars from 1800 to 1817 made it difficult to keep the price fixed. It was from 1870 to 1914 that gold was most widely esteemed as a monetary standard, largely owing to London's dominance of world financial affairs. The stability of the English government and currency made London the city of choice in which to do business. At the turn of the century Herbert Hoover, who became president of the United States in 1929, came to live and work in the city, the world centre for gold mining and finance. Hoover was one of the first mining and engineering graduates from Stanford University and a brilliant mining engineer. He made his first million dollars financing gold mines in Australia, some of which still exist today.

How standards work

The "gold standard" is simply a monetary system in which the standard unit of currency is a fixed weight of gold. Gold coins circulate as legal tender and paper money can be freely exchanged for gold at a fixed price. The detractors of the gold standard point to the fact that from 1717 to 1914, England was subject to bouts of inflation as well as deflation. Furthermore, they object to financial and economic growth being tied to the growth of gold reserves, which can be unpredictable and may not match the growth of the economy. They believe this unpredictability is too high a price to pay for the stability that gold can bring over time.

Those who believe in the gold standard point to the rise in the price of gold in British pounds by 20 per cent a year — 19,224 per cent between 1914 and 1989. During those 75 years, the world suffered through 40 years of unflagging inflation, one of the worst bouts of deflation and instability in the foreign exchange market. In fact, fluctuation in the value of currencies led to more speculation than investment in the last 20 years. The question one has to ask is which is worse: a gold standard or paper money?

A hybrid of the gold standard is the gold exchange standard, through which the monetary system of a nation is partially backed by gold internally. The currency can be converted into gold at a stable rate of exchange for all transactions with other nations. The gold exchange standard came into being after the First World War, mainly because of an inadequate supply of gold for national reserves. In fact, governments had printed too much paper money during the war and jumping back to a gold standard would have caused deflation. At that time, the gold price was quoted and determined in pounds sterling, the world reserve currency.

After the First World War, the U.S. slowly emerged as the leading economy and political power. The world recognized the emergence of the dollar as the world reserve currency under an agreement signed at Bretton Woods, N.H., in 1944. In turn, the U.S. agreed to exchange dollars at the official rate of $35 for an ounce of gold, a price it had established a decade earlier.

Is gold truly a hedge against inflation or deflation? This will be discussed in depth in Chapter 4, but a glimpse of its power can be seen in the constancy of its purchasing power over 250 years of British history. In 1717, the consumer price index in Britain stood at 8.8; today, it stands at a towering 455. If a gold sovereign coin minted in 1717 — containing 0.2354 ounces of gold — were to have maintained its purchasing power it should be trading for £50 or around $350 (U.S.) today. Who can argue that gold doesn't maintain its purchasing power?

Gold and the French monetary system

After the death of the Sun King in 1715, Louis XIV's great-grandson became king of France. Louis XV, dubbed Louis the Well-Beloved when he first ascended to the throne, ruled for 59 years but he was unable to restore the French treasury's financial health. Nonetheless, France felt the benefits of economic strength in Europe and, since the French had become wary of paper money after the demise of John Law's bank, the amount of gold in France tripled between 1715 and 1788. Most gold was earned through trade with the American and Spanish colonies. Louis XV was succeeded by his grandson, Louis XVI, in 1774. Barely 20 years old, the young king was disastrously immature and naive in the face of growing aristocratic opposition to the fiscal, economic and administrative reforms being demanded by the French parliament in the face of a deteriorating economy.

In 1789, Louis lost control of the National Assembly. It took over the affairs of France and the French Revolution began. The first move of the Revolutionary Council, on Nov. 2, 1789, was to appropriate the properties of the French clergy. This occurred against a background of economic crisis; the harvest of 1788 had been particularly poor, sparking the looting of grain shipments, attacks on markets and the pillaging of factories. Finally, in a 1789 attempt to alleviate financial pressures, the Revolutionary Council sold four million pounds' worth of property it had confiscated from the church. It issued a 5 per cent bond, known as an assignat, that was repayable in religious property. The operation failed miserably and by August, 1790, the assignat had become a bank note.

The rapid depreciation of the assignats fuelled an inflationary spiral that saw the cost of living in Paris jump 580 per cent between 1790 and 1795 and another 140 per cent in 1796. Within six years of being issued, the assignat had lost its value and the Revolutionary Council stopped issuing it. Fear and inflation were driving gold out of the country and the government imposed economic controls to try to staunch the loss. It nationalized most of the larger industries, imposing a 5 per cent ceiling on profits for wholesalers and 10 per cent for retailers. It put a freeze on wages and commodity prices.

In March, 1796, the government created a new currency, the mandat territorial. In six months, the mandat territorial met the same fate as the assignat. It had depreciated 90 per cent in value by April, 1796. By February, 1797, the mandat was fixed at 1 per cent of its original value — an official admission of bankruptcy and the end of the French Revolution's paper currency.

In September, 1797, two-thirds of the national debt was written off and one-third was consolidated in the registry of the national debt. In effect, the government was willing to pay 33 cents on the dollar to its creditors. That act further undermined the faith of the common people in their government and they hoarded their gold currency with even greater urgency. Not surprisingly, the rate of interest was as high as 7 per cent a month. The return to gold currency coincided with abundant harvests from 1796 to 1798, which depressed agricultural prices by 25 per cent to 33 per cent from prices five years earlier.

Out of this turmoil rose Napoleon — a man the country believed could restore order to France. Napoleon instituted wholesale financial reforms, including a sinking fund to cover budget deficits and war expenses. He created a Bank of France in 1800 that filled a role much like that of the Bank of England, which had been formed more than a hundred years before. In 1802, he was able to balance the budget. Finally, in 1803 he returned to a bimetallic monetary system, fixing the ratio of gold to silver at 15.5 to 1. The franc was pegged at five grams of silver that was nine-tenths pure, thereby establishing silver as the principal monetary metal. At the same time, he struck a gold coin called the Napoleon that became an instant success and to this day remains a prized collector's item.

The U.S. experience

While the French were busy using the guillotine and overthrowing the old feudal system, the American colonists were trying to create something out of nothing. Hard money was a rarity in early colonial times in North America and the little that was available was used for imports. This pushed the Americans very quickly to bills of credit or paper money.

In fact, Benjamin Franklin was an advocate of paper money and figured out very quickly that it was the best chance the U.S. had of expanding trade within the colonies when it had so little gold. This prevalence of paper at the time of the creation of the United States may explain why gold and gold coins have never had the deep symbolic significance they have had in the rest of the world. This was reinforced in 1933 when President Franklin D. Roosevelt barred all private U.S. citizens from buying, selling or holding gold except as jewelry or numismatic coins. For three generations — until 1974 when President Gerald Ford lifted the restrictions on gold ownership — Americans had very little interest in the world of gold. Gold and silver mining, which had been the engine of peace and growth in the U.S. in the 19th century, slowly died away in the 20th century. By 1980, U.S. gold production had dwindled to its lowest level in almost a century.

The history of gold as a currency in the U.S. begins with the Coinage Act of 1792 under President Washington. This act created the bimetallic standard, with the silver to gold ratio fixed at 15 to one. Gold was valued at $19.30 (U.S.) an ounce and silver was worth $1.29 (U.S.) an ounce. Forty-two years later, in 1834, the gold price was raised to $20.67 (U.S.) an ounce, a level that it held for the next hundred years — except for the four years of the Civil War when the price of gold floated freely.

In the first half of the 19th century, Russia was the leading gold-producing country. The discoveries of gold in the Ural Mountains and Siberia became the major source of the precious metal. In North America, small-scale gold mining occurred in the slate-belt of the Carolinas and up the coast to Nova Scotia. It wasn't until 1848, when gold was discovered on land owned by John Augustus Sutter in California's Sacramento Valley, that the first of the great gold rushes of the 19th century was on. The dramatic discovery on Jan. 24, 1848, came days before the United States acquired California from Mexico through the Peace Treaty of Guadaloupe Hidalgo on Feb. 2, 1848.

Sutter was unable to protect his land and within months, some 4,000 gold-hungry adventurers were prospecting the ravines and gulches. Within a year, the world experienced the greatest mass movements of population in history when a wave of 100,000 prospectors, the "forty-niners," descended on California. Between 1851 and 1855, more than 15 million ounces of gold were extracted from the hills of California as gold fever reached its peak — more gold than the Romans extracted from their Spanish mines in 300 years. Immigration in the U.S. reached a level of almost 300,000 people as men and women poured into California.

As the easily accessible mines started to peter out, the forty-niners revived an old Roman mining technique of hosing down entire mountainsides. By the end of the 1850s, most of the land was occupied and some of the miners began moving into what is now Nevada. One of them, a ragged, lice-ridden prospector with the unlikely name of Henry Thomas Page Comstock staked some placer claims in Gold Canyon close to today's Virginia City. Comstock couldn't even write his name or read the label on a whisky bottle. While working the claims with his down-and-out cronies, Comstock started to dig a reservoir for water. At about four feet below the surface, they hit gold and silver.

Within a year of his discovery, Comstock thought his find would peter out and he sold his claim for $11,000 (U.S.). Soon the richness of the Comstock ore body became apparent and speculation on the ground surrounding the Comstock became almost uncontrollable. Hundreds of parcels of land, some as small as 6.5 feet by 20 feet, were trading by the foot — almost like lakefront or oceanfront real estate. The great North American tradition of mining lawsuits was also born; no less than 245 lawsuits involving $165 (U.S.) million were launched over the Comstock in those years. Since then it has been rare to see the establishment of a new mining camp devoid of at least one lawsuit.

In 1862, a group of 37 entrepreneurs decided they could bring order to the confusion while making a bit of money for themselves. They organized the first stock exchange on the Pacific coast, the San Francisco Stock and Exchange Port. They began listing every mining company that wanted to convert their footage shares to shares of stock. From the first minute the exchange opened for business it

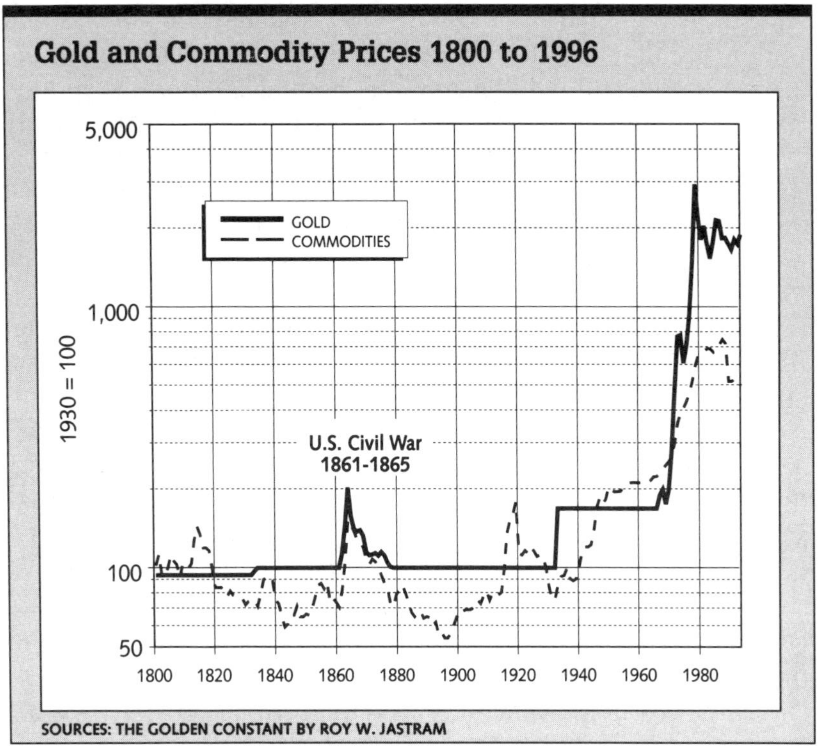

CHART I

was pandemonium. Millions of shares were traded in the first day and shares that sold for $45 (U.S.) in the morning sold in the afternoon for $790 (U.S.). Millionaires were born between breakfast and dinner.

Some of the companies listed on the exchange were worthless, but fortunes were still made on the stock play. As the easily mined ore around Comstock was slowly exhausted, the stock market play started to cool, too. John MacKay, one of the owners of the Port, allied himself with James G. Fair, superintendent of one of the mines on the Comstock. In turn, they forged an alliance with two San Francisco stock market players, James C. Flood and William S. O'Brien. These men became known as the Four Kings.

In 1867, the Ophir mine ran into bare rock and the stock market took a nose dive. Gold and silver production had dropped to a tenth of what it had been and Virginia City was quickly losing its population. The Four Kings offered $80,000 (U.S.) for the Con Virginia and the California mines adjoining the Con Virginia property. By 1873, after investing $200,000 (U.S.) in new underground tunnels and equipment, they had delineated what was to be called the Big Bonanza. By 1875, the Big Bonanza was shipping ore worth $2 million (U.S.) in profits alone every month — at a time when gold was only $20 (U.S.) an ounce. A mine today would have to make $40 million (U.S.) a month to match the Big Bonanza. During that year 2,000 millionaires were created on the stock exchange as the Comstock profit swept the market into a frenzy. The Four Kings had amassed a fortune estimated at $700 million (U.S.). In 1877, the Kings converted around $550 million (U.S.) worth of stock into cash, which they split four ways a few years later as they decided to pursue other ventures.

By 1880, the mines of the Comstock lode had paid their last dividend and one by one started to shut down. Over a 22-year period, the Comstock had produced over $1 billion (U.S.) worth of ore. John MacKay, one of the Four Kings, is remembered today in Nevada for the money he left to create the MacKay School of Mines in Reno.

During those early years, Virginia City was home to more than 60,000 people who roamed its streets drinking and shooting it up at the Bucket of Blood saloon. Virginia City, the Silver Queen, has been captured in the work of Mark Twain, who started his writing career as editor of the local newspaper.

Looking back at the market capitalization of these mines, it's hard to believe that otherwise-sane people could have bid up the stock of these companies to the incredible prices they did. The Four Kings' wealth of $700 million (U.S.) would be worth $14 billion today, surpassing the market capitalization of today's gold mining giant, Barrick Gold, which has mines with reserves of over 40 million ounces of gold — four times as much as the Comstock ever produced. The tremendous wealth delivered by the Comstock was responsible for the building of the town of San Francisco, the financing of several major railways across the U.S., and possibly, the winning of the war by the Union forces.

At the eruption of the Civil War, all banks suspended payment of gold for dollars and the U.S. treasury was quick to follow. The government, hard-pressed to keep the war going, created legal tender notes that came to be known as "greenbacks." The greenback put the U.S. on a paper-money standard for eight years. On Jan. 1, 1879, the Resumption Act resumed the exchange of paper currency into gold at a fixed price of $20.67.

Curiously, the U.S. began using the gold standard by oversight. In 1873, Congress carried out a revision and codification of the mint and coinage laws which omitted the silver dollar in its listing of future coins. When the country returned to a metal basis on Jan. 1, 1879, it found itself on a one-metal standard because gold was the only metal given the privilege of free coinage in the codification of 1873. Vast amounts of silver were being found in Nevada at the time, and western senators accused the eastern establishment of being cheaters and liars. The controversy became an issue in the 1876 presidential election when William Jennings Bryan, one of the presidential candidates, described the Act of 1873 as having put the U.S. on a cross of gold. Of course, coming from the West, he would have preferred one of silver.

During the Civil War, when the gold price floated freely, commodity prices increased by over 117 per cent and gold increased just as fast. In the subsequent period of deflation, from 1864 to 1897, the purchasing power of gold soared as long-term interest rates fell to 3 per cent. The stability of the financial system, combined with large gold and silver discoveries, led to the establishment of large-scale industries in the U.S. and the development of a large-scale railway system throughout the land.

The third great American gold rush began in the early 1870s when gold was found in the Black Hills of South Dakota. There was one problem — this was the Holy Wilderness of the Sioux, their sacred hunting grounds. The Hills came under the Sioux-United States treaty which expressly forbade prospecting or settlement by the white man. After the panic of 1873 and two years of wild speculation in railroad stocks, the economy was in serious trouble. The government was under tremendous pressure to open up the Black Hills and make the gold available.

In 1874, General George A. Custer and the 7th Cavalry accompanied a contingent of geologists, prospectors and assayers. They were looking for gold and gold is exactly what they found. The following year the government summoned the Sioux chiefs to Washington to force them to sell their sacred land. They refused. Upon the Sioux's return to their reservations, the government attacked them. However, it didn't turn out quite as expected. The Sioux and Cheyenne, led by Chief Sitting Bull, defeated the army and wiped out General Custer and his Cavalry.

Incapable of defeating the Indians by force, the government starved them to death by refusing them food and clothing in the face of one of the harshest winters in memory. On Sept. 26, 1876, the Indians signed over the Black Hills. A new gold rush was on — one that never benefited the people who had been forced to sign over their ancestral land.

George Hearst was a speculator who had worked both California and Nevada before he and two other partners moved in 1878 to South Dakota, where a new ledge had been found near Leed. For $70,000 (U.S.) they bought out the two brothers who had founded the mine and incorporated the Homestake Mining Company. The Homestake is still in production, having churned out more than 35 million ounces of gold from 300 miles of tunnels and workings of one of the largest gold mines in the world.

In 1891, it was Colorado's turn to become the site of a gold rush as the Cripple Creek district was discovered. This incredibly rich and compact district of six square miles produced over 21 million ounces of gold in a very short time. Just as in the days of the Big Bonanza, claims were being sold by the foot. One lucky prospector sold a claim for $20 million (U.S.). Again, fortunes were made overnight while gold and silver flowed East and fuelled economic expansion.

On Aug. 17, 1896, George Carmack and his native friend Skukum Charlie, discovered gold on Bonanza Creek, a tributary of the Klondike River near Dawson in the Yukon. The news hit the streets of America like a wild brush fire. In 1897, 100,000 people set out for the Klondike, crossing the White Pass, many dying on the way, in the rush to the frozen Canadian gold fields. Only 30,000 made it, and only a lucky few of those made a fortune. As people pushed farther north, discoveries were made in Nome, Alaska, in 1899 and finally in Fairbanks in 1902. The land and the climate were harsh and production peaked and faded within a few years.

This incredible era of gold discovery came to an end with the discovery of gold in 1901 and 1902 in Tonopah and Goldfield, Nev. These two mining camps produced hundreds of millions of ounces of silver and millions of ounces of gold at a time when the U.S. needed it badly. In fact, between 1903 and 1925 these mines gave Nevada more than 250 million much-needed dollars. Sitting right in the middle of the desert, Goldfield and Tonopah are aptly named the Gold Dust Twins. They were the last major precious metal discoveries in Nevada for more than 50 years.

The United States and the First World War

In 1914, with the onset of the First World War, came a financial shock. In 1915, commodity prices took off, jumping 150 per cent in less than two years while the gold price remained fixed at $20.67 (U.S.). This lopsided situation lasted until 1921 when prices fell back 33 per cent and stayed there until the beginning of the Great Depression. From 1929 to 1933, wholesale prices dropped 31 per cent while the purchasing power of gold went up by nearly 45 per cent.

In 1933, the nation's economic well-being was rocked to its foundation as thousands of banks failed. Panic spread through the U.S. and people began to withdraw their savings from troubled banks. They turned to gold as a haven for their life savings, turning over $20 million (U.S.) in paper money a week and demanding gold. To stop the panic, President Roosevelt declared a bank holiday and promptly devalued the U.S. dollar in a desperate attempt to revive the moribund economy. He did so by raising the gold price from $20.67 (U.S.) to $35 (U.S.) an ounce. To put some teeth in his economic reform the government confiscated all gold and gold coins held by individuals. Failure to remit all of your gold, except jewelry or numismatic coins, was punishable by fines of up to $10,000 (U.S.), 10 years' imprisonment and confiscation of the gold.

The desperate ploy worked. The central bank's coffers began to swell. The price was set high enough to encourage new production and the dollar was stable enough for people to want to hold the currency instead of gold. The supremacy of the U.S. dollar and its gold backing was confirmed in July, 1944, by the signing of the Bretton Woods agreement, which established the U.S. dollar as the world reserve currency. The United Nations monetary and financial conference at Bretton Woods was attended by 44 nations with the goal of putting some order in world financial affairs in light of the imminent end of the war and the massive reconstruction program that was sure to follow. Unlike the "Pax Britannica," the dollar supremacy was to be of short duration. The inflationary pressures that had started to build after the Second World War were exacerbated by the war in Vietnam, reminiscent of the inflation sparked by the American Civil War from 1861 to 1865.

In both periods, the gold price moved in step with the rise in commodity prices but reached more dramatic highs at the peak of both crises, in 1864 and 1980. Subsequently, as inflation started to wane, the gold price started to drift downward as well. The salient point is that in the American experience, gold has preserved its owners' purchasing power during inflation as well as deflation. The two short exceptions during that entire period were from 1812 to 1816, when the U.S. was at war with England when it was supported only by an extremely thin agrarian economy; and from 1960 to 1970, when the inflationary pressure of the Vietnam War was being felt in the economy yet gold was fixed at $35 (U.S.) an ounce. When gold was finally let loose in 1971, it rose with a vengeance.

CHAPTER 3

Understanding Gold's Fundamentals

ANYONE WHO HAS STUDIED economics in high school or university has been taught that the price of goods is determined by the law of supply and demand. Gold has a dual personality — it is a commodity used in electronics, jewelry and dentistry and it is the money of last resort and the reserve foundation of the world's central banks.

The law of supply and demand works on gold with a vengeance, forcing its price to bounce up and down. But which demand curve holds sway at any one time? That's the elusive question that anyone who tries to forecast the gold price must wrestle with, usually in vain. The gold market can be gripped by emotion, including panic and euphoria. Throughout history, men and women have killed, suffered untold misery and ventured to unknown lands in search of the metal of the gods. To this day, gold is money, power and fame.

Try putting that into a rational equation of supply and demand. There are times of peace and economic stability, when gold has only one use, as jewelry, and forecasting the price of gold is fairly straightforward. When gold is money, it's because the public may have lost confidence in currency, the monetary system or the economic system. That is when rational behaviour is thrown overboard and panic follows. The consequences are predictable, but not their magnitude. In 1980, a gold price of $850 (U.S.) was not rational or predictable. Is the world today producing so much gold that it can never happen again? Hardly!

The gold supply

Every year, Gold Fields Mineral Services Ltd. of London publishes what is considered to be the most authoritative work on global supply and demand in the gold industry. Gold Fields monitors the annual supply of gold to the Western industrial and private consumer from four sources:

1. new mine production
2. sales by the former Communist bloc
3. sales by central banks and international agencies
4. old industrial scrap, melted coins and jewelry
5. gold loans and forward sales.

These suppliers to the world gold pool behave in radically different ways. The world's central banks and monetary agencies sometimes act as sellers of gold and at other times as buyers, depending on monetary policy and the economic environment. It is the price of gold that prompts gold bugs to dump their old gold scrap on the market or drives entrepreneurs into the wilderness to explore and develop new mines. While the gold supply from hoarders, whether individuals or governments, can vary dramatically from week to week, the supply of gold from mines changes less.

Gold and the former Communist bloc countries

The world's fourth-largest producer of gold, after South Africa, the United States, and sometimes Australia, is the former Soviet Union. The size of the Soviet treasure chest and its annual production have been carefully guarded secrets since 1919.

However, in 1988 a Soviet bond issue inadvertently disclosed that the country's gold production between 1970 and 1985 had varied between 6.9 million ounces a year in the early 1970s and 10.6 million ounces by 1985. Gold production in the Russian portion of the former Soviet Union has decreased to 4.6 million ounces in 1995 as the economy and the availability of fuel, machinery parts, food and labour have deteriorated, especially in the Russian Far East where much of the gold is mined. In Uzbekistan, production is inferred to be steady at about 2.0 million ounces; no official figures are provided.

Prior to 1988, the only information available on the Soviet Union and its gold was the country's pattern of gold buying and selling. Over the past 40 years, annual sales have fluctuated from 15.7 million ounces under Nikita Khrushchev to a low of 1.7 million ounces, except for the five years from 1966 to 1970 when the Soviet Union was a buyer of gold. Over the past four decades, sales have averaged about 6.4 million ounces a year.

By subtracting the sales from estimated production, we can derive a domestic demand of three million to four million ounces of gold a year. That demand would have come primarily from the mili-

Gold Supply to the Private Sector

IN MILLIONS OF OUNCES

	Western mine production	Former Communist bloc sales (purchases)	Net official sales (purchases)	Gold scrap	Total supply
1950	24.3	NA	-9.3	NA	15.0
1951	23.6	NA	-7.6	NA	16.0
1952	24.3	NA	-6.6	NA	17.7
1953	24.3	2.2	-13.0	NA	13.4
1954	25.6	2.2	-19.1	NA	8.6
1955	26.8	2.2	-19.0	NA	10.0
1956	28.0	4.3	-14.0	NA	18.3
1957	29.1	7.4	-19.7	NA	16.8
1958	30.0	6.3	-19.5	NA	16.8
1959	32.2	8.6	-21.6	NA	19.1
1960	33.7	5.7	-8.4	NA	31.0
1961	34.7	8.6	-17.3	NA	26.0
1962	37.1	5.7	-10.6	NA	32.3
1963	38.7	15.7	-23.4	NA	31.0
1964	40.2	12.9	-20.3	NA	32.7
1965	41.2	11.4	-6.3	NA	46.3
1966	41.3	-2.2	1.3	NA	40.4
1967	40.2	-0.2	45.1	NA	85.2
1968	40.0	-0.9	19.9	NA	59.0
1969	40.3	-0.5	-2.9	NA	36.9
1970	40.9	-0.1	-7.6	NA	33.2
1971	39.6	1.7	3.1	NA	44.5
1972	37.8	6.8	-4.9	NA	39.8
1973	35.7	8.8	0.2	NA	44.8
1974	32.0	7.1	0.6	NA	39.7
1975	30.4	4.8	0.3	NA	35.5
1976	31.0	13.2	1.9	NA	46.1
1977	30.9	12.9	8.6	NA	52.5
1978	31.3	13.2	11.6	NA	56.1
1979	30.8	6.4	17.5	NA	54.7
1980	31.0	2.9	-7.4	15.9	42.4
1981	31.8	9.0	-8.9	7.8	39.7
1982	33.2	6.5	-2.7	7.8	44.8
1983	35.8	3.0	4.6	9.5	52.9
1984	37.5	6.6	2.7	9.8	56.7
1985	39.7	6.8	-4.2	10.7	53.0
1986	41.7	12.9	-5.0	16.5	66.1
1987	44.5	9.7	-2.3	14.6	66.5
1988	49.9	8.5	-9.2	12.1	61.2
1989	54.1	8.6	11.8	12.0	86.4
1990	56.4	12.6	0.4	16.4	85.8
1991	57.6	7.4	0.8	14.5	80.2
1992	60.2	2.0	20.1	14.4	96.7
1993	61.2	5.7	14.4	17.1	98.4
1994	61.0	3.5	2.6	18.4	85.5
1995	60.8	3.3	7.5	18.7	90.2

NA: Not available

SOURCE: GOLD FIELDS MINERAL SERVICES LTD., 1996

TABLE I

tary and space industry for its development of technology in the 1960s and 1970s. In the 1980s, the heaviest demand for gold would have been from the jewelry market. Internal gold demand has soared in the past year as Russia, the most important and populated state within the former Soviet Union, has chosen the unthinkable course of devaluing its currency in the face of rapidly escalating inflationary pressure. In fact, much of what we saw in the U.S. in 1933 is being repeated today in Russia. Instead of lining up at banks to convert paper money into gold, people are lining up at jewelry stores and buying any gold items they can get their hands on. Quite simply, they are hoarding gold. Even though the price of gold in rubles doubled in 1991, inflation of close to 100 per cent a year keeps the queues in the jewelry stores long.

Until a semblance of financial order is re-established in the Communist countries, and that could take a few years, internal gold demand is likely to stay high while production continues to decline. This would put a squeeze on the amount of gold available for export to the international markets.

In fact, since 1986 the Russians have had to dig into their official reserves to keep their export sales at the 10-million-ounce level. There are two questions on everyone's mind: How large are the Russian reserves and for how long will they draw on those reserves to maintain exports? Current Russian reserves are mostly from the Stalin era between 1930 and 1950 when gold production averaged about 3.4 million ounces a year. Total production during the two decades was probably 68 million ounces.

In June, 1992, in a presentation at the London *Financial Times* Gold Conference, the head of the Russian republic's committee for precious stones and metals stated that the Russian Central Bank had no more than 7.1 million ounces of gold reserves left. This level of reserves is much smaller than the West was led to believe. Internal consumption has been much higher than anticipated. With their reserves nearly depleted and production on the decline, Russian gold sales are becoming a much less significant factor in the market.

In the past few years, the gold market has been buffeted on several occasions by rumours of impending large-scale Russian gold sales. With its economy disintegrating and Western banks and governments reluctant to advance fresh loans, Russia has been forced to sell all the raw materials it possibly can — oil and gas, platinum, palladium, nickel, copper and, of course, gold. So far, these rumours have been only rumours. In reality, Russia has used 10 to 20 per cent of its reserves as collateral to borrow money in transactions called "gold swaps." A gold swap is a complex financial arrangement in which the Russian government borrows gold from a Western central bank and sells it on the spot market to raise cash at the same time it enters into a purchase agreement to buy back the gold at a fixed price at a specific date in the future, perhaps in a year. If the Russian government were to default on the repurchase agreement, the Western banks would foreclose on the gold put up as collateral in the transaction.

Instead of selling its gold, Russia could issue bonds backed by gold, just as France did in the 1970s. This would attract foreign investment, and decrease the supply of gold on the global market. However, such a move is unlikely.

So, what will the Russians do with their meagre gold reserves in the future? The answer to their problems does not lie in selling their reserves — the cash raised would pay for only a few weeks of imports. In any case, it is unlikely the Russian government would be willing to deplete their gold reserves completely. As it is, Russian reserves have probably been drawn down to a critical level, the level it needs to join the International Monetary Fund and be seen as a full participant in the world of central banks.

What can Russia do? In 1990, a group of distinguished U.S. bankers suggested that Russia adopt a gold standard, making the ruble convertible into a fixed amount of gold. As we've seen in the past, a gold standard is effective only when there is little inflation and a stable economy.

Under current conditions in Russia, particularly with the collapse of the centrally planned economy, such a move would certainly mean the disappearance of their gold reserves to the people within a matter of days, no matter what the price of conversion. (What is interesting, however, is the do-what-I-say-not-what-I-do philosophy of the central bankers. It also underlines the strong adherence of the U.S. central bank to the concept of gold as a monetary asset. Obviously, gold is not likely to be dismissed soon.)

Gold from the world's governments

In the gold market, the buying or selling of gold by the world's central banks, national monetary authorities and international agencies such as the International Monetary Fund is referred to as "official" transactions. In looking at these transactions, never forget that the central banks already own a third of the world's gold. From 1965 to 1995, the central banks' gold holdings have declined from a high of 1,193 million ounces to the current low of 905 million ounces.

Gold represents almost one-third of the central bank reserves of the world's industrial countries, giving them more than a passing interest in the future price of the metal. These banks hold approximately 905 million ounces of gold; the U.S. has the largest amount with 262 million ounces, most of it in its vault at Fort Knox. The holdings of the U.S. are followed by those of Germany and Switzerland, both countries with extremely strong currencies and strong balance of payments surpluses. Next are France and Italy, the inflation-prone countries that represent the third- and fourth-largest economies of Europe. The central bank reserves of the world's industrial countries are equivalent to over 10 years of current production and would swamp the gold market if they were sold. But the buying and selling of gold by any individual nation is tied to that country's economic strength and trade balance.

Through the 1970s, the U.S. and the International Monetary Fund did sell more than 112 million ounces of gold in an attempt to demonetize gold — to eliminate gold's significance as money. Over those years, the price of gold was rising and the gold of the U.S. and IMF was rapidly absorbed by the market. Over the past six years, developing nations such as Taiwan, South Korea, Indonesia, Brazil, the Philippines and Peru have been steadily raising their official gold reserves. On the other hand, a few Western countries — Canada, Belgium and Portugal — are selling. In fact, the industrialized nations have let their portion of gold reserves move steadily lower to only 21 per cent of their central bank reserves by mid-1995. Over the past 35 years, this percentage has fluctuated between 21 per cent and 70 per cent. It seems likely that the current gold position is closer to a minimum comfort level than an optimum level.

This selling has prompted economists to ask if the central banks should manage their gold more actively and, if they did, what pressure this would bring on a finely balanced market. Countries such as the United States, Germany and Switzerland, which hold between 30 per cent and 57 per cent of their total bank reserves in gold, have been content to sit tight on their hoards for several reasons. First, gold reserves are generally viewed as an indication of a nation's well-being, even though the reserves no longer play a role

Central Bank Gold Reserves

Gold (millions of ounces)	1960	1970	1980	1990	1995
ALL IMF COUNTRIES	1,083.3	1,057.9	953.1	940.5	905.4
INDUSTRIAL IMF COUNTRIES	1,000.4	941.4	813.9	795.9	763.0
United States	508.7	316.3	264.3	261.9	261.8
Germany	84.9	113.7	95.2	95.2	95.2
Switzerland	62.4	78.0	83.3	83.3	83.3
France	46.9	100.9	81.9	81.9	81.9
Italy	63.0	82.5	66.7	66.7	66.7
Netherlands	41.5	51.1	43.9	43.9	34.8
Japan	7.1	15.2	24.2	24.2	24.2
Belgium	33.4	42.0	34.2	30.2	20.5
United Kingdom	80.0	38.5	18.8	18.9	18.4
Austria	8.4	20.4	21.1	20.4	11.5
Australia	4.2	6.8	7.9	7.9	7.9
Canada	25.3	22.6	21.0	14.8	3.3

Gold (as % of total reserves *)	1960	1970	1980	1990	1995
ALL IMF COUNTRIES	63.6	41.3	57.8	28.6	21.3
INDUSTRIAL IMF COUNTRIES	69.9	47.0	66.9	34.2	29.6
United States	92.1	77.6	90.9	58.3	56.5
France	72.6	72.5	63.8	46.1	53.6
Switzerland	94.1	54.8	75.8	52.3	50.1
Italy	68.1	55.6	3.0	29.0	47.5
Germany	42.7	30.6	53.6	35.1	30.5
Belgium	78.0	53.3	72.0	48.9	30.3
Netherlands	78.3	56.8	69.0	49.2	26.0
Australia	20.2	14.9	73.4	15.8	19.2
Austria	41.4	42.2	70.2	45.6	16.0
United Kingdom	75.6	49.3	35.0	16.9	14.2
Canada	44.7	17.8	80.3	24.2	7.2
Japan	12.9	11.7	36.7	10.6	5.5

* Using market SDR valuations
SOURCE: INTERNATIONAL MONETARY FUND

TABLE II

in domestic money creation. Heavy selling of gold reserves could be seen as evidence of economic and financial failure of the government and create a run on the country's currency. (This is the case today in Russia.) Furthermore, the free-floating international monetary system is only 20 years old and central bankers, with their long memories, see it as still being in its infancy. Given the instability of the current dollar standard, prudence dictates that a large chunk of reserves remain in gold, the oldest of all the globally accepted currencies and the surest hedge against a worldwide financial breakdown.

As central bankers learn to live with the current unstable system, they are likely to begin managing their gold reserves while trying not to disturb the market. This can be done when one country swaps its gold for the hard currency of another. The swap takes place as a loan and the gold is "sold" at a discount to market price. The loan and the "interest" are paid off when the country redeems its gold by buying it back at the full market price. South Africa is an old hand at swapping gold as a way of mobilizing its gold reserves to carry it through the cash squeeze created by worldwide economic sanctions. More recently, the Russians have made extensive use of swap agreements to borrow hard currencies.

A variation on the swap is for a central bank to pledge its gold as collateral for a loan. Because gold is collateral of the highest quality, the country pledging the gold can obtain better terms than on an unsecured loan. However, history has shown that gold pledged as collateral by a weak country is usually sold to meet loan repayments. On the other hand, stronger countries, such as Italy which has often had to resort to pledging its gold, will always repay their gold-backed loans first.

In the 1980s, we have also seen the appearance of gold loans. In order to mobilize their gold reserves, central banks deposit a portion of their gold with commercial banks. The banks, acting as intermediary, then lend the gold to gold mining companies which in turn sell the gold to raise money for exploration and expansion. Gold loans provide gold mining companies with a low-cost source of financing and protect them against a fall in the gold price because the price they will receive for their gold is locked in. (This is discussed in depth in Chapter 7.) The central banks receive between 1.5 per cent and 2.5 per cent a year for their gold but the large commercial banks get only 0.5 per cent to 1 per cent and are exposed to heavy risks if the mining companies should default. At the end of 1990, 12 million ounces of gold worth $4.5 billion (U.S.) had been loaned. In the 1990s, these loans are being repaid; in 1993 alone more than two million ounces were returned to the banks by borrowers.

The emerging economic powers of the world — countries such as Japan, Taiwan and South Korea — are all at the very bottom of the list of holders of gold reserves. The countries that are most heavily in debt, such as the U.S., South Africa, the Philippines, Egypt, Turkey, Argentina and Peru, are closer to the top of the list. With this shift in economic balance, gold will probably start flowing from the debtor nations to the strong, creditor countries of the Far East just as gold and silver passed from heavily indebted Spain to England and Germany three centuries ago. In fact, between September, 1987, and June, 1988, Taiwan added 7.8 million ounces of gold to its reserves, a 140 per cent increase. After the U.S. complained that the Taiwanese were artificially reducing their trade surplus, Taiwan halted its gold purchases for a while. Less than a year later it said that it would continue its purchase of gold at a favourable time. Any change in the world monetary standard from the dollar to gold could unleash a pent-up demand not only from Taiwan but from Japan and Korea as well, as these countries dump dollars from their reserves for gold.

The question an individual investor has to ask himself is this: If the people who manage our monetary systems are believers in gold and are demonstrating it by holding millions of ounces in reserve, should an investor not also own at least a little bit of gold?

Gold scrap

An erratic component of gold supply is old gold scrap. This is made up of melted gold jewelry, old dental fillings and scrap from the computer, telecommunications and electronics industries. The availability of scrap supplies is a direct function of price. It peaked in 1980 when the gold price was at its highest and bottomed in 1984 when the price was $284 (U.S.) an ounce. These swings can have a dramatic impact on the price of gold — driving it down when hoarders of old jewelry sell their treasures to cash in on high prices and driving it up when gold prices are low and investors are nervously looking for security.

Perspective on gold production

In the recent past, financial magazines and newspapers have been decrying the tremendous growth in worldwide gold production, making dire predictions of a glut. As an investor, it's important not to lose your historical perspective. Gold production had declined steadily from 1966 until 1979 when mine production in non-Communist countries bottomed at just less than 31 million ounces. In that year, the gold price hit $850 (U.S.) an ounce, setting off an explosion in exploration and development of new mines throughout the world. This frenetic expansion in mine production went unabated for 13 years — almost doubling gold production from 1980, a 50 per cent increase from the previous peak in 1966 when production had reached 41.3 million ounces.

Predictions of a glut assumed the growth rate would continue for the next decade. As with predictions in the oil industry in the late 70s, these fears are unfounded. If gold production continued to increase at about 12 per cent a year, by the year 2000 the world would have been mining 175 million ounces annually, or about six times as much as in 1980.

But a gold mine is not an inexhaustible resource. At that rate of production, the billion ounces of existing proven, probable and possible reserves of gold in the ground would be depleted in less than six years. Just to keep up, we would have to find six Hemlo gold mines every year or an entire Carlin Trend every six months. Obviously, that is not about to happen. The 30-million-ounce gold deposit at Hemlo, Ont., was discovered in 1981. Gold was first discovered near Carlin, Nev., in the early 1960s but the discovery of 90 million ounces of gold in the Carlin Trend has taken place only since the early 1980s. These finds are unique. The previous discovery of 20 million ounces of gold in North America was made over 50 years ago at Red Lake in Northern Ontario. In fact, 1994 saw the first decrease (on both a global and Western world basis) in mined gold production since the late 1970s. Further production gains are likely to be very marginal as many of the new generation mines reach maturity. World gold mine production appears to be now plateauing and future declines in production are a very real possibility.

Gold discovery and production throughout history have occurred in cycles that have been a function of politics, price and technology. From placer mining in antiquity, quartz vein and mercury amalgamation in the Roman Empire and the discovery of sulfide flotation and cyanidation in the 19th century to the "modern" heap-leaching and autoclave processes discovered in the last 10 years, there has been a steady evolution in our knowledge that is matched by a steplike increase in worldwide production. After we have exhausted a defined technology over an area, we must await the birth of new ideas to see new deposits.

The Carlin Trend is a perfect example. It was there in the 1880s when thousands of fortune seekers swarmed through Nevada on

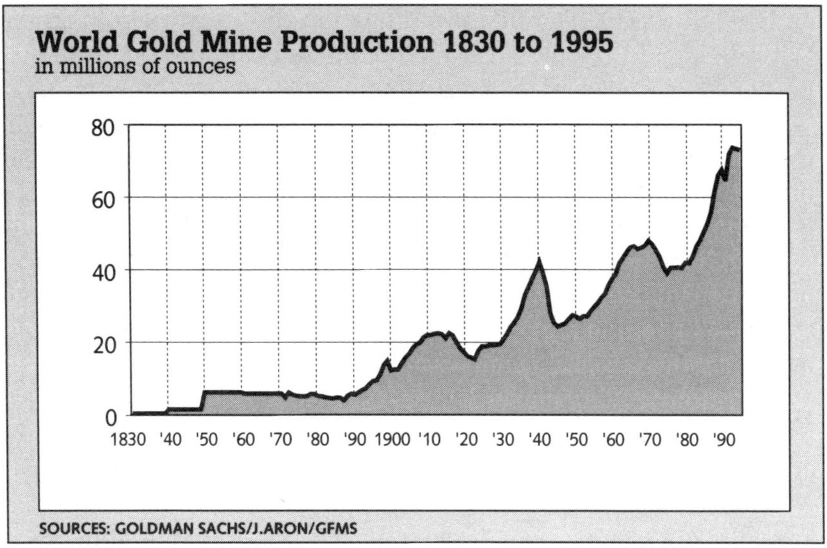

CHART II

their way from Virginia City's famous Comstock Lode to the gold and silver discoveries of Tonopah, Rawhide and Goldfields. Yet they never found Carlin. They walked across it and rode over it. A few thought they had seen something and left "gopher holes," the old-time prospectors' adits, in the ground. Yet they never found the "mother lode."

In fact, they couldn't have found it because their technology wasn't advanced enough to detect the micron-size particles of gold hidden in the rock. They couldn't see it and they couldn't pan it. They may not have found the Carlin Trend, but the old-timers didn't miss a big gold quartz vein anywhere in Nevada or California. If there's a vein of gold left untouched, it will be because it's not worth mining. Many companies and individuals have found that out at their expense in the last 10 years.

Let's look at the history of gold production throughout the last 200 years. Apart from the years between 1815 to the peak of California production in 1855, there is a remarkable degree of similarity among the various cycles of growth and contraction. The expansion phase of gold production typically lasts from 12 to 25 years, with an average of 17 years. The current boom is now in its 14th year, which means it is probably getting closer to the end of its typical cycle.

Two of the expansionary cycles were due mostly to deepening global economic and financial contraction: the periods 1883 to 1899 and 1922 to 1940. The first cycle saw the discovery of gold in the Witwatersrand in South Africa while the second boom saw the major Canadian discoveries in the 1920s and 1930s at Timmins, Kirkland Lake and Red Lake in Ontario and other smaller discoveries in Quebec and British Columbia. The 1951 to 1970 cycle was due to the large increase in South African production as capital and technology were made available to develop its large reserves. The current boom has been fuelled by two major factors: a rising gold price, brought about by deteriorating financial conditions in the reserve currency; and the application of new technology which has led to large new discoveries in North America and the Pacific Rim.

Total gold production in this cycle is, therefore, likely to rise somewhat more than that during the previous two cycles when only one of these factors was present. During this cycle, it is possible that gold production could double from its previous low. In fact, we have already seen world gold-mine production increase 90 per cent to 73.6 million ounces in 1993, compared with 38.6 million ounces in 1980. This production could be sustained for at least a decade if prices remain at or above $400 (U.S.). Interestingly, in each of the past three cycles gold production fell abruptly within five to 10 years of the cyclical high. From a 1970 high of 40.9 million ounces, Western world gold production fell to 30.8 million ounces in 1980. From 39.7 million ounces in 1940, Western world production fell to 23.6 million ounces in 1945. If that pattern repeats itself, by the year 2010 world gold-mine production could be down to 55 million ounces, or 18 million ounces less than in 1995.

It makes sense. The two best mining camps in North America, Carlin and Hemlo, both have a mine life of 20 years based on current technology and the mines' reserves. By 2010, these mines will have substantially lower production unless new theories or processes are developed to find and produce more gold from these mines.

The bottom line is simple: Gold production has increased significantly in the past 14 years and has reached a new record output that can be sustained for only a limited time. This growth is not extraordinary, but very much in line with all previous cycles as companies exploit their best reserves in the early years to pay for the high costs of bringing mines into production. Also, most of the easy gold discoveries are made in the early part of the cycle and gold production tends to fall gradually for a period of 10 to 12 years after peak pro-

Western World Gold Mine Production Since 1970

THE CHANGING MARKET SHARE OF THE LARGEST PRODUCERS

in millions of ounces

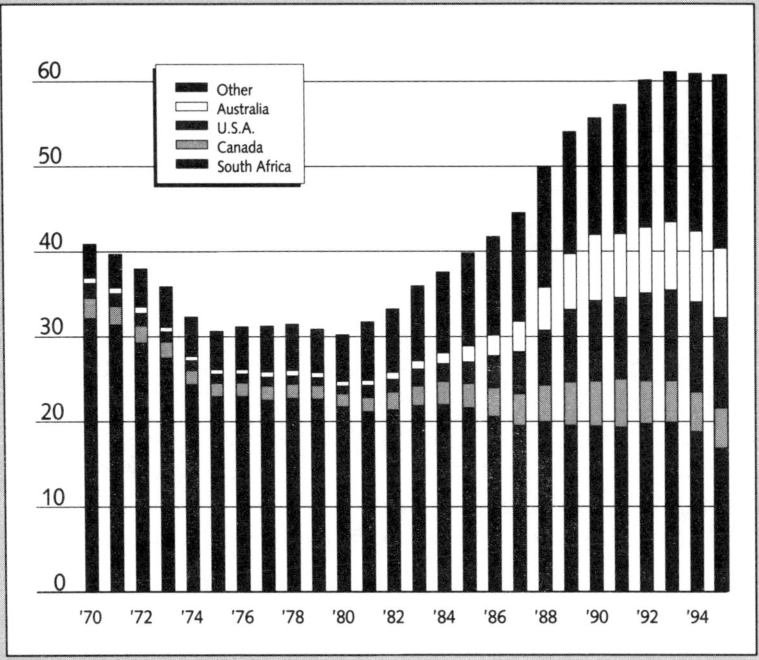

SOURCE: GOLD FIELDS MINERAL SERVICES LTD.

CHART III

duction is reached. All of these mid-life conditions are now in place. While we don't know how it will end, we have the plot and the characters. It's up to you to put your money on the best investment candidate.

The aging of South Africa's gold mines

South African gold mines have dominated world production in the 20th century, producing over 1.46 billion ounces of gold, or nearly 40 per cent of the gold ever mined in the world. There is no question that the Witwatersrand basin stands as one of the world's greatest natural resources ever discovered. From a trickle at the beginning of the century, South African production reached a peak of 32.15 million ounces of gold a year in 1970. This was accomplished as large new mines discovered in the great post-Second World War exploration boom came into production. These mines routinely mined over one ounce of gold from every ton of ore and generated enormous profits.

Today the majority of South African mines have reached middle age. By the end of 1995, production had fallen by over 40 per cent to 16.8 million ounces a year, and reserves are being depleted faster than they are being replaced. The industry is now in a very costly race to stem the rate of production decline.

Many of the problems facing the South African gold mining industry are common to any middle-aged mining operation; others are unique to the country. Specifically, the majority of the country's mines that are in production today are more than 25 years old. Mining started very close to those areas of the ore bodies that contained the richest gold grades. As these deposits are emptied of their highest-grade ore reserves, the average reserve grade starts to fall. Furthermore, the mining operations have to move farther and farther away from the shafts, thus putting even more pressure on costs.

Part of the reason for the declining grade also lies in South African mining legislation which forces the mining companies to mine at or below the average value of their declared ore reserves. This legislation was instituted to prevent mining of only the richest, or highest, grades of ore, leaving the lower-grade ore behind. This will ensure the longest possible mine life. As the gold price rose in the 1980s, the quantity of payable ore at lower grades also increased, thereby forcing companies to lower the overall cutoff grade — the lowest grade of ore that can be mined at a profit. At the same time that the grades were falling and productivity was declining, the industry has had to cope with increasing demands from workers for higher wages.

Throughout the 1980s, miners have demanded and received annual pay raises hovering around 20 per cent. Over the next decade, the South African gold industry will be under relentless pressure to contain costs as it is forced to mine deeper and pay higher wages. As for the future, the gold mines are chewing up approximately 110 million tons of ore each year. Just to replace those reserves will be a daunting task for the South African gold industry.

While the potential for the South African gold mining industry remains good for the next 20 years, profits taken out of the mines will be reduced, in some cases drastically. Instead, the money must

20 Largest Gold Mines in South Africa

Mine	Ownership	1995 Production (ounces)
Freegold	Anglo Group	2,981,000
Vaal Reefs/Southvaal	Anglo Group	2,126,000
Driefontein	Gold Fields	1,626,000
Kloof	Gold Fields	1,400,000
Western Deeps	Anglo Group	1,152,000
Hartebeestfontein	Anglovaal	810,000
Randfontein	JCI	740,000
Harmony	Randgold	647,000
Western Areas	JCI	557,000
Elandsrand	Anglo Group	497,000
Beatrix	Gencor	470,000
Ergo	Anglo Group	450,000
Buffelsfontein	Gencor	285,000
Winkelhaak	Gencor	283,000
Kinross	Gencor	274,000
ERPM	Randgold	263,000
Deelkraal	Gold Fields	212,000
Loraine	Anglovaal	212,000
St. Helena	Gencor	170,000
Blyvooruitzicht	Randgold	153,000

TABLE III

be used for a massive reinvestment program to mechanize and modernize existing operations and to find and develop new gold fields. By the turn of the century, given a stable political environment, the industry should be on a sound footing again. However, it is far from certain that the gold companies will be able to return to their former high dividend payout to shareholders. In the meantime, North American gold shares could be more attractive.

The rebirth of the United States gold industry

Gold production in the U.S. declined after the Second World War, falling to only 884,000 ounces a year by 1980. But over the past decade, production has climbed steadily to reach 10.6 million ounces in 1995, a 12-fold increase. This astonishing growth is the result of the large discoveries made in Nevada, which now account for more than half of U.S. production. California is now in second place, producing 14 per cent of the country's gold.

The Carlin Trend in northeastern Nevada continues to be the site of amazing discoveries. In 1989, Newmont Gold announced the discovery of their 20th deposit on the Trend. Called the Deep Star, it abuts the south boundary of the Barrick Goldstrike operation. In the fall of 1989, Barrick itself announced the discovery of the Meikle Mine deposit to the north of its existing operation. The discovery hole cut a mineralized zone 540 feet thick, with 0.41 ounces of gold in each ton of ore.

On the Carlin Trend, the official public reserves were estimated by Newmont and Barrick to be approximately 70 million ounces, but it appears that these mines will produce far more gold than expected, possibly as much as 100 million ounces.

The Battle Mountain trend in north-central Nevada is also the site of several large-scale mining operations, including the Fortitude, Round Mountain, McCoy/Cove and Marigold mines. It is also on that trend that the latest discovery of gold has occurred. Early in 1992, Placer Dome announced the discovery of the five million ounces Pipeline deposit near its Cortez operation. This new find has sparked renewed interest in Nevada and the state remains the most prolific gold province in North America. The Getchell Trend, which has been mined for almost 40 years, has recently come alive with the Chimney Creek, Rabbit Creek (now combined to form the Twin Creeks mine) and Getchell mines which have combined resources of over 25 million ounces of gold. Getchell Gold's discovery of the five-million-ounce Turquoise Ridge deposit in 1995 and early indications coming from Powder Hill indicate the best may yet be to come for the Getchell trend.

Exploration efforts are being expanded to neighbouring states, such as Idaho, Montana and Washington, where very little exploration has been done in the past. As for California, which used to be the dominant gold-producing state in the country, environmental issues and lobbies have bogged down the development of all but the most promising projects owned by large companies with very deep pockets and patience.

Smaller gold mines have also made a great contribution to American production. There are at least 50 mines across the U.S. producing less than 100,000 ounces of gold each year. However, there are

20 Largest Gold Mines in the United States

Mine	State	Ownership	1995 Production (ounces)
Goldstrike	Nevada	Barrick Gold	2,032,000
Newmont Carlin	Nevada	Newmont Gold/Mining	1,635,000
Bingham Canyon	Utah	Kennecott	525,000
Twin Creeks	Nevada	Sante Fe Pacific Gold	424,000
Homestake	S. Dakota	Homestake Mining	403,000
Round Mountain	Nevada	Echo Bay/Homestake/Case	344,000
Jerritt Canyon	Nevada	Independence/FMC Gold	327,000
McCoy/Cove	Nevada	Echo Bay	310,000
McLaughlin	California	Homestake Mining	242,000
Lone Tree	Nevada	Sante Fe Pacific Gold	228,000
Mesquite	California	Sante Fe Pacific Gold	193,000
Getchell	Nevada	FirstMiss Gold	178,000
Bullfrog	Nevada	Lac Minerals	176,000
Castle Mountain	California	Viceroy Resources/MK Gold	156,000
Rawhide-Denton	Nevada	RTZ/Kiewit/Kinross	121,000
Pikes Peak	Colorado	Independence/Golden Cyc.	115,000
Bald Mountain	Nevada	Placer Dome	114,000
Florida Canyon	Nevada	Pegasus Gold	111,000
Cortez	Nevada	Placer Dome/Kennecott	111,000
Ridgeway	S. Carolina	Kennecott	111,000

TABLE IV

few mines of this size still in the development stage. The U.S. gold mining industry is entering the late 1990s with over a hundred mines in production, the majority of its capital expenditures behind it and a life expectancy of at least 15 to 20 years. Because higher grades of ore are always mined in the first years, the industry should enjoy large cash flows over the next five to 10 years.

The gold boom in Australia

In 1988, Australia outpaced Canada to become the world's fourth-largest producer behind South Africa, the United States and Russia. Australian gold production reached 8.2 million ounces in 1995, more than twice the previous record of 3.8 million ounces established in 1903. It is also 14 times the gold produced in 1980. A number of factors are responsible for the growth of the past decade.

First, the last gold boom in Australia occurred almost 100 years ago. With the recent introduction of large open-pit mining and heap-leaching technologies ideal for the Australian climate, there has been a considerable jump in the number of mines which can now economically produce gold. Exploration, which had been quiet for a long time, was given a healthy boost when the price of gold soared in the early 1980s and the Australian dollar remained weak against the U.S. dollar. Also, gold mines in Australia were exempt from taxation until 1991.

With the introduction of a tax on the gold mining industry, companies accelerated mine development to maximize cash flow before being hit by the tax. Major companies are expanding production by building large-scale plants, pushing mines to their maximum physical capability and maximizing output by processing the higher-grade portions of their reserves as fast as they can. The combined effect of "picking the eyes out" of these ore bodies was expected to dramatically reduce the economic life of some of these mines and production was expected to drop at a much earlier time than would normally be expected.

However, strong equity markets in 1992 and 1993 have provided fresh exploration and new capital funds to the industry and resulted in the discovery and development of a new generation of mines such as Kanowna Belle, Mount Todd, Henty, Bronzewing, Mt. McClure and Cadia Hill.

The boom of the 1980s is reminiscent of Australia's first gold boom of 1880 to 1903. During both periods, Australian production soared rapidly as scores of small, high-grade projects reached production early and profits were maximized by processing the highest-grade ore at the highest production level sustainable. For some reason, the Australians have a go-for-broke approach to mining, placing return of capital ahead of mine life and overall profitability. If you look at the average mine life in Australia, you would find that it is noticeably shorter than in North America.

Canada's golden shield

Some of the richest gold deposits in North America are in Canada's vast Precambrian Shield, with its veins of gold along the Porcupine-Destor, Larder Lake and Cadillac faults, where spectacular chunks of gold are often found. It is on this gold-rich fault that the mines of Timmins and Kirkland Lake in Ontario and between Rouyn-No-

20 Largest Gold Mines in Australia

Mine	Ownership	1995 Production (ounces)
Super Pit	Gold Mines of Kalgoorlie/Homestake	539,000
Boddington	Posgold/Acacia/Newcrest	388,000
Telfer	Newcrest Mining	387,000
St. Ives	Western Mining	341, 000
Mt. Leyshon	Mt. Leyshon Gold	237,000
Granites	North Flinders Mines	221,000
Granny Smith	Placer Pacific/Delta Gold	219,000
Kidston	Kidston Gold	206,000
Plutonic	Plutonic Resources	166,000
Kanowna Belle	North/Delta Gold	163,000
Hill 50	Western Mining	149,000
Agnew	Western Mining	144,000
Peak	CRA	138,000
Bluebird	St. Barbara Mines	127,000
Bronzewing	Great Central	124,000
Sons of Gwalia	Sons of Gwalia	119,000
Big Bell	Posgold	113,000
Red Dome	Niugini Mining	111,000
Yilgram Star	Gasgoyne/Orion	109,000
Hedges	Alcoa of Australia	105,000

TABLE V

randa and Val d'Or in Quebec are found. Until 1985, this country was the world's third-largest gold producer behind South Africa and Russia. But over the past decade it has slipped into fourth place. This has not been because gold production has declined, but because of larger increases in gold production in the U.S. and Australia. In 1991, gold production in Canada peaked at a record 5.6 million ounces, but has since declined to 4.8 million ounces in 1995. The giant Hemlo gold field in northern Ontario, the largest gold discovery in Canada in more than 50 years, produces 20 per cent of all the gold mined in Canada. Three mines are operating at Hemlo: Golden Giant, David Bell and Williams. All three mines achieved maximum production in 1990 and 1991 as both mill capacity and mine grade reached their peaks. For the rest of the 1990s, production from Hemlo will be stable at close to one million ounces of gold a year.

Several smaller mines came into production in recent years, including Holt McDermott in Ontario, Colomac in the Northwest Territories and the SNIP and Eskay Creek mines in British Columbia. There are 35 to 40 smaller mines in Canada, each producing less than 100,000 ounces of gold a year. Two of the nine larger mines in Canada, Campbell Red Lake and Dome, have together been producing over 500,000 ounces of gold every year for over 50 years. They are not young mines, but they still have a good deal of life left in them. Both are undergoing significant expansions and a new open pit mine has been developed at the Dome. In the rush to bring new mines to fruition, several mining companies, aside from being too optimistic, have been severely undercapitalized as well as handicapped by a shortage of qualified personnel. As a result, a substantial number of new mines have experienced start-up problems while others have been outright failures.

The Nickel Plate mine in British Columbia became a disappointment when initial reserves had to be downgraded after mining showed the grades were far more erratic than originally thought. The tailing project of ERG Resources in Ontario never reached the original design capacity before being terminated. Finally, at the Magnacon mine the mining grade was much lower than once expected and the mine was shut down early. On the disaster side of the ledger, the Tartan Lake, McLellan and Puffy Lake mines in Manitoba; Mount Skukum and Ketsa River mines in the Yukon; and the Golden Rose and Kerr mines in Ontario, all had to be shut down during 1989 as grades and tonnages fell short of expectations.

In the Northwest Territories, the Colomac mine started up in 1990 to be shut down by July 1991 as continued low gold prices rendered the operation uneconomic. A new lease on life was given to Colomac by a new management team who restarted the mine in June, 1994. In Quebec, the Bousquet No. 2 mine began operation in mid-1990 along with the Silidor mine. The SNIP mine in British Columbia started up in early 1991 while Eskay Creek, with three million ounces of gold and 100 million ounces of silver, had a very successful start of production in 1995.

The end of the 1980s brought to an end the tax incentives offered by the federal government to encourage Canadians to invest in new mining ventures. Dubbed the flow-through tax scheme, individual

20 Largest Gold Mines in Canada

Mine	Location	Ownership	1995 Production (ounces)
Williams	Ontario	Teck/Homestake Mining	405,000
Campbell Red Lake	Ontario	Placer Dome	324,000
Dome	Ontario	Placer Dome	256,000
Golden Giant	Ontario	Battle Mountain Gold	234,000
Bousquet 1 & 2	Quebec	Barrick Gold	220,000
Doyon	Quebec	Barrick Gold/Cambior	219,000
Eskay Creek	B.C.	Prime Resources	197,000
Lupin	NWT	Echo Bay Mines	172,000
LaRonde	Quebec	Agnico Eagle	167,000
David Bell	Ontario	Teck/Homestake Mining	159,000
Snip	B.C.	Cominco/Prime Resources	128,000
Con Mine	NWT	Miramar	123,000
Detour Lake	Ontario	Placer Dome	121,000
Colomac	NWT	Royal Oak	118,000
Hoyle Pond	Ontario	Kinross Gold	92,000
Giant Mine	NWT	Royal Oak Mines	91,000
Nickel Plate	B.C.	Homestake Mining	91,000
Kiena	Quebec	Placer Dome	87,000
Hope Brook	Newfoundland	Royal Oak Mines	82,000
Pamour	Ontario	Royal Oak Mines	80,000

TABLE VI

investors could write off up to 133 per cent of their investment in Canadian exploration against their tax bill. The mining flow-through tax shelters raised $3 billion between 1983 and 1989 for gold exploration in Canada. The death of the tax incentives has had a severe impact on junior exploration companies who have relied almost exclusively on them to raise capital. Exploration activity in Canada has declined dramatically, a situation that is reflected in the lack of any major discoveries since Eskay Creek in 1989. However, by late 1995 it was becoming evident that equity investors who had made money in offshore exploration ventures were willing to again risk more capital to explore back home.

Canadian gold production received a much-needed boost when Eskay Creek came into production in early 1995, but it will continue to fall gradually since the number of significant gold discoveries has fallen off in the past four years.

The Pacific Rim's "ring of fire"

The decade of the 1980s has also seen the discovery of major gold ore bodies in the "ring of fire," a chain of islands stretching from the south of New Zealand northward through Fiji before swinging west and north through Vanuatu and the Solomon Islands and, finally, Papua New Guinea and Indonesia. These islands are located along the contact point of the Australasian and Pacific tectonic plates, which stimulate volcanic activity. It has been known since the 1880s that Papua New Guinea has gold resources. In fact, the birth of one of today's largest gold mining companies — the Canadian firm Placer Dome — can be traced to placer mining in Papua New Guinea. Located there also, the fabulously rich Porgera project, owned equally by Placer Pacific and MIM Holdings, and the Renison Goldfields produced over 1.5 million ounces of gold in 1993, although the mine is now maturing and production had declined to 850,000 ounces in 1995. Finally, the smaller but still very large projects of Misima and Hidden Valley are also both likely to produce 300 thousand to 500 thousand ounces of gold a year.

The granddaddy of all Papua New Guinea's deposits has to be Lihir Island owned by Rio Tinto Zinc and Niugini Mining. With over 40 million ounces of gold in reserve, it is thought to be the largest gold deposit ever found outside of South Africa. The project's development poses some serious challenges to RTZ. Its ore is highly complex and the volcano from which it came is still hot. The cost of putting Lihir into production is likely to exceed $1 billion (U.S.).

If there is any region in the world where massive discoveries are likely to be made, it is in the "ring of fire." The area has been barely touched by modern exploration technology, but the geology of the region and the amount of money now being spent on exploration could make it a significant player in the gold world in the 1990s.

The massive potential of the "ring of fire" is currently being demonstrated by the ongoing exploration news coming from Busang, located on the island of East Kalimantan, Indonesia. Busang means "hill" or "ridge" and is located 150 kilometres inland from the east coast. In early 1995, a small Canadian junior exploration company called Bre-X Minerals Ltd. uncovered what appears to be an elliptical-shaped deposit up to 7.5 kilometres long by three kilometres wide. Drilling is ongoing but recent engineering estimates based on work to date in mid-1996 indicate an in-situ open-pittable resource of about 47 million ounces. For perspective, this is a larger number

20 Largest Gold Mines in the Rest of the World

Mine	Location	Ownership	1995 Production (ounces)
Grasberg/Ertsberg	Indonesia	Freeport McMoran C&G/ Gov't/Bakrie	1,310,000
Ashanti	Ghana	Ashanti	937,000
Porgera	PNG	Renison/Placer/Highland/Gov't.	849,000
Yanacocha	Peru	Newmont/Buenaventura/BRGM/IFC	552,000
Ok Tedi	PNG	BHP/Inmet/Gov't.	482,000
Kelian	Indonesia	CRA/Buana	369,000
Kori Kollo	Bolivia	Battle Mountain/Zeland Mines	339,000
Misima	PNG	Placer/Gov't.	331,000
Igarapé Bahia	Brazil	CVRD	324,200
La Coipa	Chile	Placer Dome/TVX Gold	282,000
Hishikari	Japan	Sumitomo	263,000
Teberebie	Ghana	Pioneer/Gov't.	235,000
Morro Velho	Brazil	Minorco/Bozano Simonsen	224,000
Syama	Mali	BHP/Gov't./IFC	197,000
El Indio	Chile	Barrick Gold	192,000
Omai	Guyana	Cambior/Golden Star/Gov't.	175,000
Mahd Ad-Dahab	Saudi Arabia	General Petroleum & Mineral	170,000
Morro do Ouro	Brazil	RTZ/TVX Gold/Montana Power/AAIC	162,000
Fazenda Brasileiro	Brazil	CVRD	151,000
Mt. Muro	Indonesia	Aurora Gold	138,000

TABLE VII

of ounces than Barrick Gold's entire reserve base. A recent tour by mining analysts has led to speculation of a potential for 150 million ounces which could make this the largest gold find since South Africa's Witwatersrand basin was discovered at the start of this century. This discovery has caused Bre-X's stock value to soar and, in a little over a year, the company's value has reached $5 billion (U.S.). This is a higher value than all but a few of the major gold producers. This success story has understandably spawned a lot of "me too" Indonesian exploration plays and excitement on the equity market. The other great example of Indonesia's gold potential comes from Freeport's Grasberg copper mine in Irian Jaya. In 1995, over 1.3 million ounces of gold were produced as a byproduct of this massive copper mine.

Unfortunately, all of these golden promises may never be fully realized due to the complex and backward political system in some of the islands. In Papua New Guinea, Bougainville, another great copper-gold operation, has been shut down since early 1989 and is one of the most obvious casualties of internal political warfare. Quite apart from this internecine warfare between hundreds of tribes living on the various islands, there is a clash between 20th-century technology and entrepreneurship and a people who don't necessarily accept the governments or the new economic and social order that is being imposed upon them. It is unlikely that this will be resolved in the near future, which means the mining of the region's gold will be hampered. From the investor's standpoint, it would be wise to have only a small percentage of one's portfolio invested in the region.

Brazil's garimpeiros

Brazil reached new production highs when it produced slightly more than three million ounces of gold in 1988. Almost 80 per cent of production comes from the so-called "informal sector," the garimpeiros who work small placer operations. The formal gold mining companies account for only 20 per cent of the country's gold production. One lesson from the California gold boom of 1847 to 1855, which was much like today's Brazilian gold rush, is that most of the easily accessible deposits are usually worked out within 10 years. The discovery of gold attracts thousands of prospectors, adventurers and merchants who descend on an area to make their fortunes. In the California gold boom, 100,000 prospectors flocked to the California mountains; close to one million garimpeiros are now working the deposits of the Amazon Basin.

Furthermore, just as in California, the frantic activity of the garimpeiros is creating serious environmental concern. They've created giant holes, like the hole at Sierra Pelada, that have become unstable due to soil erosion and overmining. The pit walls are crumbling, sliding down to the bottom, burying people who dare work in the mine. More damaging, the garimpeiros have used mercury amalgamation to recover the alluvial gold. Through carelessness, ignorance or mere nonchalance, the mercury has spread through fish into the Amazon food chain. The mercury contamination of the Amazon River has been found to be significantly higher than permitted by the World Health Organization. While the Brazilian government formally banned the use of mercury in gold production in June, 1988, the garimpeiros, who can easily find mercury on the black market, have largely ignored the edict.

Because of the general state of the economy in Brazil, gold production has already fallen by over 30 per cent in the last five years. The formal sector continues to increase production, and a new mining code along with privatization measures undertaken by some of the large landholders, such as CVRD, will increase the formal sector's role. Furthermore, major international companies have been spending serious exploration dollars in Brazil but so far have been coming up blank, in part because the jungle cover makes it difficult to readily explore the area. Overall, Brazilian gold production will probably grow slowly from the current low level of 2.2 million ounces a year.

The resurgence of Chile's gold mines

Chilean gold production is dominated by the large El Indio mine now owned by Barrick Gold. Located high in the Andes Mountains between 14,800 feet and 16,200 feet, El Indio is in some ways comparable to the Nevada discoveries in the 19th century. With grades running in the thousands of ounces per ton in some areas, the mine continues to be a golden marvel. The whole country is waking up from a long period of underinvestment first brought about by the Communist regime under Salvador Allende and then by the prolonged malaise under the dictatorial rule of General Augusto Pinochet. The country has tremendous geological potential and is now being actively explored by more than three dozen international companies. In 1991, Placer Dome and TVX brought the La Coipa project into commercial production. With exploration on the rise and a more favourable political environment, it would not be surprising if Chilean gold production increased considerably from the current level of 1.6 million ounces a year. But Chile is first and foremost a copper province and it is very unlikely that it will develop into another Nevada.

The awakening of Peru

Till the early 1990s, Peru was simply too dangerous for most companies to consider sending geologists into the field, as Marxist guerrillas were active in many areas. However, Chile's example, combined with a new pro-business president and a decline in rebel activities, has vastly improved the climate so that today, Peru is a major centre for international exploration activity.

The example of Peru's potential has been Newmont Mining's success at the new Yanacocha Mine in northern Peru, which produced 500,000 ounces in 1995 and is being further expanded. But the best endorsement of Peru has to be Barrick Gold's mid-1996 offer to buy out a junior exploration company called Arequipa Resources for almost $1 billion, based on a promising property portfolio and a limited number of drill holes.

Global mine production

Worldwide gold mine production is levelling off at a pace that will be nearly double 1980 production. Any further increases will have to come from significant new discoveries over the next five years. While this is clearly not impossible, it is not likely to happen. The world has already seen billions of dollars spent on gold exploration in the past 10 years with tremendous results. But even a discovery such as Busang represents the replacement of only one year of global gold-mine production. More massive discoveries are needed. We can expect diminishing returns from any exploration activity as each new dollar is spent farther and farther from an existing prospect or a marginal known ore body. But no one really knows when or where the next Witwatersrand or Carlin Trend will be found.

Western world gold consumption

On the other side of the gold market, the demand for gold is made up of three distinct and different components. The central banks, which are prime hoarders and suppliers of gold, are also major contributors to gold demand. Second, there is the demand for gold for fabrication in jewelry, electronics, dentistry, medals and metallic coins. The third component is the investment demand for gold bullion and gold coins. These markets exhibit entirely different supply and price relationships.

Gold investment activity has an unconventional, upward-sloping relationship with the price of gold — as the price of gold rises, so does demand. What other commodity are you aware of that people rush out to buy at ever higher prices? Gold jewelry, on the other hand, follows the conventional supply-price relationship. Demand for jewelry made from high-karat gold, which represents as much as 60 per cent of the fabricated gold products, follows an unusually

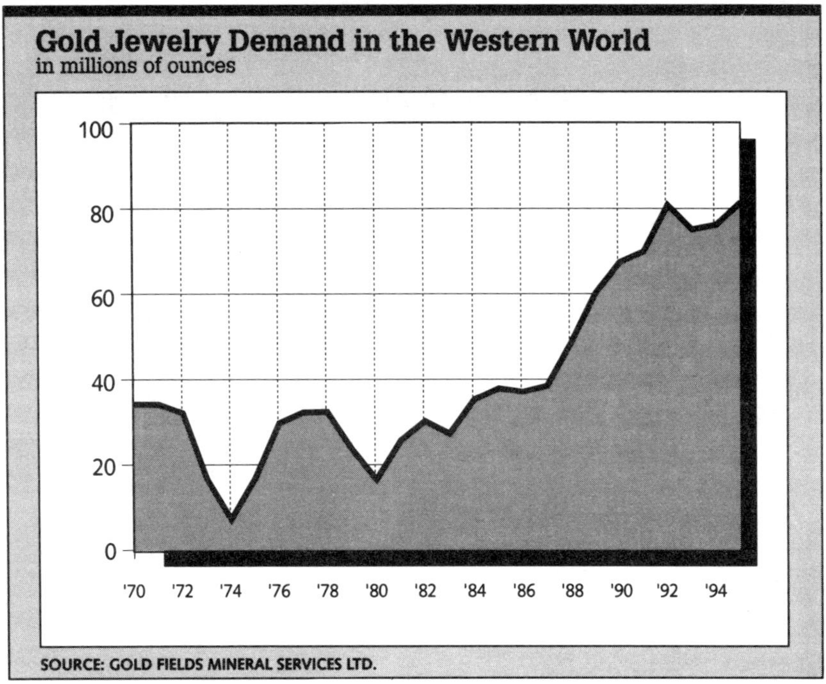

CHART IV

well-defined linear relationship to the price of gold — when the price of jewelry rises, demand falls.

Global demand for fabricated gold rose strongly in the past decade and a half, from 30.4 million ounces in 1980 to an estimated 96.7 million ounces in 1995. This strong growth was driven mostly by the insatiable appetite for gold in the Far East and consistently low gold prices in both U.S. dollars and local currencies. There has been a resurgence of demand from the Middle East, China and the Russian Federation. This unusual demand for fabricated gold, especially in the last three years, has been responsible for keeping the price of gold from falling below $330 (U.S.) at a time when the supply has reached new highs.

Gold in jewelry

When the price of gold hit its peak in 1980, the demand for gold jewelry dropped to a low of four million ounces that year. But over the past decade jewelry has been the mainstay of gold demand, topping 81.6 million ounces in 1995. Demand for jewelry has a dual personality. In developing countries, gold is bought as an invest-

Gold Fabrication Demand in the Western World

IN MILLIONS OF OUNCES

	1986	1987	1988	1989	1990	1991	1992	1993	1994	1995
Developed countries										
Jewelry	18.7	18.5	21.3	25.8	27.8	28.3	29.7	28.6	28.6	28.9
Electronics	3.8	3.8	4.0	4.1	4.4	4.5	4.2	4.5	4.8	5.2
Dentistry	1.5	1.4	1.5	1.5	1.6	1.6	1.8	1.7	1.8	1.8
Other industrial	1.6	1.7	1.7	1.8	1.8	1.8	1.9	1.9	2.0	2.1
Medal sales	0.1	0.2	0.2	0.3	0.3	0.3	0.2	0.1	0.1	0.1
Coin sales	9.6	5.3	2.8	2.8	2.9	3.9	2.5	3.1	1.9	2.4
Subtotal	35.4	31.0	31.6	36.4	38.7	40.4	40.3	40.0	39.1	40.5
Developing countries										
Jewelry	19.6	21.2	28.8	36.1	38.7	40.8	50.4	46.7	47.8	52.7
Electronics	0.2	0.3	0.3	0.3	0.4	0.4	0.4	0.5	0.6	0.7
Dentistry	0.1	0.1	0.1	0.2	0.2	0.2	0.2	0.2	0.2	0.2
Other industrial	0.2	0.2	0.2	0.3	0.3	0.3	0.7	1.1	1.2	1.2
Medal sales	0.3	0.3	0.4	0.4	0.4	0.6	0.7	0.7	0.7	1.0
Coin Sales	1.6	1.2	1.3	1.5	0.9	0.6	0.4	0.5	0.6	0.4
Subtotal	22.1	23.3	31.2	38.7	40.9	42.9	52.8	49.6	50.9	56.4
Total	57.4	54.3	62.8	75.1	79.6	83.3	93.1	89.6	90.2	96.7

SOURCE: GOLD FIELDS MINERAL SERVICES LTD. 1996

TABLE VIII

ment, not simply for decoration. The rise in consumption is particularly evident in the Far East, where people prefer jewelry made of 22- or 24-karat gold. Also, India has become more prosperous in the 1980s and has more than doubled its jewelry consumption over the decade. The most dramatic rise rests within the Pacific Rim countries. These countries have more than tripled their jewelry consumption in the last 10 years to about 26 million ounces in 1995.

The industrial countries are predominantly a market for jewelry of lower-quality gold. This market recovered throughout the 1980s as economic conditions improved and has remained fairly stable in the 1990s at around 28 million ounces a year.

In the coming decade, jewelry consumption will continue to be dominated by the U.S. dollar gold price. Should the U.S. dollar continue its downward trend against currencies of Japan and Germany, the price of gold in these countries will make it even more attractive and could spur sales. However, a stronger U.S. dollar gold price would cause jewelry demand to drop. General economic conditions will have a secondary effect on demand for gold for jewelry, but will be particularly significant in developed countries where jewelry popularity depends on disposable income.

Jewelry demand will continue if currency rates remain stable and the price of gold hovers around $375 (U.S.). If the price of gold climbed to $600 (U.S.), jewelry demand would fall by at least half of the current level.

Gold in electronics

Nearly six million ounces of gold are used every year by the electronics industry, making electronics the most important primary industrial user. Gold's superior physical properties, including its excellent electrical conductivity and resistance to corrosion as well as the ease with which it can be worked, have found extensive applications in the printed circuit boards, microchips and connectors required in a variety of electronic products. But the use of gold in the electronics industry depends on the health of the industry itself and was severely affected by the downturn of 1985 and the 1981-82 recession. Furthermore, during the course of the 1980s the industry has begun to use less gold in each product it makes, employing silver, copper and palladium alloys instead. The industry has also become more selective in its gold plating while reducing the thickness of gold coatings.

These structural changes have worked their way through the industry and gold usage can be expected to grow in line with the growth of the electronics industry. Overall, gold consumption in the electronics industries in the 1990s is likely to be stable at five to six million ounces a year. The increased demand from new electronics products is likely to be offset by some loss in the defence and aerospace industries.

Gold in dentistry

Gold has been used in dentistry for well over four thousand years. The Pharaohs of Egypt recognized that gold's strength, resistance to corrosion and its malleability make it ideal to plug a bad tooth. Recently, gold has been facing stiff competition from other dental alloys such as platinum and palladium and the increasing trend toward ceramics. From an average annual consumption of 2.4 million ounces in the 1970s, gold use in dentistry has fallen to an average of 2.0 million ounces in the 1990s. In 1995, gold use in dentistry remained at 2.0 million ounces a year, with two-thirds of that used in the U.S., Germany and Japan.

Even though gold is still superior in its reliability and durability, continued reduction in the use of gold in dentistry is likely to persist. Gold is more expensive and dental insurance plans are reducing their coverage amounts. Decreased consumption in developed countries may be tempered by a gently rising trend in developing countries such as Korea, where gold use in dentistry is still seen as a sign of wealth and remains cheaper than the alternatives. Over the 1990s, the consumption of gold in dentistry is expected to remain at current levels.

Other industrial and decorative uses

Gold demand for industrial and decorative uses other than jewelry, electronics and dentistry has been relatively constant for the past 20 years. From a peak consumption of 2.5 million ounces in 1979, demand fell to only 1.7 million ounces by 1982. However, consumption has since steadily climbed to the current 3.3 million ounces a year. The U.S. and Japan take more than half of this gold, using it mainly in large architectural and decorative work as well as for personal accessories such as gold watches, pens and costume jewelry.

In architecture, gold's reflective properties are finding increasing appeal, particularly with the new environmental conscientiousness against the heavy use of electric power in air conditioning. Gold plating in windows reflects the sun's rays and reduces the need for air conditioning. The use of gold on large office buildings may increase, but decorative gold plating remains the largest single component of this sector. In fact, one ounce of gold can be hammered down to a single sheet covering 30 square metres, almost 1,000 square feet, or made into a hair-thin wire that can stretch for a mile.

In France, in celebration of the 200th anniversary of the French Revolution, there was extensive refurbishing of the glorious monuments erected in the 17th and 18th centuries with completely new gold cladding. As any visitor to Paris can tell you, the effect is particularly stunning on a sunny day. Over the 1990s, it is likely that gold consumption in this sector will reflect economic conditions.

Official coins and medals

Official gold coins and medals, such as the Canadian Maple Leaf, or imitation coins are often considered to be one segment of gold demand. But in reality they respond to quite a different demand-price relationship. The demand for medals and imitation coins is closely related to jewelry demand, particularly in developing countries where they appeal to the same buyer. On the other hand, the demand for gold coins moves with the dollar gold price along with investment demand.

Demand for medals and imitation coins suffered a severe decline during the 1980s. From an average annual consumption of 1.1 million ounces in the 1970s, demand dropped to an annual average of 643,000 ounces in the 1980s. Much of this fall reflects declining sales in the Middle East due to weak oil prices throughout the 1980s. Recently, there have been some positive signs of a re-emergence of the Middle East market, but it is likely to prove subdued for as long as oil prices remain low. At barely 1 per cent of the total gold demand market, this sector is not significant in overall demand.

The official coin market is really a segment of investment demand. Gold coins can be bought by the small investor who can purchase gold in denominations that he can afford. The coins can be easily carried and sold. The average annual consumption rate in the 1970s was approximately five million ounces. However, this figure masks some very strong years, such as 1978 and 1979, when demand reached 10.6 million to 10.9 million ounces. The 1980s saw a slight increase in average annual demand of 5.3 million ounces. When compared to expanding mine production, gold coin demand represents less and less of total gold demand as it is gradually being squeezed by demand for gold jewelry and bullion bars, particularly in the Far East.

This erosion of interest in gold coins, particularly in industrialized countries, is a reflection of the general deflationary trend of the 1980s. This became particularly clear after the October, 1987, stock market crash. Gold coin sales for 1990 fell to a low of 3.8 million ounces but rebounded to 4.5 million ounces in 1991.

Over the next decade, gold coins are going to continue to play the investment role that they have played over the past 20 years for the individual investor and will likely represent 10 per cent of overall gold demand.

Investment demand

Gold bullion demand exhibits a pattern that is contrary to the most common law of economics. Instead of demand dropping as the price rises, gold bullion demand has soared with every major gold price rally. In 1980, when gold reached its highest price of the decade, investment demand jumped to 10.9 million ounces. Yet in the following two years, as gold prices fell, investment demand plummeted while hoarders dumped 8.6 million ounces of gold into the market in 1981 and 6.4 million ounces in 1982. The pattern continued when gold rallied in 1983, sparking investment demand of 10.9 million ounces, just 32,000 ounces shy of the previous record level. Looking at the entire decade of the 1980s, you will find that net investment demand comes to a grand total of zero ounces — there has been as much selling as there has been buying.

Actually, much of that can be blamed on gold loans, not the buying and selling of skittish individuals. The production already presold by the producers in the late 1980s will not have to be sold again when these loans are repaid in the early 1990s. It is estimated that as much as 10 per cent to 15 per cent of the next four years' production has been presold in this manner. (Gold loans will be discussed in detail in Chapter 7.)

As for individual investors, the pattern that we have seen in high-karat jewelry demand is starting to emerge for gold bars. The rising wealth of the Far East, particularly Japan and Taiwan, is allowing investors to build their investments in gold. In Japan, the individual gold accumulation program, started over 10 years ago by Tanaka Bank and adopted by other Japanese banks, has grown dramatically in the past two years. Bank customers are encouraged to invest in gold with the same ease they might use to deposit their savings into a savings account. There are now more than 300,000 accounts open with an average of 10,000 yen being deposited into each account for the purchase of gold every month. At current gold prices, this adds up to a total gold off-take of over one million ounces a year.

With inflation remaining subdued in North America, investment demand has been low for several years. This lack of inflation, combined with a high real rate of interest, has made owning gold less attractive than in the early 1980s. In Japan, on the other hand, the price of gold in yen is at a 10-year low while the real rate of interest has remained stable. This makes gold very attractive to Japanese investors.

Overview of global gold supply and demand

During the 1980s, there was strong growth in the global supply of gold. This growth was spurred by a relatively high real price for gold, the development of new exploration technology and the application of new production processes including heap-leaching, bulk mining and autoclaving. Gold production in the 1990s will continue to rise for at least another three years, although at a much lower rate, at which time it is likely to taper off and start to decline. This scenario is likely to occur no matter what happens to the gold price throughout the decade. In fact, should the gold price fall precipitously, gold production would probably increase as miners scramble to cut costs and increase the grade to the mill to stay profitable. On the other hand, the immediate impact of a strongly rising gold price would be a decline in production as more marginal ore would then become profitable.

On the other side of the market, the demand for gold is driven by a split personality. Jewelry demand, which accounts for 70 per cent to 80 per cent of average annual demand, moves with the dollar gold price. When the price of gold in dollars is low, jewelry demand will usually put a floor on that dollar gold price. Of course, the demand for jewelry itself is governed by worldwide economic conditions which also have an impact on the floor price of gold. It is gold bullion demand that intensifies volatility in the gold market. Investment demand kicks in to push prices higher as the gold price rallies and disappears at the bottom of cycles to deepen the fall in the gold price. This side of gold demand is erratic and unpredictable, being driven by a series of factors which will be examined in the next chapter.

Gold bullion demand plays only a minor role in global gold demand or supply, yet it has provided the gold market with the roller coaster price movements of 1973, 1974, 1979 and 1980, as well as the two bull markets of 1982 to 1983 and 1985 to 1987. As well, it was gold bullion demand that caused the contraction in gold supply over 1981 and 1982. This pattern is likely to continue in the 1990s and any large changes in the dollar gold price will depend on disturbances in international economics and politics.

CHAPTER 4

Gold, Governments and the Economy

GOLD RESPONDS TO MANY more pressures than the simple forces of supply and demand, unlike any other commodity in which you can invest. As an investor in gold, you cannot ignore the activities of governments, political unrest or economic forces such as inflation, interest rates and the strength of the U.S. dollar. These have an overwhelming impact on the future direction of the price of gold and, therefore, on the decisions of gold producers to expand their mining operations and the desire of anyone to buy or sell gold, whether he or she is an investor, jeweller or computer manufacturer.

Can governments fix the price of gold?

In fact, the price of gold was fixed for centuries: Britain fixed the gold price from 1717 to 1914, the U.S. took over in 1934 and kept it fixed for another 36 years until mounting inflation pressure forced it to allow gold to establish its own price in the marketplace in 1970. But what about today? Could the U.S. reassert its worldwide financial supremacy by fixing the gold price?

The U.S. and Canada are suffering under the strain of massive budget and trade deficits and the mountains of national, corporate and personal debt are starting to crumble. Inflation is stuck at 4 per cent to 5 per cent a year, which may seem harmless after the inflation of the early 1980s but it is still too high to produce long-term financial stability. Even at this rate it takes only 10 years for the value of your money to depreciate by 50 to 60 per cent. Under these precarious economic conditions it would be monetary suicide for the U.S. to try to relink its currency to gold; it could result in a severe recession, if not a depression. Since either scenario would be political suicide, and painful for all of us, it is highly unlikely the U.S. will return to the gold standard.

It isn't impossible for governments to influence the gold price through their central banks, however. Their influence just doesn't last long; it would be like trying to stop the tide with sandbags. Why would governments, particularly the U.S., intervene in the workings of the free market at all? Governments manipulate the price of gold for the same reasons they intervene in the currency market — mainly to maintain an orderly market. In 1985, when the Japanese yen launched an assault against the American dollar, it marched from as high as 260 yen to the dollar to a historic high value of 123 to the dollar less than two years later. There was very little the U.S. government could do beyond smoothing the volatility. Corporations and individuals have far more money with which to sway the value of currencies than the foreign funds the U.S. government holds in its reserves.

If the currency market is about to turn or there is some hesitation one way or another, governments can take advantage of the indecision by strategically moving with vigour and giving the market an impetus to move one way or the other. But government cannot buck the trend of public demand for long.

Anybody less than 60 years old in Canada or the U.S. has known principally one economic condition — inflation. Very few people who actually experienced the Great Depression of the 1930s are left in the active work force or in politics. The survivors are well into retirement but still willing to recount the time when everything collapsed, from wages to real estate and commodity prices. Yet it was precisely at that time that gold was revalued from $20.67 (U.S.) an ounce to $35 (U.S.) an ounce. The U.S. central bank was able to print new money and bail out a banking system and economy that was near bankruptcy.

Gold serves a role during a depression when there isn't enough money and credit to fuel the economy, and in times of inflation when there is too much money. Indeed, over the past 20 years it has become apparent that the most important factors affecting the gold price are:

- total world money supply
- real rate of interest
- exchange value of the U.S. dollar
- monetization of debt
- worldwide economic activity
- commodity prices
- political tensions

Total world money supply

Historically, under the gold standard the money supply is fixed in relation to the amount of gold available in the central banks. An increase in gold supply at a time of full employment and maximum economic activity would generate inflation by feeding the demand for goods. The simple debasement of the currency would produce inflation by pushing up the real cost of goods. A loss of gold reserves would immediately manifest itself in a loss of currency, curtailment of economic activity and deflation.

In the fiat paper system now in use worldwide, the creation of money is a decision made by a few central bankers. In effect, the value of your currency is in the hands of a few men and women not only in your own country but also in other countries. While most of these people are not elected, they are appointed by politicians who have to seek re-election. You may recall George Bernard Shaw's words: "If you must choose between placing your trust in government or placing your trust in gold, then, gentlemen, I strongly advise you to place your trust in gold."

In the early years of the paper system, the central banks maintained a tight grip on money creation through regulation of the banking system. Not so today: After 14 years of deregulation, there have been fundamental structural changes such as disintermediation of the credit markets — a way of bypassing the formal banking system to create new sources of money — and securitization of assets by banks — the bundling of debt into investment packages to create securities such as mortgage-backed securities. As a result, the links between money, economic activity, inflation and gold have become much looser. Furthermore, as international trade among countries escalates, the U.S. economy itself is more dependent than ever on economic activity worldwide.

Over the last 20 years, central bankers have been painfully aware that inflation has been the greatest threat to economic health. Since early 1990, the growth rate of money creation in the U.S. has fallen to a 30-year low, sparking concern that the central banks, particularly the U.S. Federal Reserve Bank, could be going too far in the battle against inflation.

The U.S. has become the world's largest debtor nation. It has accumulated a federal deficit of close to $5 trillion, and its annual interest on that debt for 1994 alone is over $300 billion. Budget deficits have been running at $100 billion throughout the 1980s and in the 1990s the budget deficit has averaged over $200 billion. Even though the Gramm-Rudman amendment originally called for a balanced budget by 1990, the U.S. will continue to build its deficit unless drastic cuts in spending are made. The economic plight is repeated in Canada, where the central bank has squeezed out inflation but at a terrible cost to the economy.

There are more people working in North America than at any time in history. Inflation since the early 1980s has been relatively subdued due to intense global competition. The U.S. and Canadian economies grew steadily from 1983 to 1990, the second-largest expansion in history. In 1987, we saw a stock market crash reminiscent of 1929, yet the economy continued to expand. As the new decade rolls in, North America faces three possible economic scenarios — deflation, growth without inflation or more inflation.

The last half of the 1980s was remarkable: The world experienced seven years of modestly inflationary growth in sharp contrast to the stagflation — economic stagnation combined with inflation — of the 1970s when the world's strongest economies were synchronized in their troubles.

The world was unusually lucky in the 1980s in the timing of economic growth of each country. When the U.S. and Canadian economies rebounded in 1983, the rest of the world was still deep in recession. By 1985, the U.S. economy cooled just as Japan and Germany started growing. In 1990, the European economies were strong while the North American economies were entering a recession. If this scattered global growth can be sustained, gold will probably continue to trade mainly as a commodity with the price being set by jewelry demand and economic growth. Gold as an investment would remain unattractive and the price would likely stabilize in a fairly narrow bracket of $350 (U.S.) to $400 (U.S.) per ounce.

What if the growth can't be sustained? If the world sinks into true global deflation, the price of gold would rise dramatically as worthless paper money is converted into a hard currency — gold. The price to which gold would be propelled would depend on the magnitude of the collapse. If it were restricted to only North America, gold would react only modestly, perhaps reaching $600 (U.S.) an ounce. If the entire global economy slid into depression it could reach dramatic new highs of over $1,000 (U.S.).

After a few years, as commodity prices, interest rates and economic conditions began to stabilize, the price of gold would start falling until it reached the purchasing power it has been able to maintain for centuries.

Gold and inflation

Could the world again suffer the disastrous inflation of the early 1980s? Could the producers of the horror movie *Friday the 13th* make a sequel? It can happen again but, just as in the movies, even though the villain is the same — inflation — the plot is always somewhat different. The central banks today are governed by people who do not want to repeat the errors of the 1970s. In the face of a recovering economy experiencing mild but still damaging inflation, they have few alternatives. If they tighten money supply to impede inflation they risk throwing the economy into a new recession that could force U.S. unemployment to climb to over 10 per cent. As in the past, gold will rise in price as monetary policy eases and fall as it tightens.

As a gold investor you should be aware of changes in the money supply. The money supply is the total stock of money in the economy. Too much money in relation to the stock of goods tends to push prices up, causing inflation. Too little money pushes prices down and causes unemployment.

The price of gold is heavily influenced by the U.S. money supply, especially that segment of the money supply called M1. The M1 is made up primarily of currency in circulation and deposits in chequing accounts. The world money supply is measured by adding up the M1 of the seven countries known as the Group of Seven and applying a weighting factor in proportion to their gross national products. The money created, or not created, by the U.S., Japan and the other countries can generate non-inflationary economic activity, stagflation or hyperinflation. The economic result will depend on the liquidity being generated in relation to the underlying economic and fiscal policies and the employment conditions. If the liquidity is drying up, it will reduce economic activity and decrease inflationary expectations.

The problem in trying to forecast the gold price from these economic scenarios is that the timing is uncertain. At times the money supply leads the gold price by a few months while at other times they are coincident. But over many months they move in the same direction. The question, of course, is how do you forecast money supply? The decisions of the central bankers are predicated on their views of the economy and expectations for the future. But their views are not perfect. The ultimate goal of every central bank is to generate economic growth without inflation. But if you look at their track record, there is a lot of room for improvement!

Real rate of interest

In looking at the state of the economy, the real rate of interest is measured by deducting the annualized rate of inflation over the last three months from the imputed interest rate on a 90-day government treasury bill. If inflation has been running at an annual rate of 4 per cent over the last three months while the imputed annualized return on a 90-day T-bill is 9 per cent, the real rate of interest is 5 per cent. For the past nine years, real rates of interest have been substantially higher than at any time since the 1930s. These high rates are not found in North America alone. German interest rates have been pushed to historic highs due to the heavy demand on capital created by reunification.

When global liquidity is being squeezed, as has been the case for the last three years, real rates of interest remain high. This creates a poor investment climate for gold, since bullion's main drawback is that it doesn't pay interest. Therefore, gold is more attractive at lower real rates of interest. In contrast, in the 1970s, when inflation was outpacing the return on 90-day T-bills, gold was very attractive.

Not unexpectedly, the higher real rates of interest of the past decade have dampened the volatility of gold prices. Every time the price of gold has moved up since 1981, people or institutions who invest in bonds or T-bills have been very quick to demand higher returns at this hint of rising inflation. As a result, the real rate of interest has expanded until owning gold was less attractive than switching to government T-bills. This recurring fear of inflation, along with the demands of lenders for high real rate of interest, has been one of the main forces keeping gold under $500 (U.S.) for the past 10 years.

The impact of the value of the U.S. dollar

Because gold is bought and sold in U.S. dollars, the exchange value of the U.S. dollar against the Japanese yen, the German mark or the currency of the purchaser is very important. In 1981, when the yen traded above 230 to the U.S. dollar and gold was close to $650

Gold and the Economic Environment

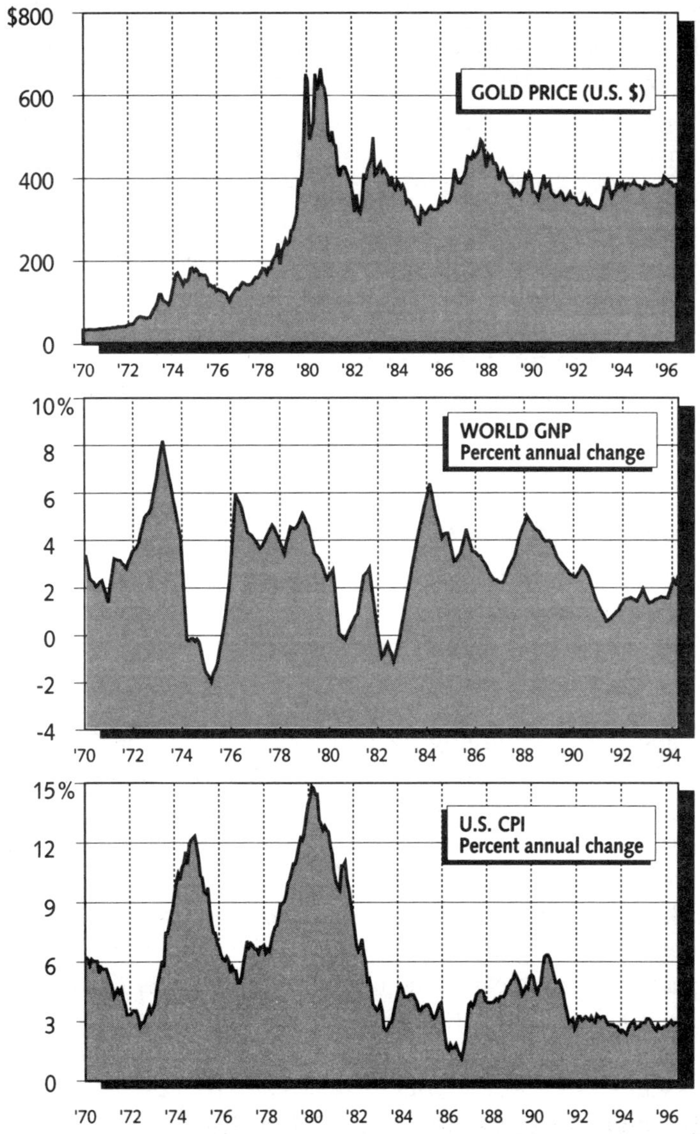

SOURCES: DATASTREAM; INTERNATIONAL MONETARY FUND; U.S. DEPARTMENT OF COMMERCE

CHART V

(U.S.) an ounce, it took over 150,000 yen to buy an ounce of gold. In the fall of 1995, with the yen trading at less than 90 yen to the dollar and gold at $385 (U.S.) an ounce, it takes less than 35,000 yen to buy the same ounce of gold. For the investor with U.S. dollars, it would be the same as gold dropping from $650 (U.S.) to $150 (U.S.).

The exchange rate also has an immediate impact on the price of gold because gold remains the ultimate world hard currency and an alternative to the world reserve currency, the dollar. It took only three years after fixed rates of exchange were abandoned in 1970 for the U.S. dollar to lose 65 per cent of its value against the Japanese yen and German mark. In those three years, the price of gold rose from $35 (U.S.) to $180 (U.S.) an ounce. From 1974 to late 1976, the dollar rallied against the yen while it stabilized against the mark; gold weakened during that time, dropping to $120 (U.S.) by 1976.

During the following three years, the dollar fell again to new lows while gold reached an all-time high of over $850 (U.S.) in January, 1980, at the same time that the dollar was bottoming against the German mark. The dollar then went through a six-year bull market which was marked by a steep bear market period for gold, which bottomed in 1982 and 1985 at about $285 an ounce. The year 1985 marked the end of the dollar rally in terms of both the Japanese yen and the German mark and the start of a steep decline which terminated in late 1987 at the same time gold hit its cyclical peak of $500 (U.S.) an ounce. The dollar then rallied against both currencies for two years before slumping again in 1991 and 1992 to the level reached in 1987. If the dollar breaks to new lows it could start a run on the currency which would encourage gold demand as Americans switch their paper money to real money.

While there is an inverse relationship between the gold price and the exchange rate of the dollar vis-à-vis the yen or the mark, it is far from perfect. The yen peaked in late 1978 against the dollar but the gold price did not peak until early 1980. In 1983, the gold price staged a strong rally to $500 (U.S.) while the dollar was in a bull market against both the yen and the mark. Unfortunately, the exchange value of the U.S. dollar cannot be used to predict short-term changes in the price of gold.

Looking at the relationship between the yen, the mark and the dollar again, we see that there are two points that are readily apparent: First, the dollar has been in a downtrend against the yen and mark for the last quarter century. This decline, or devaluation, of the U.S. dollar is reminiscent of the fall of the British pound, then the world currency, in the 1930s and 1940s against the dollar itself.

Second, once an intermediate trend has been established by the dollar it tends to last two to five years. The yen has seen three sharp bull markets against the U.S. dollar; each has been of about two years' duration — 1971 to 1973, 1977 to 1979 and 1985 to 1987. Each of these bull markets was followed by a three- to five-year rally by the U.S. dollar. However, the dollar rally that started in 1988 seems to have been aborted after only two years as the dollar resumed its fall against the yen and the mark in 1990. This is very bullish for gold as it gets cheaper in these currencies.

Monetization of debt

Throughout the 1980s, it has been predicted that the massive federal fiscal deficits and attendant debt creation could only lead to the devaluation of the dollar, a rapid increase in inflation and record high gold prices. While we did see $500 (U.S.) gold briefly in 1983 and 1987, inflation has been subdued since the early 1980s. What happened?

Part of the answer lies in how the debt is created. It has little impact on inflation if the debt is created by government borrowing, since the government is spending money that already exists rather than creating new money. However, if the government cannot borrow enough money it can require the central bank to cover its debt with newly printed dollar bills. This process, by which the central bank purchases government debt in return for dollar bills, is called the monetization of debt.

The degree to which the government resorts to the monetization of debt is another indicator of the long-term behaviour of inflation or deflation and its effect on the gold price. In 1958, the U.S. government began a 20-year program of monetization of debt. In 1970, after more than 12 years of inflationary pressure, the U.S. government was forced to free-float the dollar. The value of the dollar plummeted while gold shot up from $35 (U.S.) to over $90 (U.S.) in only a few months. This debt monetization cycle reached its peak in early 1977, but continued at a good pace until early 1980 when Paul Volcker was named chairman of the U.S. Federal Reserve Board. Volcker stepped on the brake of the money-printing machine with both feet and engineered the most severe recession the U.S. had known since before the Great Depression.

This deflationary process continued unabated until January, 1990, at which time the ratio of the Federal Reserve debt holding to the debt outstanding had fallen to a 50-year low. Is this good or bad? By mid-1992, inflation was much lower than anybody would have expected eight to 10 years ago, but the world economy was brought to the brink of a depression.

Since the monetization of debt tends to lead both gold and inflation by two to three years, it was to be expected that inflation would continue to be subdued until 1992-93. Any rise in the price of gold could be limited by the disinflationary impact of the fiscal policy of the past 12 years. However, we have turned the corner. The U.S. Federal Reserve started to monetize debt in the spring of 1991 in the face of an extremely weak economy and the lowest growth in money supply for over 50 years. How far they will carry this round of monetization will, in part, determine the ultimate end of inflation and the peak price of gold.

One thing is certain: Not to have started this monetization process would have been suicidal for the U.S. for it would have led the economy into a 1930's-style depression. This would have resulted in the complete loss of confidence in the financial system caused by bank closures, massive write-downs on loans from soured corporate takeovers and write-offs of loans to the Third World. Foreigners and U.S. citizens could lose faith in the U.S. dollar and shy away from purchasing American debt. At that point, if the U.S. government panics and tries to engineer a comeback by printing money, the gold market would respond very rapidly and gold prices would jump. When private investors saw the growth in U.S. debt monetization from 1966 to 1968 they purchased about 112 million ounces of gold that was being sold by world central banks at $35 (U.S.) an ounce. Realizing that they were in danger of losing all their gold reserves, the central banks closed the gold purchase window, freed the price and devalued the U.S. dollar.

Europe today is at the mercy of the German Central Bank which, out of fear of inflation, is keeping interest rates so high that it is preventing economic recovery elsewhere, particularly in the U.K. and France. While it is expected that Germany will win the battle against inflation, it would be tragic if it lost the war and precipitated a global crisis.

Worldwide economic activity

Since gold is an international commodity, its price is also closely tied to the strength of the world economy. The relationship between global money supply and the world gross national product (GNP) or industrial production can be seen in Chart V. Money creation is followed within 12 to 18 months by a rise in GNP, while a decrease in money will be shadowed by a drop in world GNP. The world industrial production is itself mirrored a year or so later by world exports; interestingly, exports seemed to peak at almost the same time as the peaks in the gold price in 1974, 1980 and 1987. The only time the relationship did not hold was in 1983, when gold peaked but world trade did not hit its high until the end of the following year.

There are very good reasons why gold and exports will peak together at a late stage in the economic cycle. In the early stage of a recovery, the unemployment rate is still high and the pressure on prices is lower because there are ample raw materials and labour available. Meanwhile, there is ample industrial capacity and the level of imports and exports is relatively low. As demand picks up, an increase in production follows; the demand for raw materials increases and the available labour starts to shrink, producing the first signs of inflationary pressure.

As more countries join in the economic good times, raw materials prices are pushed up and inflationary pressure increases worldwide as producers around the world begin searching for materials and labour at the same time. This boom is coincidental with the peak in employment and industrial activity. The people who are employed can afford to pamper themselves, perhaps with a gold necklace or watch. Jewelry demand starts to build and investors, skittish about inflation, hoard a bit of gold bullion. So the price of gold is pushed up, just as it was in 1974 and 1987.

While there is a relation between world trade, industrial production and gold prices, it's one where money growth is associated with expanding industrial production and world trade. There isn't a direct relationship between exports and gold which we can use to predict gold prices.

Gold and the price of oil

The clearest example of the relationship between gold and the price of other commodities in an inflationary environment could be seen at the time of the Civil War in the U.S. This was the only time in

American history prior to 1970 that the gold price was allowed to fluctuate freely. As discussed in Chapter 3, throughout those 20 years, gold marched in step with the movement in price of a basket of commodities. Because of the pressures of the war and its demand for commodities such as iron, copper and lead for war materials, commodity prices rose steadily. In the 1970s, gold rose from its fixed depression low of $35 (U.S.) to over $850 (U.S.). For a while, oil and gold moved together as precursors of inflation, moving steadily up. Before long it became obvious oil was just another commodity with a long elasticity curve.

When the 1981-82 recession hit, the countries of the Organization of Petroleum Exporting Countries (OPEC) found themselves in the unenviable position of having to reduce output by 50 per cent and still see prices drop from over $40 (U.S.) to $10 (U.S.) a barrel. Oil has recovered to around $20 (U.S.), where it has held more or less steady for the past five years. Gold dropped to $285 (U.S.) an ounce in 1985 before recovering to hover at $350 (U.S.). This mimicry convinced many people that the price of gold and oil should always trade in step. But there are major differences between the two commodities. In inflationary times, gold behaves like a commodity; in deflationary times, gold behaves like the strong currency it is — not as a commodity. This abrupt difference can be seen in the numbers of barrels of oil you could buy with one ounce of gold over the last inflation-deflation cycle of the 1920s and 1930s.

Gold was fixed at $20.67 (U.S.) an ounce until 1933 and at $35 (U.S.) until 1974. But during the Second World War, an ounce of gold would have bought as little as 10 barrels of oil. In 1980, at the most recent inflationary peak, that same gold would have bought only 20 barrels. As inflation began to ebb and the depression of the 1930s came into full force, the ratio of oil to gold soared to 40 to 1. History seems to be repeating itself as the ratio consistently moves higher. The "normal" ratio seems to be 20 to 25 barrels of oil to an ounce of gold, but in periods of extreme conditions, particularly deflation, it tends to go much higher. Should the world experience another severe recession, the ratio could reach the same 40-to-1 ratio seen in the 1930s. This implies prices of $10 (U.S.) to $15 (U.S.) for a barrel of oil and $400 (U.S.) to $600 (U.S.) for an ounce of gold.

Political tensions

For most people, the price of gold is seen as a barometer of international anxiety. But over the past years the eruption of conflicts in the Middle East, the Falklands and Afghanistan as well as a scattering of tense political situations around the world have not really moved the gold price as political tensions did in the 1970s. This raises questions over the role of gold as a haven in times of political tension, but Roy Jastrum in his 1977 book *The Golden Constant* has convincingly documented what he calls the "Attila effect." Historically, he says, gold has served as a financial refuge in political, economic and personal catastrophes. Then he goes on to give a few examples:

- The Latifundia passed gold bars secretly to their heirs which survived Barbarian invasions to become nobility under the Merovingien kings in the fourth century.
- White Russians fleeing from the Bolsheviks survived on treasures they carried.
- Austrian refugees, fleeing from the Nazis, often owed their survival in a new country to the golden jewelry they could carry with them.

The main point of the Attila effect is that anyone who fears the collapse of his country's government or currency will try to protect part of his wealth, and possibly save his life, by hoarding gold.

During the 1970s, particularly at the height of the oil crisis, the Arab world felt threatened by the resentment of countries which were being starved for oil by the OPEC cartel. Oil prices were extremely high and the Middle East was awash in petrodollars the Arabs believed could be made worthless by a collapse of the American dollar. To protect this wealth, the Arabs plunged into the gold market — a market that was already heated by inflation and political anxiety.

This is in stark contrast to the 1980s, with the softening of political tensions between the superpowers and the cessation of conflicts around the world such as the wars between Iran and Iraq, Vietnam and Cambodia and in Afghanistan. There has been a sharp drop in oil prices brought on by stable demand and increased production. There has also been a 10-year slump in gold prices. The Attila effect is usually confined to a specific country and will affect the gold price on a worldwide scale only if the magnitude of the demand for gold in that country overwhelms global supply. Most of the conflicts of the past decade have been local and the demand for gold bullion modest.

Over the next five to 10 years, the effect might be felt in three countries: China, Russia and South Africa. China's booming trade with the West has strengthened its internal economy, pushing inflation at a much faster pace than the government would like. Increased demand for gold by the Chinese, who have a historic affinity for the metal, can be glimpsed in the heavier flow of gold from Taiwan to the mainland. More significantly, China may be on the verge of political turmoil. The Chinese leadership structure has been in place for over 20 years and is growing old and ineffective. Its political clumsiness shocked the world when the gradual political reform of the past few years was stopped dead in Tienanmen Square in June, 1989. When the changing of the guard finally occurs, a power vacuum could create serious internal turmoil. Should a national conflict erupt, the price of gold could escalate dramatically as 20 per cent of the world's population is sent scurrying for gold.

The disintegration of mining in Russia

In the summer of 1991, I spent two weeks in Russia assessing the state of Russian mineral production. In the company of 14 other mining executives, I flew first to Moscow to meet the people responsible for the sale of the country's metal production. Our most significant problem was language. It was not simply translation that proved troublesome. On both sides, the ideas expressed were so foreign that it was difficult for either us or the Russians to understand the other side's position. We listened to one Russian official for an hour trying hard to convince us that "with your money and our brains, we'll go far." We were not persuaded.

Our tour of Russian mines did little to change our view. The first stop was Magadan, an eight-hour flight via the North Pole and eight time zones from Moscow. A city of 25,000 people, Magadan is the capital of the Russian Far East, a region which produces about a third of all Russian gold. The one-way fare from Moscow was 165 rubles (about $5 [U.S.] at the official exchange rate of 32 rubles per dollar). It may sound cheap, but during the eight hours we were fed only cold chicken and two cups of water. The drinks were served in plastic cups which were handed out, collected and handed out again.

Magadan was only a stop on the way to Susuman, another 150 kilometres north. We were fortunate to be visiting in summer. The average temperature in January is -48°C. In fact, the coldest recorded point on earth is only 200 kilometres west of Susuman. The province of Magadanskaya itself is thinly populated and most of its 45,000 citizens work in the gold mining industry. The province's annual gold production peaked at 3.4 million ounces during the Second World War and has declined over the years to two million ounces.

The climate is harsh; in fact, it's very similar to Alaska. The earth, covered with permafrost at -10°C, must be thawed using a 15°C water-injection well on a four-by-four-metre pattern; the process takes 30 to 45 days. The overburden is removed by a drag line and the gold-bearing gravel is processed by dredge or by hydraulicking before it's put through a sluice box.

We had been invited to visit one underground and three surface gold mines. At the first mine, the drag line that had been set up to remove the overburden was down for maintenance. Workers explained that it would be up later that afternoon. At the next mine, the dredge wasn't working. Again, we were told it was down for maintenance and would resume operation that evening. At the third mine, a hydraulicking plant had malfunctioned. In fact, not one of the open-pit mines we saw that day — a Monday — was producing gold.

The underground mine was still under development. The mill was half constructed with what appeared to be a 200-to-300-ton-per-day ball mill on its foundation. But the entire facility looked abandoned. Not one person was working. We were told that they were waiting for a shipment of parts. (A scarcity of working equipment seems to be the norm in Russia. During our tour, we saw hundreds of construction cranes idle because of lack of money or material. Complaints about equipment breakdowns were endless. To remedy some of the problems, the Russian Far East Gold Enterprise recently purchased a hundred Caterpillar D-9 bulldozers. They were to be shipped from Seattle. Unfortunately, these attempts to alleviate equipment problems are undermined by the problem of finding hard currency — and Caterpillar would not ship the equipment until the money was in the bank.)

The underground Susuman mine was chasing a vein that was six inches to three feet in width with a grade of only 0.25 to 0.35

ounces of gold per ton. Such a mine would not be economic in North America, especially in Alaska or the Northwest Territories. In fact, I doubt whether any of the placer operations we saw would be economically viable in the West. The Russians can sustain the operation only because of low wages.

The highest-paid Russian gold-field worker, an underground miner, earns 1,700 to 1,800 rubles per month (less than $50 [U.S.]). By comparison, the lowest-paid black South African miner is paid 700 rand per month (more than $200 [U.S.]) as well as room and board.

In North American mines, the most highly prized position — the position of greatest responsibility — is probably that of hoistman. In Russia, it is always hoistwoman. Women play a prominent role in the Russian work force; however, we were also told that there have been too many accidents in which drunken men dropped the cage, killing other miners. In fact, all of the important jobs were held by women. Even in the gold room and the bullion pour we found women, always armed with guns.

Man or woman, the productivity of the average Russian worker is low. At Karamken, our next stop, there are three shifts per day plus blasting time. Technically, workers are on duty for about six hours. But there are lunch and coffee breaks, and the time needed to get to and from the stope. The workers actually work for only four to 4.5 hours a shift, a stint reduced by half because of lack of equipment.

Karamken is about 110 kilometres north of Magadan. There we toured a gold and copper mine that has been in production since 1978. This mine has a rated capacity of about 1,000 tonnes per day, employs 600 people and is supposed to operate 330 days a year. The day we visited nothing was working and nobody was in sight. In fact, half the mill was torn down. Its motors were being rewired, pipes were cut in various places, and the mill pinion was being resurfaced. Officials said the mill would be functioning by the end of the week. I doubt the mill was working by the end of the month.

Underground about 25 veins were being worked in an area extending five to seven kilometres. The veins ranged in width from 10 centimetres to — it was claimed — six metres with the average grade approximately 0.25 ounces per ton. Not even the best operators would be able to get much tonnage out of the vein we saw. Indeed, in any market economy this operation, too, would probably be closed.

We flew on to Norilsk, a city of 250,000 located well inside the Arctic Circle. Despite its remoteness, Norilsk has enormous strategic importance. It produces all of Russia's platinum, 60 per cent of its nickel and 40 to 50 per cent of its copper. In fact, the area generates as much export revenue as the entire Russian gold industry. The climate is forbidding. There aren't any roads or railroads to the mainland so all supplies must be flown in or shipped by freighters that have been reinforced for ice conditions.

Until 1958, Norilsk was a gulag; writer Alexander Solzhenitsyn was interned there for a time, some two million people are said to have died. Today, 25,000 workers are directly involved in metal production and tens of thousands of others work in related occupations. Mineral output is flat, we were told, and there are no planned increases. However, ample reserves are expected to see the mine well into the next century. After a tour of the area and a brief survey of the geology, I would endorse that assumption. In fact, the area's total potential production seems to be two to 2.5 times that of the entire Sudbury complex in northern Ontario.

The underground Octobersky mine, the flagship operation, is a real jewel box. Standing 45 metres high by 500 metres wide and running 1,000 to 1,200 metres in length, it has three different types of ore bodies; the bottom one has the highest-grade ore. On average, Octobersky grades 26 per cent copper, 2.5 to 6 per cent nickel, and one to two ounces of platinum group metal per ton. If you can't make money with that, you can't make money with anything. The average ton would bring in at about $2,000 (U.S.), the equivalent of five to six ounces of gold. The mine is so profitable that it can afford to import foreign equipment. In fact, all of the equipment — from the Garner Denver drill to the Mitsubishi transports — was foreign.

An amazing 11 shafts have been sunk to serve the mine and keep production at required levels. One entire shaft is used strictly for moving heavy equipment. In North America, such equipment is dismantled, slung under the cage, lowered, and then reassembled. In Octobersky, the equipment shaft is wide enough to lower the entire, unassembled pieces of equipment.

Due to inefficiencies, Octobersky maintains a one-month stockpile of ore in front of the mill. (In North America, the maximum stockpile would be three days' production.) However, on the day of our visit every piece of equipment we saw was working. The mining method itself is a modified room-and-pillar in which the entire roof of the stope is cemented in order to get 100 per cent extraction. It's an expensive process, but with ore that rich we would likely do the same thing in the West.

Russian mining practices are generally similar to our own, although they seem lax on health and safety standards. One serious problem is that the richer the ore, the higher the sulphur content — as much as 34 per cent. This means Russian smelters release three million to four million tonnes of sulphur dioxide every year; the pollution from the Norilsk smelters is slowly destroying the environment within 150 kilometres of the town. There are no easy answers here. Current technology can capture the sulphur in sulphuric acid but there aren't any overland routes to the south and ocean transport of sulphuric acid is banned. The mine operators have no choice; they must release the sulphur into the atmosphere. One day, we had an inversion over Norilsk and the air was thick with the yellow fumes of sulphur dioxide.

Our next stop was at the milling operation of Talnak. This operation was less impressive. Constructed less than 13 years ago, four of its 12 mills were out of action. New equipment is hard to come by; old parts lie discarded everywhere — on the floor, on the ground, all around the town. Talnak would be a junk dealer's paradise. Most of the mill's pipeline and piping was built with titanium steel, designed to last a hundred years. But when the technology changes, as it does every few years, they don't remove the old pipe. It's easier to build new piping on top of the old but they end up with as many as four layers of pipe of which only one is operational.

Our last stop was a visit to the three smelters in Norilsk — two for nickel (one old, one new) and a 10-year-old copper smelter. Built by Outukumpu of Finland, the copper smelter has been well-maintained and the people who run it are well trained and efficient. More processes could be automated but I was impressed. However, the old nickel smelter, built 50 years ago by concentration camp workers, is a disaster. It employs more than 4,000 people to produce what Falconbridge does with a quarter as many workers. The manager said he wanted to shut the plant but could not; the country needs the hard currency. Eventually, they will have no choice. The mine's best ore will be depleted within seven years.

According to the technical manager, 95 per cent of production is state-ordered; revenues go directly to state coffers. The remaining 5 per cent is left to the enterprise itself to pay workers. Wages are rising fast. In 1990, the average wage was 760 rubles per month but a successful strike more than doubled wages to 1,700 rubles a month. Another strike could increase wages a further 20 to 25 per cent. The inevitable result is obvious; inflation is running rampant.

Looking at Russia and its prospects for the next decade is frightening. The gold industry is clearly in serious trouble. Between 1930 and 1970, the bulk of gold came from the placer gold fields of the Far East. That source is slowly reaching depletion. A fair amount of exploration has been done but if the deposits we saw are the best they can do, they are in trouble.

Although some Russians are optimistic, I remain skeptical. It's obvious that mineral production is in decline, and that this decline would be aggravated by mine closures if and when the country shifts to a market economy. Take Norilsk, for example. The smelters would have to be closed. Their construction would never have been approved if a proper environmental assessment system existed. Cleanup operations would be extremely expensive; the pollution extends over a 500-square-kilometre area. The smelters would have to be rebuilt in the south, close to ports and phosphate ore bodies (for fertilizer). But that would probably eliminate the jobs of 200,000 people at a cost of more than $2.5 billion (U.S.). The area's mineral richness makes it economically worthwhile, but what will they do with the people? In the Far East, the situation is even worse. Not one operation would survive a shift to market economics. That means 200,000 to 500,000 people would lose their jobs.

There isn't enough money in the world to bail the Russians out of their predicament. They have three major strikes against them: Capital stock is hopelessly outdated; the level of education is low; and, after 74 years of communism, there is little sense of a work ethic or accountability. I wouldn't invest two cents in Russia over the next 10 years.

Political turmoil in South Africa

South Africa is a country of unprecedented natural beauty. There are the beaches around Cape Town, the vineyards of Paarl, the desert of the Orange Free State, the mountains of the north and the incomparable African bush of Kruger National Park — it's very easy to fall in love with the country. Unfortunately, this beauty has been tarnished by the injustice of apartheid. After decades, that injustice is finally being addressed. The election of Nelson Mandela as president in April, 1994, marked the beginning of a new era in South Africa.

However, the early euphoria is more than likely to be followed by some disappointments as the road to equality proves to be longer and more arduous than it might seem. In the end, it may turn out to have been far easier to dismantle apartheid than to share political power.

The fundamental problem is one of education. Even though South Africa enjoys the infrastructure of a developed country, the world of the vast majority of its population is that of a Third World nation. For democracy to work, the country will have to direct vast sums of money to its education system, particularly to the education of the blacks. Even this will take time, probably generations, and time is not a commodity that the present government has much of.

Whether or not the white South African can relinquish absolute power in the next decade remains to be seen. Because of the universal chaos that has befallen the introduction of so-called democracy in the African continent, white South Africans have a deep fear of even sharing power let alone giving it up entirely, as they will under the one-man, one-vote rule.

However, in the end the demography of the country clearly dictates that it will be a black-dominated country. Whether it will happen without bloodshed remains to be seen. A revolution in South Africa would produce a reverse Attila effect. It is not the internal demand for gold that would push up the world price of gold but the potential disruption of gold supply to the international market caused by mine closures or sabotage. For the sake of all South Africans, let us hope this will never happen.

CHAPTER 5

Is Gold a Prudent Investment Today?

IT HAS BEEN OVER TWO decades since the United States removed restrictions against private ownership of gold. Yet there remains a great deal of doubt, even distrust, of gold as a prudent investment, especially among the managers and trustees of U.S. pension funds. In the spring of 1988, I went on a marketing tour for Beutel, Goodman Precious Metals Ltd. to promote its precious metal management capabilities to 20 of the United States' largest pension funds. We were well prepared, with thorough studies showing that gold was a separate asset class that enhanced the returns and reduced the volatility of any portfolio. Almost everywhere we went the response was the same. The managers of the funds were generally intrigued, in some cases they even owned some gold stocks in their personal portfolios, but none of them would dare present the concept to their board of trustees. Gold is too volatile, they said. It doesn't pay interest. Gold stocks are too expensive by traditional measures. Finally, we don't understand gold.

These investors may scorn gold, but their scorn is irrational. In October, 1987, the Dow Jones industrial average lost 26 per cent of its value in two trading sessions. Gold would have to drop from $400 (U.S.) to $300 (U.S.) to match this. Almost every pension fund owns oil stocks — a few even own oil in the ground — yet oil doesn't pay any more interest than gold. Other pension funds own real estate, including raw land and timberland, or invest in junk bonds and high technology ventures. Yet they remain skeptical of gold, despite the fact that the U.S. government continues to hoard 260 million ounces of the metal.

On the following pages, I have summarized the main points of a study that Beutel, Goodman commissioned on gold and gold stocks as investment vehicles for institutional portfolios. The purpose of the study was to prove mathematically to the quantitatively in-

The Size of the World Gold Market

	Value (U.S.$ billions)
Gold bullion:	
Above-ground reserves 4.0 billion ounces	1,520
Annual production 73.0 million ounces	28
Total	1,548
Gold equities:	
North America	38
South Africa	17
Australia	15
Total	70
Gold options and futures:	
Trading volume	553
Total gold market:	**2,171**

TABLE IX

clined analysts that gold has a place and a role in an investment portfolio.

Whether he manages a multimillion-dollar portfolio or a few personal investments, the cautious investor's first concern is that the market should have the size and liquidity to enable him to trade freely. As a point of reference, the New York Stock Exchange (with the Dow index at 5700 in mid-1996) has a market capitalization of $6.0 trillion (U.S.); the Tokyo Exchange (with the Nikkei index at 20,000) has a capitalization of $2.4 trillion (U.S.). The gold market has a capitalization of $2.2 trillion (U.S.) divided into three components: gold bullion, gold equities, and gold futures and options.

The above-ground reserves of gold — all the gold that has been mined — now stand at four billion ounces and have a value of approximately $1.5 trillion (U.S.). This is around 70 per cent of the gold market, about one-third of it held by official institutions such as the central banks of countries around the world and agencies such as the International Monetary Fund and the Bank of International Settlement. Another 50 per cent is owned by individuals as jewelry that is either worn or tucked away under the mattresses of nervous investors. The remaining 20 per cent is in the ornaments and treasures of museums and churches or is used in architecture or industry.

Those reserves of gold grow very slowly. Global production in 1995, including that of the Communist countries, was only 73 million ounces, which builds the above-ground reserves by less than 2 per cent a year. This new gold has a value of around $28 billion (U.S.) at today's gold price of around $380 (U.S.). The second component of gold market capitalization is gold equities, which are divided into three groups:

TSE Gold and Precious Minerals Index

Stock symbol	Company name (1)	% Weight on composite (2)	Current price (3)	Shares (mm)	Capitalization ($C mm) (4)
Gold and Precious Minerals Index		**11.00**			
ABX	Barrick Gold (84%)	3.12	$38.25	358.5	$13,713
PDG	Placer Dome	2.85	32.00	239.4	7,661
TEK.B	Teck Corporation CL B	0.77	27.40	92.0	2,521
ECO	Echo Bay Mines	0.46	14.05	130.5	1,834
HEM	Hemlo (56%)	0.27	17.00	100.1	1,702
TVX	TVX Gold	0.53	10.50	160.0	1,680
FN	Franco Nevada (83%)	0.32	42.00	34.8	1,462
EN	Euro-Nevada	0.27	27.90	43.2	1,205
K	Kinross Gold	0.33	9.85	116.7	1,149
CBJ	Cambior	0.28	17.75	60.1	1,067
AGE	Agnico-Eagle	0.25	20.90	39.9	834
AQP	Arequipa	0.18	28.10	28.4	798
PRU	Prime Resources (49%)	0.12	10.20	76.1	776
RYO	Royal Oak Mines	0.17	5.30	140.1	743
ABZ	Aber Resources Ltd.	0.17	20.10	35.4	712
PGU	Pegasus Gold	0.16	16.25	40.9	665
GSC	Golden Star Res. (85%)	0.07	18.50	24.6	455
BGO	Bema Gold	0.11	5.80	76.6	444
DMM.B	Dia Met Minrls Cl B (59%)	0.06	20.00	21.6	432
MAE	Miramar Mining Corp.	0.13	6.80	56.8	386
G.A	Goldcorp Cl A SV	0.13	11.15	30.0	335
VOY	Viceroy Resource Corp.	0.05	7.40	45.3	335
LTL	Lytton Minerals	0.07	3.20	99.7	319
GLG	Glamis Gold	0.09	9.60	26.5	254
CAL	Caledonia Mining	0.07	6.60	28.8	190
WFR	Wharf Resources (50%)	0.04	8.55	19.2	164
RAY	Rayrock Yellowknife (80%)	0.08	8.00	19.7	158
					41,992

(1) Percentages in brackets indicate available float on which relative index weights are calculated.
(2) Calculations as of June 30, 1996
(3) Prices as of Aug. 31, 1996
(4) Canadian dollar capitalization based on entire capitalization rather than on float capitalization.

SOURCE: TORONTO STOCK EXCHANGE

TABLE X

Gold and Its Correlation Coefficients

	Gold	Gold equities
S&P 500	0.054	0.304
Small stocks	–0.015	0.295
Gov't bonds	–0.016	0.042
Corp. bonds	–0.024	0.050
Treasury bills	–0.046	–0.089
Real estate	–0.046	–0.089

SOURCE: JEFFREY F. JAFFE

TABLE XI

1. North American equities, including all of the gold stocks listed on the Toronto Stock Exchange and New York Stock Exchange. In mid-1995, the outstanding shares of these companies had a value of approximately $38 billion (U.S.).

2. South African gold companies, which have a market capitalization of about $17 billion (U.S.). South African capitalization was substantially higher 10 years ago when the rand was three to four times more valuable than it is today.

3. Australian companies, with a market capitalization of approximately $15 billion (U.S.).

The shares of all of the publicly traded gold mining companies therefore exceed $70 billion (U.S.).

Finally, gold can be traded as futures and options on exchanges around the world and around the clock in New York, Chicago, Tokyo and Hong Kong. Contracts representing close to 1.3 billion ounces of gold are traded on these exchanges during an average year, making it a paper market that is 20 times bigger than the bullion market itself. Activity on these markets has mushroomed in the 1980s; the big gold players find it more liquid than the bullion market itself. As a result, the futures and options markets are likely to lead any future gold price movements. The Japanese especially are more likely to use these markets to quietly establish gold positions and not tip off the market that they are buying gold before taking delivery. At $380 (U.S.) for an ounce of gold, the total annual value of the turnover in the futures and options markets is $550 million (U.S.).

Gold as an asset class

The first goal of the study commissioned by Beutel, Goodman was to establish whether gold was a separate asset class which deserved a place in every investment portfolio. Table X shows that gold tends to behave differently from most other investments. Because gold goes up in price when other investments are dropping — or down when other investments are going up — it can be used as a "hedge" against abrupt changes in the value of a portfolio.

The behaviour of investment vehicles is measured in what is called correlation coefficients. A negative number means the investments move in a contrary fashion; a positive number means they behave in the same way. The correlation between the behaviour of gold and Standard & Poor's composite index of 500 U.S. stocks is a negligible 0.054; it's negative against small stocks, government bonds, corporate bonds, treasury bills and real estate. On the other hand, the behaviour of gold equities is similar to the behaviour of S&P's 500 and the small stocks index, although their fall in an overall market decline will be cushioned if gold prices are stable or rising. However, gold stocks tend to be more volatile than the general market, primarily because a rise or fall in the gold price has a dramatic impact on the profit margins of the producer. Gold equities have a negative correlation with both treasury bills and real estate but show no significant relation with government bonds and corporate bonds.

On Black Monday — Oct. 19, 1987 — while the stock markets around the world plummeted, the price of bullion actually rose. The TSE composite index dropped 11.14 per cent, but the gold stocks in the TSE gold subindex only lost 8.8 per cent. It was a temporary reprieve. Bullion kept climbing in price, but within days gold stocks were decimated. By mid-November, they had dropped 44.3 per cent from their August peak. In the weeks that followed, bullion kept moving until it finally peaked at $503 (U.S.) in December and gold stocks spun around to regain 37.5 per cent of their losses.

Impact of gold on diversified portfolios

To test the hypothesis that some gold should be beneficial to a portfolio's performance, we incorporated gold into different portfolios and measured both the performance and volatility of these portfolios. We established four portfolios, ranging from an aggressive portfolio containing 55 per cent common stocks and no long-term government bonds to a conservative portfolio containing 35 per cent common stocks, 5 per cent small stocks, 5 per cent international equities and as much as 35 per cent in long-term bonds. First, the performance of these portfolios was measured; then each portfolio was adjusted by reducing the stocks and bonds proportionately and adding gold.

The return for the portfolio with 5 per cent or 10 per cent gold is higher than the same portfolio without gold. The return from the most aggressive portfolio rises from 12.87 per cent to 13.24 per cent and 13.59 per cent by adding 5 per cent or 10 per cent gold. In the most conservative portfolio, the impact of the gold is even more dramatic: The rate of return over a year jumps from 10.6 per cent to 11.51 per cent, an improvement of 0.9 per cent a year. That's understandable. The conservative portfolio's lower initial return is bound to gain more from the boost provided by a higher-return, higher-risk investment mix.

The most surprising finding is that even though gold is a volatile investment, when added to a portfolio the volatility of the entire portfolio actually decreases. In the aggressive portfolio, the standard deviation — the statistical measure of the degree of volatility of a portfolio — decreases from 3.73 per cent to 3.6 per cent when you add 5 per cent gold, dropping even further to 3.51 per cent when you add 10 per cent gold. The standard deviation in the most conservative portfolio decreases from 2.73 per cent to 2.61 per cent.

This leaves the indisputable conclusion that gold can be beneficial to a portfolio when added in amounts of 5 per cent to 15 per cent. It can increase your yearly return and decrease your monthly standard deviation. Having 5 per cent to 10 per cent of your portfolio in gold is not new to the Europeans; they have held 3 per cent to 15 percent of their portfolios in gold for decades, if not centuries. Everywhere you travel in countries like Switzerland, France or Italy, banks will predominantly display gold coins and prices in their front windows. Most of the large European financial institutions which manage clients' money use gold and gold equities in their portfolios.

In the United States, the ban on private gold ownership over the past three generations has left investors with a lack of understanding of gold equities. The relative stability of the dollar as the reserve currency up until the early 1970s and the absence of political tension threatening the economic stability of the North American continent have combined to nurture an overwhelming apathy toward gold. So far gold has not become an integral part of U.S. institutional portfolios. Private individuals, on the other hand, have begun hedging, primarily through gold mutual funds which have grown to a value of $5 billion (U.S.).

However, there is some hope for U.S. institutions. Indeed, their interest in following the gold sector is demonstrated by their attendance at various gold conferences presented by the major American brokerage houses in recent years.

Gold equities versus gold bullion

Gold is more volatile than other investments and gold stocks are more volatile than the bullion itself; the value of gold equities climbs higher and falls lower than the bullion. This characteristic of gold stocks is measured by a mathematical expression known as "beta," which expresses the deviation of one index versus the other. Gold stocks tend to have a beta of one to two, which means they are one to two times as volatile as gold itself. This was particularly evident in 1982, when gold bottomed in June then surged more than 45 per cent over the next nine months. The gold equity market bottomed in August and staged a strong rally which pushed gold equities up by 90 per cent to their highest level in the past 30 years.

The beauty of a high beta stock is that in a rising market you can get more bang for your buck. By properly using gold equities, you can increase the performance and decrease the volatility of your gold portfolio. You have to keep in mind that it works both ways; on the way down you should own as few stocks as possible while holding more of your portfolio in bullion.

Portfolio allocation

So far we have established that:

- The gold market is large enough to qualify as a legitimate asset class for investment.
- Gold bullion and gold stocks can be used effectively to diversify your portfolio since they tend to move in opposite directions than most other investments.
- Therefore, if you add gold bullion and stocks to your portfolio you can increase your total return while decreasing your total risk.

It seems to me that we have just defined a legitimate and prudent investment. The next step is to actually build a gold bullion and stock portfolio that fits your circumstances. The decision process to accomplish this can be simplified by using a portfolio allocation

Gold Portfolio Allocation in Alternative Environments

			Gold bullion outlook		
			Positive	Neutral	Negative
Gold equity outlook	Positive	Bullion	10%	20%	30%
		equity	90%	80%	70%
		% invested	15%	11%	7%
	Neutral	Bullion	55%	50%	45%
		equity	45%	50%	55%
		% invested	11%	8%	5%
	Negative	Bullion	70%	60%	50%
		equity	30%	40%	50%
		% invested	8%	5%	3%

TABLE XII

matrix. A matrix is really just a methodical, decision-making process you can use instead of the impulsive, seat-of-the-pants approach that too many investors seem to adopt in the gold market. To put the matrix in place, the first question you have to answer is how much of your assets should be invested in gold instruments.

If you are an employee of a large Canadian company, it is likely that a small part of your pension fund is already invested in gold equities. Most Canadian pension fund managers try to mirror the Toronto Stock Exchange 300 composite index, which has approximately an 11 per cent gold content. This gold content is just too big to be ignored by any Canadian money manager. In the U.S., gold stocks are such a small part of the New York equity market that they can easily be overlooked without making a bit of difference in the performance of a pension fund.

As an individual investor, you should think of gold bullion as your insurance against two potential kinds of economic problems: deflation and inflation. It's clear that you should have some insurance, but what is the right amount? From our studies, it appears that 8 per cent to 10 per cent gold is an optimal level for a balanced portfolio.

The decision to hold more or less than 8 per cent must be based on your view of the investment climate, future economic activity and your own comfort or discomfort. If most of your wealth is tied up in real estate — your house, condominium, a piece of land in the country — you'll do well during times of inflation as your real estate climbs rapidly in value. But in times of deflation, you may have trouble selling any of this real estate if you need to raise cash in a hurry. Depending on your outlook for inflation or deflation, you may choose to have as little as 3 per cent gold or as much as 20 per cent. Look at your assets, determine how they will fare under various inflation or deflation scenarios and use gold as an insurance policy against a specific risk. This will give you the minimum and maximum amount of gold you should own in your portfolio.

For example, you may have assets worth $300,000 — made up of a house worth $150,000, a retirement plan, some treasury bills and $80,000 in a stock portfolio. Even in the worst economic crisis, as long as you own your house free of a mortgage, nobody will take it away from you. You don't need gold to ensure that you have a place to live. It may go down in value, but that doesn't really matter. On the other hand, your stock portfolio is clearly at risk. If you want to protect half of your $80,000 portfolio and believe that gold would triple in price in a crisis, as it did in 1979 and 1980 when it jumped from $275 (U.S.) to $850 (U.S.), you would need around $13,500 in gold bullion and equities to cover your $40,000. This would be 17 per cent of your portfolio. If you live in a place like Beirut, from which you might have to flee, you may want to hold more gold.

The second decision to make is the ratio of bullion to equities within your precious metal investments. Your matrix can be as simple as the one shown in Table XII, which illustrates the allocation of a portfolio in different economic and market conditions.

Let's say you've just finished reading the latest edition of *The Wall Street Journal* with its forecasts on interest rates, the stability of the American dollar and the future of the U.S. economy. If you conclude that the outlook for stocks is neutral to negative but the outlook for gold is neutral to positive, according to the allocation matrix you should have around 8 per cent of your assets in gold, roughly 60 per cent in bullion and 40 per cent in gold equities. An allocation matrix is important because it gives you the discipline to review the market and the condition of your portfolio every month or even every week.

Once you have determined what percentage of your assets should be in gold and whether you should hold bullion or equities, the next step is to carry out your plan. But what should you buy, when should you buy and where do you buy it?

CHAPTER 6

What Should You Buy?

IF YOU ASPIRE TO BE A successful investor in any field, you must accept that nobody can make decisions for you better than yourself. But to do that you have to spend the time to review, analyze, select and monitor the appropriate investments for your portfolio. Depending on the type of investor you are and the size of your portfolio you may have to devote one to six hours a week to this task.

The investor

This book has been written by an investor for investors. I believe the only way to build wealth over a lifetime is to buy good, undervalued assets and have the patience to see them reach full value with time. If you are in a hurry to make money, this book isn't for you. I haven't yet found the secret to making millions out of thin air.

The main objective of an investor is to preserve or increase his capital in real terms — in other words, to earn an after-tax rate of return which is greater than the rate of inflation. If you're not beating both inflation and the taxman, your wealth is slowly disappearing even though you have more money at the end of the year than at the beginning.

The vital characteristic of a successful investor is having the ability to identify "fundamental value" in the bullion or equity market, the patience to hold on to an investment and the courage to sell when the investment has risen in price until it is overvalued. This type of investor keeps his transaction costs low because he is not constantly flipping from one market favourite to another. He doesn't get whiplashed by the gyration of the market because he keeps his eyes firmly on the ball and not the pitcher.

The trader and the speculator

Speculating is simply a fast-forward kind of trading activity. For a trader to make money, he has to hold a large amount of gold or stocks because he's in the market for only a short period of time and will probably be exposed to only small changes in price. But a large position means one thing only — large risk. And if you are borrowing heavily by indulging in the options and futures markets, you are boosting your investment to the status of speculation. You may be lucky once or twice, but there are very few elderly, rich traders or speculators. Use the pillow rule to determine whether you're investing or speculating: If you can't sleep with your head firmly on your pillow, you're probably speculating.

If you don't have the time, patience or inclination to manage your gold portfolio, you still have two choices: Buy gold bullion and put it away or buy into a gold mutual fund. In either case, you should do at least enough research to determine where to buy and how to hoard your bullion or which gold fund is best suited to your particular needs. Once you've done that, you can turn on the autopilot and simply check now and then to make sure everything is going according to plan.

Gold bullion

Once you've decided you should own some gold bullion, you'll have to choose among the different ways of holding gold. You can hold it yourself or let someone else — a banker or a dealer — hold it for you. There are several ways to own gold: gold bars, through gold proxies such as gold certificates, gold passbook accounts at financial institutions and storage programs offered by financial institutions that sell, handle and store gold. My advice is to keep it simple. Deal exclusively with a financial institution that has a good reputation and that you know well. The bullion you buy should be in a size small enough to be easy to carry and to sell. Gold comes in one-, two-, five-, 10- and 100-ounce wafers and in one-kilogram bars. The affluent can even buy the standard 400-ounce bars used for government and bank transactions.

Bullion investors should stick to gold bars of 0.9999 quality processed by a reputable refiner, preferably one recognized around the world. Each bar should be clearly stamped with the refiner's name and a number certifying that it has been registered. You should also stick to bullion bars of at least one ounce to avoid the premiums paid on smaller bars. These premiums represent a manufacturing charge to cover the cost of making a smaller bar. However, you have to weigh the economy of the larger bars against the ease of carrying and selling wafers of gold.

Once you've bought your gold, store it in a place where it will be safe but still easy to get at if you need it in a hurry. Remember, you are buying gold as insurance. If you want your insurance policy to be of value when you need it, make very sure you purchase it from a reputable dealer. There aren't any bargains in the gold world. Nobody sells gold at less than market value; shopping around may uncover small differences but you shouldn't neglect your security or your peace of mind.

The leading gold-dealing financial institutions in Canada are the Bank of Nova Scotia and Deak International. In the United States, the most prominent are J. Aron & Co. and the Republic National Bank of New York. There are also a number of good regional bullion dealers that aren't included, so if you know of one don't hesitate to use it. But shop around and make sure you get what you pay for. If you use a dealer to store your bullion, make absolutely sure that the firm is in good financial condition.

If you intend to buy bullion and just put it away, you can avoid the risk of bad market timing by setting aside a certain amount of money every month and buying gold at regular intervals. This technique is known as dollar-averaging. This way, you won't be buying all your gold at the lowest price during a cycle, but neither will you buy it at the top of the market. However, there will be times when your gold bullion will be worth less than the average price you paid. Just remember, you are buying this insurance policy to protect yourself against economic or political crisis for the long run, not for a quick gain in the short run.

Look at these occasions of lower prices as a time to buy more gold to reduce the average cost of the bullion you own. You won't have to worry about the stock market, the currency market, the economy or commodity prices. In fact, your real hope should be that you will never have to turn to your gold insurance since it will be needed only when everything else you own is in jeopardy. Bullion doesn't pay interest or dividends, nor does it grow or expand by itself. That's the price you pay for tranquillity.

A Comparison of Bullion Coins

Country	Coin	Size	Purity
Canada	Maple Leaf	1,1/2,1/4,1/10 oz.	0.9999
U.S.	American Eagle	1,1/2,1/4,1/10 oz.	0.9167
	Double Eagle	1 oz.	
South Africa	Krugerrand	1,1/2,1/4,1/10 oz.	0.9167
Mexico	Centenario	1.206 oz.	0.9990
Australia	Golden Nugget Koala	1,1/2,1/4,1/10 oz.	0.9990
China	Panda	1, 1/2 oz.	
Austria	Corona	0.96 oz.	0.9000
U.K.	Sovereign	0.2354 oz.	0.9167
France	Britannia Napoleon	1,1/2,1/4,1/10 oz.	0.9167

TABLE XIII

Bullion coins

Bullion coins are issued and guaranteed by at least 15 countries including Canada, the United States, China and Australia. These official coins are legal tender in all of these countries, so counterfeiting would be a criminal offence. Despite this, the legal tender value is almost always far below the actual worth of the gold in the coins and they seldom circulate as "money." The one-ounce American Eagle has a face value of $50 (U.S.), yet with gold at $380 (U.S.) an ounce it is obvious that no one would use the coin to pay for groceries.

Bullion coins don't have any numismatic or collectors' value since they can be struck in limitless amounts. Because of their convenience in portability and affordability, as well as their status as legal tender, these coins carry a price that is slightly higher than the price of bullion. This difference in price is called the premium. Before you purchase your coins you should contact several reputable dealers to make sure you're getting a fair deal.

As an investor wondering which coin you should buy, remember that an ounce of gold is an ounce of gold; it doesn't matter where it comes from. The most popular coin over the last 20 years has been the South African Krugerrand. South Africa has issued 43 million coins since it issued its first Krugerrand in 1967. In 1987, the U.S. government decided to impose sanctions against South Africa by banning the sale of the one-ounce Krugerrand in America. What happened to the value of this coin? Not much. In the U.S., the coin began selling at a discount instead of a premium. This discount represents the cost of melting down the coin and turning it into new coins or bars. The gold wafer or coin in your pocket may once have been a Krugerrand. You cannot know — which is one of the beauties of gold. Once it has been melted, its origin cannot be traced. The sanctions were lifted in July, 1991.

The coin you choose will depend on your personal preference, dictated somewhat by the premium you are willing to pay for a particular coin. If you buy a Canadian Maple Leaf or an American Eagle, you'll have to pay a premium of 4 per cent to 5 per cent, an extra $15 to $20 per ounce of gold. These premiums can be even higher in periods of scarcity. When the American Eagle was first issued, the dealer premium reached 9 per cent — an extra $36 if the gold cost $400 an ounce. Also, the premium is higher on smaller coins than on larger ones. If the premium is 6 per cent on a one-ounce coin, for example, it could be as high as 25 per cent on a coin that weighs only one-fourth of an ounce. When you sell your coins you will not recoup all of this premium as the dealer takes the profit on the difference between his buying and selling price.

If your investment decisions are not coloured by your patriotism, buy the coins with the lowest premium. Both the Krugerrand and the Mexican Centenario sell at barely 2 per cent above the cost of bullion.

Taxes, storage and other considerations

Despite the fact that the Canadian Maple Leaf and the American Eagle are legal tender, they are considered by governments to be real property just like your house or your car. Therefore, they are subject to capital gain or capital loss treatment for income tax purposes when sold. Furthermore, most states and provinces have imposed a sales tax on coins. Only the province of Alberta and the states of Nevada, California and Florida exempt coins from sales tax. If you are planning to invest a lot of money in gold coins, it might pay to buy in a tax-free jurisdiction while you are there or to buy the coins and have them shipped to these jurisdictions for storage. If you live in a province that taxes gold coins, you cannot avoid the tax by ordering the coins from a tax-free jurisdiction and having them shipped to you. In Canada, the introduction of the 7 per cent GST has added a level of complexity as it is not applied to the Maple Leaf but it will be applied on the American Eagle.

If you keep your bullion or coins in banks or facilities set up to hold precious metals, you will pay yearly storage fees of 0.25 per cent to 0.50 per cent of the value of the stored gold. These include insurance on your gold at current market value. If you decide to use a bank to safeguard your precious metal, you have two choices: You can store it "unallocated" or "fully segregated." There is a critical difference between these two types of storage. In an unallocated metal account your gold is pooled with that of other clients; in a segregated account your gold is kept distinctly separate. You are given an account number with your bullion allocated to that account.

The distinction between the two types of safekeeping accounts is crucial in the event that the financial institution holding your bullion declares bankruptcy. The unallocated metals account is simply a liability on the institution's balance sheet and can be used to pay creditors in the event of bankruptcy; you become one of the creditors without any priority over the asset you own. The gold in a segregated account is definitely yours — it does not appear on the bank's balance sheet and cannot be used to pay the bank's or financial institution's debts.

Of course, the price for this higher form of security is higher fees. Until your gold hoard reaches a certain dollar value you might be better off renting a safety deposit box or putting the gold in a strongbox at home. If you use a safety deposit box, remember that the contents of the box are not insured by the bank. How could they insure the contents when they don't know what you put in your box? However, you can purchase a homeowner's or tenant's property insurance rider which will cover the contents of your safety deposit box.

Wherever you keep your coins, be sure that you always handle them with care. If the coins are scratched or dented, you will still get the gold value when you sell, but you could lose all of your premium. If the coin dealer feels he cannot sell the coin because of the damage, he may even charge a melting fee.

Numismatic coins

Gold coins minted by governments and sold for their bullion are a different investment from a gold or silver coin that is rare and of limited quantity. These numismatic coins can be fun and emotionally rewarding to collect, but as gold investments they are a poor substitute for the bullion coins. The reason is very simple. The value of a numismatic coin is in the rarity of the coin; the gold content represents only a fraction of its selling price. The $20 (U.S.) St. Gaudens gold piece was minted between 1908 and 1928 but was selling in July, 1991, for $1,350 (U.S.) to $1,400 (U.S.), four times the value of its gold content. An Indian Quarter Eagle of the same period was selling for $4,100 (U.S.) to $4,500 (U.S.), even though only a fraction of its content is gold. The value of numismatic coins can fluctuate wildly. For example, the St. Gaudens coin was selling for $4,000 (U.S.) to $5,000 (U.S.) in 1989 while the Quarter Eagle fetched $10,000 (U.S.) to $13,000 (U.S.). If you had bought these coins back in 1989 you would have suffered a loss of 70 per cent of your investment — not a pleasant prospect. To look at it another way, gold bullion would have to drop from $375 (U.S.) to $112.50 (U.S.) for you to suffer a comparable loss.

The second major problem is liquidity. The numismatic coin market is small and is controlled by a restricted number of dealers. When you buy a coin, you are buying retail; you must sell to the dealer at wholesale price. The difference in the price at which you buy and sell is called "the spread." The spread depends on the popularity of the piece and the ease with which the dealer can sell it.

Look at the Quarter Eagle gold piece. In July, 1991, a dealer would have sold you this coin for $4,500 (U.S.) while he would have bought it for only $4,100 (U.S.), a 10 per cent difference — the spread. Actually this wasn't too bad; the market for numismatic coins had cooled yet the Quarter Eagle remained a relatively sought-after piece. In 1989, the spread was closer to 30 per cent. It can take a long time for an investor just to recover the spread, let alone ride out the wide fluctuations in prices.

Numismatic gold coins are better left to the serious coin collector who has the knowledge and patience to hold the coins for five to 10 years. Even then, these collectors are not "investors," but people who collect coins for their beauty, rarity and historical interest.

Mutual funds

A mutual fund is a pool of savings that belongs to many investors. This pool is invested by professional managers in a broad portfolio. A mutual fund can be invested in many different types of investments — common stocks, foreign stocks, bonds, mortgages, treasury bills and real estate are the most common.

Mutual funds are for individuals who do not have the time or the expertise to manage their own portfolios and for investors who do not have enough money to create a diversified portfolio. When you buy shares of a mutual fund, you are purchasing a share of a portfolio and hiring the expertise of the management team that has been running this portfolio. Before you take the plunge, take a few hours to do your homework. As an investor, you want to know if a particular fund is likely to meet your expectations in the long run. In both the U.S. and Canada, there is a considerable amount of literature on mutual funds and a little weekend reading should give you enough background to narrow the search to three to five funds.

The next step is to request prospectuses and the latest quarterly reports of the funds that interest you. The prospectus explains the investment objective of a fund. Some funds, such as the Central Fund of Canada, have to be 90 per cent invested in gold or silver bullion, while others cannot invest in South Africa. A few set limits on the amount of cash that can be held. Once you've read the prospectus, study the fund's portfolio. Look at the proportion of gold bullion, gold equities and cash. Look at each of the components and determine whether the bullion is mainly gold or silver and if the equities are speculative exploration companies or senior blue-chip companies. What you are trying to establish is whether the fund, as it is structured and managed, is likely to meet your long-term objectives. Is it the kind of portfolio you would have built yourself given the money or the opportunity? If it is, then it will likely meet your expectations and let you sleep at night.

Let's say that you have found more than one fund that meets your criteria. The next step is to look at the quality and philosophy of the management teams. Look at each fund's track record over the past three, five and, if possible, 10 years. Make sure that the managers who were responsible for the performance during that time are still in place; you may not want to put your money on a horse with a new jockey.

Before going any further, we should differentiate between the two main types of funds: open-end funds and closed-end funds. The vast majority of mutual funds are open-end. Their main attribute is that they are highly liquid and can be purchased or sold at any time at the net asset value per share (NAVPS) on the day of purchase or sale. This NAVPS is the total market value of the investments held in the fund's portfolio divided by the number of shares outstanding. The price you pay or receive is the NAVPS that day; there isn't a discount or premium to that value. The purchases or redemptions of the shares or units are done directly through the fund company or their agents, often mutual fund brokers. Profits generally flow through to the investors directly and are not taxed at the fund level. As with other open-end mutual funds, some do not have a load, or fee, for purchasing the funds while others will charge either a front-end or back-end fee.

Closed-end funds, as their name implies, sell through an initial public offering of a fixed number of shares. After this, the fund is closed and the shares of the fund are traded on an exchange. The shares can only be purchased or sold if there are willing buyers and sellers. Because closed-end funds are corporations, the profits are fully taxable just like any other corporation. Because of the potential tax liability as well as difficulty selling the shares in a down market, most closed-end funds tend to trade at a discount to their net asset value. When the stock market is strong, the discount tends to narrow. Occasionally, these funds trade at a premium to their net asset value. When trading closed-end funds you will have to pay a brokers' commission.

An investor interested in long-term performance should probably buy and hold an open-end mutual fund. If your investment horizon is short term, then the closed-end fund may be more appropriate, especially if the fund is trading at a large discount.

Portfolio managers will adopt different management styles, depending on the type of fund they are managing. In both closed-end and open-end funds a manager will try to maximize returns, but in an open-end fund the manager will want to be able to meet any unexpected redemptions. Therefore, as a manager of both types of mutual funds, I tend to keep a portfolio of highly liquid securities and more gold bullion in an open-end fund than I would keep in a closed-end fund. In the closed-end fund I do not have to meet any unexpected redemptions and I can afford to take higher risks. I can purchase more private placement securities that can't be traded for six or 12 months as well as more junior companies that are riskier but promise a higher return over time. As a result, the closed-end funds tend to be more volatile and therefore more suitable for an investor willing to live with the higher risk.

If you decide to put your money into a gold fund, you will not be alone. As of mid-1996, there were approximately 120 gold or gold-related funds worldwide. These funds had a total value of approximately $11.5 billion (U.S.). Only 1 per cent, or about $120 million (U.S.), of that was invested in bullion and 6 per cent, or $720 million (U.S.), was in cash. The rest, almost $11 billion (U.S.), was invested in equities. Of the $11 billion invested in gold equities, 52 per cent was in North American gold equities, 24 per cent was in South African gold equities, and 15 per cent was in Australian gold equities. The most popular gold equities in the gold funds were Barrick Gold, followed by Placer Dome, Anglo American, Western Mining, Newmont and Freeport Copper & Gold.

Hedging and the use of futures and options

A recent information circular on futures trading started with this sentence: "The first step in successful futures trading is deciding how much money you are willing to lose on each trade." This admonition underscores the fact that 90 per cent to 95 per cent of investors who have speculated on the commodities futures exchanges have lost their investments.

The concept of futures contracts dates back to the early and mid-1800s in the U.S., when farmers and their customers began to write contracts for future delivery of their farm produce — wheat, corn, soybeans. The contracts locked in a price that would be paid in the future when the produce was delivered. These contracts met the needs of the producers for a guaranteed income from the crop and the needs of the consumer who wanted to be protected from unexpected increases in the costs of goods. Futures contracts began trading on the Chicago Board of Trade and later the concept was adopted by the New York Metals Exchange, which eventually merged with several other commodities exchanges to form COMEX, which eventually became the leading futures exchange in the world.

The futures market can be used by gold producers or consumers in a business practice called hedging. Most gold-producing companies use the futures exchange at one time or another, particularly if their cost of production is relatively high, to secure the gold price they need to stay profitable. On the other hand, the consumers of gold can protect themselves against rising gold prices. Jewelry manufacturers, for example, purchase their gold in July and August for manufacturing in September and October and delivery in time for the Christmas shopping season. Through the futures market, a jeweller can protect himself against the inherent volatility of gold prices by buying gold at a time when he or she believes the price is reasonable. The gold can then be delivered when it's time to begin fashioning it into jewelry.

The individual investor who neither produces nor takes delivery of his gold is strictly a speculator trying to take advantage of fluctuations in price. The undeniable appeal of the futures or options markets is the ability of turning a few hundred dollars into a fortune; the undeniable risk is the loss of 100 per cent of all the money you're gambling, if not everything you own. The risks differ in the futures and options markets, however.

A futures contract is a commitment to deliver or take delivery of a specified amount of gold during a specified future month at a price agreed upon in the trading pit of a commodity exchange. The gold futures market is not for the timid; a contract on the Chicago Board of Trade is for 32.15 ounces while on the Commodity Exchange in New York one contract represents 100 ounces of gold. When you purchase a contract, your broker will ask you for a margin deposit, usually between 5 per cent and 10 per cent of the value of the underlying gold. If the market swings against you, you'll be asked to put up more money to keep pace with your losses. You'll also have to pay commissions and a premium that reflects current interest rates, the expectations of the marketplace and the cost of storing the gold.

Buying an options contract gives you the right, but not the obligation, to buy or to sell a certain quantity of gold at an agreed price for a certain period of time. If you buy a "call" option you have the right to purchase; a "put" option gives you the right to sell. The price you pay for an option is called the premium, which is determined by a number of factors including the time left to expiry, the intrinsic value of the option, the volatility of the market and carrying charges. Unlike the futures market, where your risk is unlimited, in the options market your risk is limited to the premium you've paid. If the price of gold does not move as you've anticipated, you can let your option expire worthless, as most do. Gold bullion options trade on the Montreal, Vancouver and American stock exchanges where the contracts represent 100 ounces of gold.

The futures and options market is a zero-sum game; for every $1,000 made by one person, somebody else loses $1,000. One side always wins, the other side always loses. This is not the case in the equity market, where you can buy a stock for $5, sell it for $10 and no one loses. When a major producing company hedges its future production of gold it is transferring the risk of future price movement to the purchaser of the futures contract, the speculator. What are your chances against such formidable adversaries? These companies have dozens of economists, traders and engineers who spend their days studying the world's economic environment and its impact on the gold price. If a company sells to you a futures contract agreeing to deliver 10,000 ounces of gold in one year in return for $400 (U.S.) an ounce and the price of gold has risen to $425 (U.S.), you will have made $250,000 (U.S.). The mining company, which has sold its gold at $400 (U.S.) an ounce, has the $4 million (U.S.) it felt was a fair price. However, where will you be if the gold price is down to $375 (U.S.) an ounce? The mining company still gets its price, $4 million (U.S.), but you're out $250,000 (U.S.).

Gold equities

For an investor analyzing the purchase or sale of gold, the fundamentals boil down to one thing — price. It's not as simple when buying shares in a gold mining company. When you buy gold equities, you're buying gold that hasn't yet been mined. Making an astute investment will demand an understanding not only of the forces that drive gold prices but also a grasp of the workings of the stock market and the fundamentals of the stock — the company's reserves, production costs, earnings, dividends and management.

These fundamentals often require careful homework and a bit of legwork — a trip to a company's mine is not out of the question for an institutional investor. These fundamentals will be covered in detail in Chapter 7. This first glance into the world of gold equities will be taken through the eyes of the technical analyst. Technical analysis is the study of the price movement and trading volume of both stocks and the stock market by plotting charts or graphs, without regard to the multitude of factors that influence the price of a stock. A cynic once said buying stocks by technical analysis was like driving a car by looking through the rearview mirror. It is true that the past is hardly a perfect map of the future, but it can give you some benchmarks or hints of change that might keep you on track and out of trouble.

Technical analysis captures the behaviour of the stock on a chart, giving you information you can use in making your own decisions to buy or sell a stock. I have kept the discussion of technical analysis to a few simple techniques which I'll illustrate with charts and graphs, but I encourage anyone who intends to do more trading, or the speculator, to read a book devoted to technical analysis.

Before I go further, be warned that you should be leery of technical analysis. Most traders and speculators use very sophisticated trading programs, all based on the same theories that have been computerized, regurgitated and fed to everyone at the same time. Often, once a trend is established, it tends to feed on itself, becoming a self-fulfilling prophecy. This happened in the late 1970s and early 1980s when the gold price was set by the traders on the New York Commodity Exchange. Demand for gold for jewelry was at a historic low, yet the price of gold was driven to historic highs by traders and speculators. The paper market took over until sanity returned.

You can use technical analysis by following a few relatively simple rules.

Rule 1: The trend is your friend

If there is one thing that technical analysis should teach you, it is to recognize a trend, its direction and its vigour. If the market is going up, every stock you own is likely to go up, some more than others. If the market is going down, even the strong companies you own will go down. It comes down to one simple notion: Go with the flow.

Look at the London gold price graph. This graph charts the daily London morning fix expressed by a bar for every week. The bar represents the high and low price over the week. You can see three distinct trends. From 1983 to early 1985, the gold price was in a downward trend that took it from $510 (U.S.) an ounce to $285 (U.S.). The price then broke through the major trend line — the line that skips across the peaks — to start an upward trend. This took gold to $503 (U.S.) an ounce by December, 1987, before it moved into a bear market and broke through the lower trend line in May, 1988. Fortunes are made at the point when the trends reverse, when the gold price reaches its bottom or top and turns around. In January, 1993, gold hit its lowest price since 1985 before starting a major uptrend.

The technical analyst's most effective tool in identifying these major reversal points is the moving average. A moving average is a

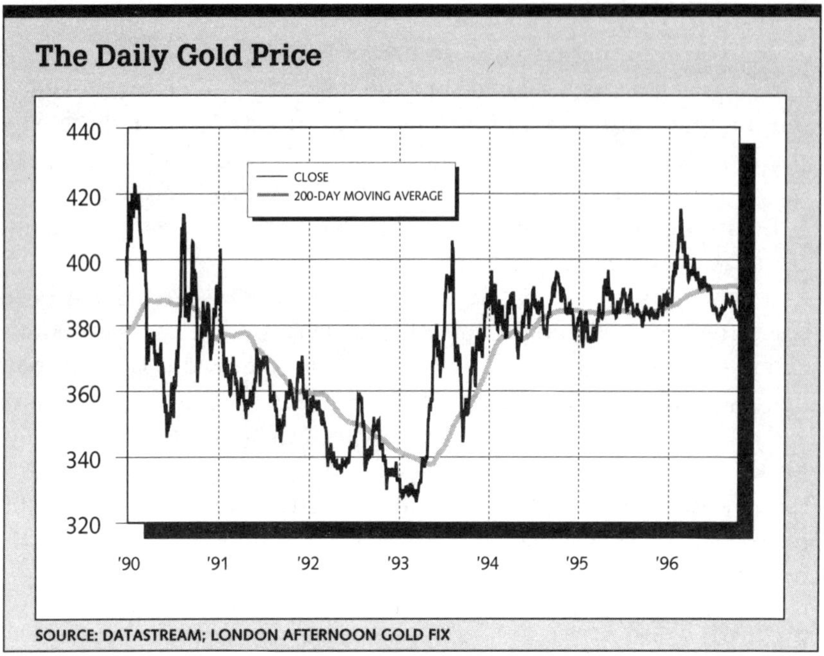

CHART VI

way of smoothing out the fluctuating values of a stock by averaging its price over a period of time as short as a few days or as long as several years. This will filter out the day-to-day fluctuations and allow you to see the trends. In the gold market, the 200-day or 40-week moving average is the most reliable indicator of a confirmation in trend change.

If you don't have the time to calculate and chart the moving averages, you can subscribe to reports published every week or every other week. You can also ask your broker for the reports of the technical analysts on staff. Read these reports carefully. When interpreting their work, technical analysts often colour their writings with their own judgment, a judgment that can be shadowed by their expectations of the market. It can be difficult to separate fact from personal judgment. If you have been reading or dealing with the same analysts for a period of time, you will begin to recognize their biases and will be able to make your own interpretation.

Rule 2: Beware of your biases

In late 1983, Echo Bay started on a four-year upward trend even though the price of gold kept falling throughout 1983 and 1984 before finally turning up in late 1985. The company seemed unable to do anything wrong. Acquisitions and discoveries kept boosting the company's stock. At Beutel, Goodman & Co. Ltd. we had loaded our portfolios with Echo Bay stock in late 1983, paying less than $4 a share. We started selling in early 1986 when the stock hit $10. The stock had already more than doubled in price, it was more than fairly valued and we couldn't see any new projects on the horizon that would increase the company's value. It was obvious the chart was still in a rising trend — and a very steep one at that — but we were jittery. We were too early. The stock was still in a rising trend, the gold price itself was in an upward trend and Echo Bay management bought the McCoy/Cove mine from Tenneco. Together, these provided the impetus for the stock to almost quadruple. The stock hit $40 less than two years later.

From 1987 to 1992, Echo Bay management was unable to stop the company's slide. In May, 1992, Echo Bay shares had dropped to as low as $6.90 a share, almost one-sixth of the 1987 peak value. The stock price has been driven down by falling gold prices and by Echo Bay's problems with the Sunnyside mine and the McCoy/Cove mine, where early reserve estimates have had to be lowered, and another write-off of their Muschocho and Alta Bay investments. But the company is still doing relatively well; it's producing as much gold as ever, it has repaired its balance sheet, and I'm sure management will resolve its problems. When the tide turns, it may be a good stock for a portfolio. But before you invest, do your homework. Read the annual and quarterly reports, look at the balance sheet and figure out the real value of the company. You may agree or disagree with the opinions of the analysts but, as an investor, you have to make your own decisions.

Rule 3: Look for support and watch the resistance

There are times in the market when values are so compelling that the price of a stock cannot drop any further because too many investors will recognize the value and begin buying. This can be seen in the chart of Rayrock Yellowknife Resources Inc., which seems to have an ascending support level, first at $6, then $6.50, and finally, at $7. Each time the buying power came in to support the stock's price. On the other hand, except for a brief few months in 1987 when euphoria carried the stock to just over $14, Rayrock had never been able to muster the market power to keep itself above its $12 resistance level for too long.

If the stock breaks through either its resistance or support level in a decisive fashion, you can expect it to either climb to much higher ground or to plummet. Indeed, in early 1994 the stock decisively broke through the $14 level to climb to a high of over $19. Sudden shifts are usually caused by a major change in the company's fortunes; there may be new management, a discovery or new plans to expand the company rapidly. Conversely, should it break through the support level, people will see the stock as not performing and will dump it.

On the same chart, you can see another technical formation — the triangle. The changes in price from the 1987 top at $14 through 1988 and 1989 show descending peaks which, when combined with the ascending support line, create a triangle formation. This formation is always broken eventually. If the price begins to move up it is very bullish; if the break occurs on the downside it is bearish.

If you come to the conclusion that Rayrock is worth $10 a share and you can see that there is tremendous support at $6, you know that you will probably not be able to buy the stock for much less than $6. If you are patient, you can wait for the stock to drop to the $6 support level, pick it up and then wait for the stock to climb back up to the price you think is fair value. Despite this homework, it's important to keep your knowledge of the company up to date; a sudden change in its fortunes could have a dramatic impact on the market performance you expect. Should the company make a discovery, for example, your valuation of the company might jump to $14 instead of $10.

Rule 4: Watch the trading volume

Finally, you should keep an eye on the volume of stock that is traded. Stock prices are not only determined by detailed technical and fundamental analysis, they respond to the law of supply and demand. If demand is high, the number of shares of the stock being traded will be larger and the price of the stock is probably being pushed up. If you look at the chart you will see that all the major moves have been made when volume reaches higher-than-normal quantities. The converse is also true. As the volume starts to decrease, the stock price is likely to decline, reflecting erosion of demand. Be aware of trading volume but don't be deceived; a change

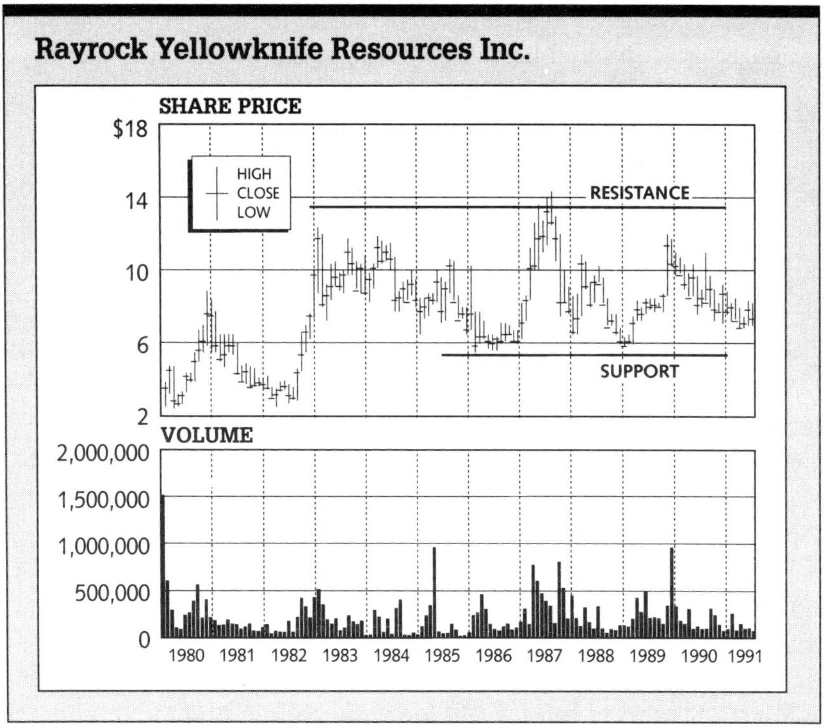

CHART VII

in volume could be one person making a very big mistake. Do your homework before making any moves.

The analysts and the brokers

In 1980, when I joined the investment counselling firm of Beutel, Goodman as a mining analyst, close to 80 per cent of my work was in analyzing base metal mining companies. Gold mining analysts did not exist; there were really only a few gold mining companies worth analyzing. Of the 15 top-ranked gold mining companies in 1992, only one existed in its current form in 1980 — Homestake Mining. Lac Minerals and Pegasus were junior companies. Companies like Teck, Placer and Newmont Mining were known strictly as base metal companies. Echo Bay, American Barrick, Amax Gold, Battle Mountain Gold, FMC Gold, Freeport McMoran Gold and Hemlo Gold were all created in the mid-1980s.

There were serious problems getting information. Gold mining had practically disappeared in the 1960s and 1970s in both Canada and the U.S.; few people were knowledgeable about gold mining and the vast differences with base metal mining. An investment manager or individual investor wanting to know anything had to go out into the field, visit the emerging gold camps and gather the information first-hand before making an informed judgment.

One trip I remember quite vividly was to Cullaton Lake in February, 1981. Cullaton Lake is located in the Northwest Territories, 300 air miles north of Lynn Lake, Man. When our little party of five people arrived at this desolate mining camp, the thermometer was hovering around -30°F at midday. By late afternoon the wind was blowing fiercely from the west and the temperature dropped to more than -45°F. You couldn't stay outdoors more than three minutes without your nose turning white and you were warned not to go outside where you could become quickly disoriented in the sea of white surrounding the mine. Only the local Inuit could find their way in and out of this frozen hole without risking their lives.

The year before, the price of gold had hit $850 (U.S.) and as we sat at Cullaton Lake it was just beginning to slip below $600. You couldn't spend money fast enough to bring mines into production and that was what was happening here. More than $32 million had already been spent to buy and ship by air the material, equipment and men needed to bring a 300-ton-a-day mine into production. Yet all this money was being predicated on the results of no more than a dozen drill holes. The holes were so good that the geologists felt there had to be an ore body down there. With the price of gold falling, the mine needed more capital to get into production as the company was fast running out of money. The current reserves stood at about two years of mine life, but there were indications that the potential was quite significant.

We ended up arranging the financing to complete the installation of the mine and mill, but to our disappointment no more gold was found and the mine ran only for about two years before shutting down. In the meantime, the Canadian federal government brought in the flow-through tax scheme. Subsequently, more than $50 million was spent at Cullaton trying to identify new reserves, but none were found. The sobering realization from this was that it would have been cheaper to buy gold than to try to mine it at Cullaton Lake.

Cullaton was a disappointment uncharacteristic of the industry in the early days. The Canadian gold mining industry expanded throughout the decade with the discovery of new ore bodies. This growth was reflected on the Toronto Stock Exchange, where the TSE Gold Index grew to represent as much as 10 per cent of the TSE 300, up from 1 per cent in 1981. This growth was matched by a proliferation in the number of brokerage houses and analysts following gold mining companies.

In Canada, where the tradition of mining is very strong and mining still plays a significant role in the Canadian economy, both the number and quality of analysts increased rapidly. There isn't a major brokerage house in Canada that does not have at least one, if not two or three, gold mining analysts. Even the smaller, boutique houses have to follow gold and the mining industry to keep up with the demands of clients.

In the U.S., the push for distinct gold mining analysts did not come until the mining companies themselves achieved sizes that made it possible for large American brokerage houses to recommend specific gold stocks. However, there is still an enormous amount of educating to be done in the U.S. before institutions fully understand the gold mining industry.

The research material published by the major brokerage houses is prolific and of exceptional quality. Firms like Donaldson, Lufkin and Jenrette, Goldman Sachs and Merrill Lynch in the U.S. and Nesbitt Burns, Scotia Capital, Gordon Capital, First Marathon and Bunting Warburg in Canada are a few of the companies that publish comprehensive, detailed analysis of the top 15 to 45 companies in North America. There are also smaller investment houses, such as Yorkton Securities, Canaccord Capital, and C.M. Oliver, that concentrate on junior gold mining companies or specialize in the emerging companies listed on the Vancouver and Toronto stock exchanges.

Canadian mining analysts tend to have a technical background, often in mining or geological engineering, as well as solid business credentials. Their New York or American counterparts tend to be business graduates who have become mining analysts. As a result, there can be a difference in reports, especially of ore reserve calculations and feasibility studies. The depth of reporting in financial statements depends on the exchange on which the company is listed and the country of incorporation. Junior companies listed in Vancouver have in the past faced far less stringent reporting standards than a company listed in Toronto or New York. Furthermore, reports on possible reserves are shadowed by the geological interpretation made by the mining company's management. An analyst without enough technical knowledge may not be able to discern fact from fiction when he is reading an inexperienced, optimistic or exaggerated report.

Breakwater Resources was caught when it bought 20 per cent of Noramco Mining in 1988. I was on the board of directors of Breakwater and we relied heavily on the company information circulars released when Noramco went public and two published reports from major brokerage firms. Noramco had already spent over $100 million on exploration and development, there were three mines with proven reserves on the drawing board, it had $30 million in cash and the stock was trading at around $6 a share. Not long after coming to market, Noramco's stock traded as high as $16 a share. With 15 million shares outstanding, the company had a market capitalization of over $225 million at that time. After Breakwater took control of the company it was realized that the three "mines" in the prospectus were really exploration projects with no defined minable ore reserves, even though the prospectus clearly stated that there were minable ore reserves. None of the 50 or 60 exploration projects, on which the company had spent millions of dollars, had even geological reserves. A few didn't even have properties that were known to contain gold. The people handling the technical aspects of the company had not followed industry practices and only a detailed, painstaking property visit could have prevented the mistake that was made.

Another mining company which has been stung is Western Mining of Australia. Western Mining spent over $450 million from 1987 to 1988 to buy four publicly listed gold mining companies. One of the acquired companies, Seabright Resources of Nova Scotia, was considered an emerging gold producer. But after spending $90 million to acquire Seabright, Western had to downgrade the reserves and grades of the two main deposits. The projects never yielded significant amounts of gold. Western sued for misrepresentation and omission of public documents filed with the regulating bodies, but it was rebuked by the courts with the ruling that Western should have done its homework.

The opinions of analysts should be impartial, but it's not always easy to get all the information needed. Much of the information analysts must use is interpretation of geological formations and assay results. Every analyst also draws on personal experience, both with mines and people in the industry. In the end, you can have two analysts with two very different opinions of a mine or mining company. Get to know the analysts by reading their reports, comparing their opinions and understanding their viewpoints.

Analysts' biases

Most analysts, whether they watch mining or any other industry, are inclined to the buy side of the market. They are far more likely to recommend that you buy a stock than they are to recommend that you sell. Why? Because the mining companies are valuable clients of the brokerage firms. In the past five years, gold mining companies have generated hundreds of millions of dollars in brokerage commission through mergers, acquisitions, equity issues, and gold bond issues. Even the analyst who sits behind the "Chinese wall" knows who is buttering his bread.

These "Chinese walls" are the securities regulations designed to restrict the flow of knowledge from one group within the company to another. This prevents the firm from using inside information in its decisions to buy or sell stock. It would be quite inappropriate for the firm to buy stock knowing that another department is structuring a merger or acquisition. If a brokerage firm is involved with a company that it is recommending to investors, it must tell investors on the back of its reports. A quick look can tell you if there is a potential bias in the firm's recommendation. This is particularly possible if the company is underwriting a public issue for the client firm. There is enormous pressure on the sales force and the analysts to sell a new issue and it's up to you to accept or reject your broker's or analyst's sales pitch.

If you're confused by your analyst's recommendation to buy, hold or sell, don't worry. You're not alone. Most reports are written with the long-term investor in mind. However, the analyst may also decide to include his short-term view for the traders. Perhaps a gold company's growth prospects over time are excellent, but the outlook for the overall stock market and for gold may not be good. So the analyst may tell the trader to sell, but advise the long-term investor to hold. It's important to read the report, understand the values that are attributed to the company and make your own decision to buy, hold or sell a stock.

CHAPTER 7

Gold Shares: What's So Different About Them?

TO MOST INVESTORS, PRIVATE as well as institutional, the weighing of the value of gold shares is a nebulous mix of finance and engineering that's closer to alchemy than financial analysis. It's difficult for the average investor to understand the emotions that erupt with the discovery of gold and the consequent surge in price not only of the company that made the discovery, but also of the companies that operate in the vicinity.

Man has been using gold as money for thousands of years, but the commercial business of finding, developing and producing gold is only about 150 years old. There's really nothing magical about gold mining; it's little different from any other mining venture — be it copper, zinc, nickel or any other metal. You must develop an understanding of the mine's resources, production methods, financial health and management capabilities. But because gold is money, there are a few peculiarities, particularly in the financing and selling of gold, that do set it apart from any other business — not only other mining businesses but other commercial enterprises as well.

Discovery costs

The lifeblood of any mine is its reserves. The day the very first ton of ore is mined, that particular ore body starts to die. Therefore, in order to survive, a mining company must spend money to replace the reserves that it mines. Two of the elements that set a mining company apart from other companies are the costs of finding and replacing each ounce of gold and the number of years that its reserves are likely to last — known as the mine life. This mine life is essentially the total reserves of the mine divided by the annual rate of production.

Over the past 20 years, the average cost of finding an ounce of gold in America has been approximately $25 (U.S.). At a gold price of $400 (U.S.) an ounce, that $25 (U.S.) would be the same as finding a $20 (U.S.) barrel of oil for less than 30 cents. There is, of course, only one place in the world where oil may still be found for as little as 30 cents a barrel — in Saudi Arabia which has the world's largest reserves.

But $25 (U.S.) an ounce is only the average cost of finding gold; there are companies that spend less and others that spend far more. Obviously, the lower the finding costs the more the company that owns those reserves should be worth. The finding cost is predicated on a number of technical factors, such as the particular geology of the area, the location and nature of the deposit and the extent of the gold within the deposit. There are several geological classifications of deposits, but as an investor you should be familiar with the three main types of gold deposits found in the world — placer deposits, veins or lodes, and bulk or porphyry deposits.

Placer deposits

Placer deposits were the first form of gold deposit to be found and exploited by man. Gold is heavy — six times heavier than most rock — and if it is dislodged from the rock by water erosion it will soon sink to the bottom of the stream. The gold can be found in the nooks and bends of an ancient river bed where the water has slowed. Sometimes the rivers are still flowing; in other instances, the rivers have dried up and the deposits lie on river beds that have been covered by gravel and rocks. The first known gold rush, the 1849 gold rush in California, was sparked by the discovery of placer gold at Sutter Creek. Placer gold also sparked the Klondike gold rush and today, along the Amazon, hundreds of thousands of Brazilians are mining placer deposits in the depths of the Matto Grosso jungle.

In 1986, I went on a tour of gold mining operations in Brazil. After a two-and-a-half-hour flight from Rio de Janeiro over a solid green carpet of jungle we landed in a godforsaken outpost in the middle of the jungle. The town had dusty streets, clapboard houses, and a saloon and dance hall complete with gun racks at the door. The only concessions to modern life were small pickup trucks and electricity. Life for the Brazilian garimpeiros is just as miserable as it was a hundred years ago in the mining camps of Nevada. They toil 10 to 12 hours a day on their concessions for meagre returns, fighting disease, jungle animals, humidity and claim jumpers.

The ingenuity of the garimpeiros is without equal. Much of the Brazilian placer gold has found its way to the bottom of large fast-moving rivers. To recover that gold they use a barge, on top of which is installed a suction pump and a small sluice box — the screen that separates the gold from the dirt. The whole thing can be operated with two people on the barge and a diver. The barge floats down the river, stopping and vacuuming the river bed. If the pickings are good, the garimpeiros install themselves for as long as the river pays. There's no way of knowing where the gold will be in a placer deposit or how much gold exists. The diver spends up to 10 hours a day underwater, vacuuming the bottom of the river. His air comes from pumps that are old and inefficient; whenever he is underwater he breathes air mixed with engine fumes and oil. After eight months on the job most divers are either retired or dead. Why do they do it? Because they get to keep 25 per cent to 50 per cent of the gold found. The owner of the barge keeps the difference.

When I switched from the mining to the investment business 10 years ago, one of the senior partners in the firm told me I could invest in any mining deal I thought was attractive, but to avoid placer deals. The advice had not been forgotten when in July, 1983, Galaxy Minerals, Inc. raised $11 million from the Canadian public to acquire and operate a placer gold deposit at Livengood, Alaska, about 80 miles northwest of Fairbanks. The company had prepared a superb 40-page prospectus on its placer deposit. The ore reserves had been compiled and approved by a prestigious Canadian geological consulting firm and the plan of operation had been carefully designed by the best people in the field. The board of directors was composed of reputable people, including several mining men. Most of the equipment and people were already in place, gold production was about to start and profits were practically in the bank. With some hesitation, we decided to pass for two reasons.

First, the money being raised was to be used to repay the previous owner/operator of the property, who had spent over $22 million (U.S.) and had yet to make money. Second, after all that money had been spent, consultants estimated reserves to be barely above 100,000 ounces. With $22 million (U.S.) already spent, the cost of finding the gold had already reached $220 (U.S.) an ounce. Mining would probably end up costing $250 (U.S.) an ounce in total, leaving little room for profit.

A month later, mining at Livengood hit bedrock, much sooner than expected. This was devastating, since it meant the much higher grades of ore that had been expected were not there. Placer mining in Alaska lasts only from June to October and by the end of mining season Galaxy had been able to process only 85 per cent of the projected gravel because of permafrost, equipment problems and smaller-than-expected reserves. The fatal stumble was over the gold that was actually recovered. In its prospectus, the company and its consultants had estimated production would amount to 25,000 ounces in its first season. It mined only 11,300 ounces. Within six months the company, incorporated in Colorado, sought protection under Chapter 11 of the U.S. bankruptcy code. After several unsuccessful attempts at finding partners to continue operations, the company was declared bankrupt and its stock exchange listing was terminated in June 1984, only 11 months after the initial offering.

What could have gone so wrong despite the calibre of people and advice? The first problem lay in the placer mining knowledge of the people involved. Placer mining technology and knowledge all but died with the California and Yukon placer camps at the turn of the century. What we have today are hard rock geologists and engineers interpreting placer deposits. During the previous two years, the original operator had mined almost 403,000 cubic yards of gravel for just over 6,000 ounces of gold. This represented an average grade of 0.015 ounces for each cubic yard. Yet when the consultants calculated the reserves of the remaining gravel as 0.041 ounces a yard — nearly three times the two-year sample — they weren't questioned.

To protect yourself when investing in companies with placer deposits, you're more likely to stay out of trouble if you heed these warnings.

Caveat 1: Placer deposits are notoriously erratic. Since the gold has been deposited in the bends of rivers, it is exceedingly difficult to predict exactly where it is. Often the company is exploring ancient river beds that have been covered or eroded over the centuries. Where pay gravel is predicted, more often than not there is only dirt. If 50 feet of gravel is predicted, chances are good that only 25 feet will be found.

Caveat 2: Placer deposits have short lives. It takes thousands of years for a little bit of gold to be deposited on a river bottom, yet it can be scooped up quickly with today's technology. Most placer gold rushes have petered out within 10 years of their discovery because the reserves are depleted so quickly.

Recent debacles may be proof that after 140 or so years of placer mining in North America, there isn't much placer gold left. Placer mining is really best done as a mom-and-pop venture. On a small scale, and given a decent placer deposit in the Yukon or Alaska, a family of four can make a living panning for gold. As for commercial placer mining, there is only one large placer mine left in North America. Yuba Gold in California has been around for over 100 years, producing 30,000 ounces of gold a year — unfortunately not at a great deal of profit in the past three decades. As many as 50 to 60 small placer mines in the Yukon and Alaska are each producing between 2,000 and 5,000 ounces of gold a year.

A vein deposit

In Canada, it's called a vein. In the U.S., they talk about a lode or ledge, and in South Africa they refer to reefs. In every country the deposit being talked about is the same — an opening or crack in the earth's crust filled with gold-rich rock. The more dramatic the geological event that caused the crack or fissure, the richer the deposit that is likely to be formed. The golden mile of Kirkland Lake in Ontario has produced over 24 million ounces of gold since 1910. The famous Comstock Lode in Virginia City, Nev., has produced 15 million ounces of gold and 750 million ounces of silver. In South Africa the Witwatersrand basin has produced hundreds of millions of ounces of gold and will likely continue to produce gold for decades.

The vein type of deposits can vary in size from a few feet in length and only an inch wide to unimaginably rich veins several thousand feet in length, hundreds of feet wide and as deep as 12,000 feet. The gold in a vein can be easier to measure than in a placer deposit, but still cannot be predicted with certainty. In Kirkland Lake, only one drill hole in five is expected to provide an ore with enough gold to make it worth mining and most of these deposits are vertical to near vertical. In exploration, vertical deposits present two problems — they can be easily missed and if you drill down the vein you'll have no idea how wide it is. It's easier to measure a vein that slopes.

The depth of the vein is also important. It's not too difficult to drill veins near the surface, but as the vein target becomes deeper, drilling costs increase dramatically. As an investor, you must know these geological facts before you can determine the credibility of a company's promises. I vividly remember a junior exploration company with a California mine that drilled down the throat of a vein and came out with spectacular drill hole results. When the geologist looked at the deposit and found little gold surrounding the drill hole, the stock plummeted and buried itself 10 feet below ground.

Bulk or porphyry deposits

Gold deposits can also be formed when gold-imbued liquids rise from the earth's centre along a fault in the earth's crust. When the liquid hits a strata of porous rock, it will spread throughout the rock and form what is called a bulk or porphyry deposit. Most large open-pit mines, such as the McLaughlin mine in California and Round Mountain mine in Nevada, are bulk deposits. They are somewhat easier to drill and far easier to prove than either placer or vein deposits. Once a hole has hit gold-bearing ore, you can drill holes every 300 feet, then every 100 feet, 50 feet and finally as close as 15 feet in very small erratic deposits. The entire ore zone can be proven by drilling from the surface in a fairly short period of time and the reserves can be considered proven, with some of the periphery as probable.

Any geologist reading this book will take a dim view of the way I've classified gold ore bodies, since I've ignored the distinction between the event that has led to the rock's formation and the event that has brought the gold into a particular type of rock. For the geologist, the distinction is quite important because it enables him to pinpoint potential ore bodies. As an investor, you don't need this knowledge any more than you need to know how a computer is built before you can invest in IBM. Every investor has to rely on the company to tell him what's going on. However, when you're dealing with a junior company, you have to realize that the predictions of future mining activity will be based on the judgment of one individual. If that person is wrong, or doesn't tell the whole truth, you won't know until it's too late. That's another reason to screen your junior portfolio investments carefully. But even big companies have been known to make mistakes in calculating ore reserves. In December, 1988, Echo Bay estimated its gold reserves at McCoy/Cove in Nevada to be more than 10 million ounces. In December, 1989, it revised this estimate to less than 5.5 million ounces, a 45 per cent drop.

The cost of developing a gold mine

The cost of finding, and then of developing, a deposit depends heavily on its location. A vast area of northern Quebec, including the newly discovered Casa Berardi gold camp, is in a marsh that's almost impossible to travel over during the summer. This confines drilling to the winter, when the ground is frozen. In northwestern British Columbia, there aren't any roads or power and the winters are so fierce that sometimes as much as 60 feet of snow falls over the winter. The drilling season is confined from late May to barely the end of September and has to be supported entirely by helicopter, which is rather expensive.

The rugged, forested frozen expanse of northern Canada contrasts sharply with the deserts of Nevada and Mexico, where the deposits can be easily reached with a pickup truck and the weather is usually clement. Obviously, the costs of working these mines are dramatically lower. In South America, you learn to cope with totally different problems. Chile has a long and proud reputation as a mining country; in the rest of South America labour is cheaper but the productivity is low and technical competence negligible. The difficulty of getting equipment and spare parts is compounded by local restrictions on imports and by duties, paperwork and, very often, bribes.

Finally, exploration costs are affected by the type of drilling equipment that is used. Drilling a flat deposit in soft rock can be as low as $7 (U.S.) a foot, while drilling through hard rock to a vein deep in the ground can run higher than $35 (U.S.) a foot.

In the end, companies like Newmont Gold can explore their Carlin Trend acreage and increase their reserves for a cost that is slightly less than $4 (U.S.) for every ounce of gold found over the past 10 years. In Canada, the average cost of finding an ounce of gold is $65 (U.S.) an ounce if you include the large, rich Hemlo mines. The Hemlo mines make up more than half the gold discovered in the past 10 years; if you remove Hemlo from the statistics, the cost of finding an ounce of gold in Canada rises to $100 (U.S.).

As an investor, you can easily determine a company's costs of finding an ounce of gold by analyzing its annual report — the first step that every investor must take to evaluate a gold mining company. All you have to do is divide the number of ounces of gold added to the company's reserves by the amount of money spent on exploration in that year. It is quite clear that if the cost of finding an ounce of gold is higher than the selling price of gold, there is little hope for that particular company. Indeed, you should not forget that after a company has found gold in the ground, it must make the capital expenditures and pay the operating expenses to remove the gold and extract it from the rock.

As a general rule, a company that can find gold for less than $20 (U.S.) an ounce in the ground is doing very well. At $20 to $40 an ounce, the company is above average but will have to strive to earn the most profit it can from its operation. If the gold costs more than $50 an ounce to find, the company is not likely to be in business for long unless it already has many years of reserves.

Costs of operation

In North America, the total cost of producing one ounce of gold in 1995 was approximately $292 (U.S.). This is made up of cash costs of around $233 (U.S.) and depreciation of $59 (U.S.) per ounce. If the price of gold is $380 (U.S.) an ounce, the mining company has an operating profit margin of around 39 per cent before depreciation.

When a company discusses cash costs in its annual report, it is talking about all the expenses that the mine incurs to extract and produce the gold from a deposit. As a matter of policy, these costs will include definition drilling, development drilling, blasting, hauling, hoisting, crushing, screening, grinding, cyanidation, pressure leach, gold precipitation, tailings dams, environmental reclamation and water pumping. For the large mining companies, these costs are always included in financial statements. However, there is room for interpretation and possible abuse. Depending on whether the mine is in operation or still being developed, some of the costs of exploration and development can be capitalized instead of expensed. If this is done, the reported cost of producing an ounce of gold will be lower than it is in reality. This accounting sleight of hand is likely to be used if a mine has high operating costs and the cost of developing new reserves is unprofitable at current gold prices.

The place to look for any indication of trouble is in the funds flow statements in the quarterly and annual financial statements. Mining companies have several ways of reporting how they spend their money. As an investor, you cannot look only at the income statement to know the company's real operating or exploration costs. All work already expensed will be incorporated in the cash costs and net earnings generated by the company. Any work in addition to the above that is being capitalized will be shown as using up cash in the funds flow account. It's important to find out the nature of these expenditures. If the company is sinking a new shaft in a new area of the mine with proven reserves, the accounting method is entirely justified. So would be the prestripping of a new open-pit zone. It could mean trouble, however, if the development of already-accounted-for reserves is capitalized: It doesn't represent the true situation at the time of the financial statements.

All of these cash costs are incurred to move and process the tons of ore that contain the gold. Each ton of ore could have as little as 0.02 ounces of gold, as in the RTZ Moro's de Oro mine in Brazil, or as much as several hundred ounces of gold, like some of the ore in Lac Minerals' El Indio mine in Chile. Before you can figure out the cash cost of an ounce of gold, there is one last factor to take into consideration — the gold recovery factor in the processing plant. The technique that has been used to recover the gold and the form in which the gold is present in the ore makes a great deal of difference. The gold recovery will vary from as low as 50 per cent in a heap-leaching operation to as high as 99 per cent from ore that is shipped directly to the smelter. The mill recovery factor is usually spelled out in the company's annual report and is one of the least variable factors of a mining operation.

Once you have all of these numbers, it becomes fairly simple to calculate the cash costs of producing the gold in dollars per ounce. Take the ore grade reported by the operator and multiply by the recovery rate to arrive at the effective gold content. Divide this into the cost of mining and processing each ton of ore. Take the following example: It costs $20 (U.S.) to mine and process each ton of ore. There are 0.12 ounces of gold in each ton of ore and 82.5 per cent of the gold can be recovered. The cash cost of producing each ounce of gold will be $202.02. The calculation: $20 divided by (0.12 multiplied by 0.825) = $202.02.

The reality of the mining business boils down to knowing the cash costs. If you know those, you know the company's profit margin. It doesn't matter whether you have very low-grade or very high-grade ore, what counts is the profitability of each ounce. In the past 10 years, we have seen the development of a promising new technique in the gold industry called heap-leaching. It has been touted as the salvation of the gold industry, but this exuberance ignores three significant facts:

- Heap-leaching can only be used on a small percentage of gold ore.
- The recovery factor is lower than other standard recovery techniques.
- Heap-leaching only works in warm weather.

It can't be denied that heap-leaching is generally inexpensive, mainly because it's an earth-moving operation. In its simplest form, ore is drilled, blasted and trucked to a pad resembling a giant asphalt parking lot where it is dumped in a heap. The heap is sprinkled for days with a weak cyanide solution that dissolves the gold particles. The solution bearing the gold — now referred to as "pregnant" — is collected in ditches around the pads and passed through carbon columns which absorb the gold. The columns can be refined and the gold collected. In Nevada, heap-leaching can cost as little as $2.50 (U.S.) per ton.

Heap-leaching makes it possible to extract gold profitably from ore of a very low grade. On Nevada's Carlin Trend, Newmont Gold can recover 60 per cent of the gold from ore that has only 0.015 ounces of gold in each ton. If the gold price is $400 (U.S.) an ounce, the gold recovered from each ton will be worth $3.60 (U.S.) — a profit of $1.10 (U.S.) for each ton of ore, a 44 per cent profit margin.

Underground mining is far more costly and capital intensive. Hemlo Gold can get 96 per cent of the gold from ore with 0.40 ounces of gold per ton, making each ton of rock worth $134 (U.S.) if the price of gold is $350 (U.S.). Even though its mining costs are $50 (U.S.) a ton, compared to heap-leaching's $6 (U.S.), it remains very profitable.

The point of all this is that you cannot judge the profitability of a mine simply from the grade or the method of mining and recovery. The only way to compare the operating expenses of mines is to bring them all down to a cash cost for each ounce of gold.

Capital costs

The mining business has always been a very capital-intensive business requiring patience and deep pockets. The extraction of gold from the earth is almost never a simple affair. The capital costs in gold mining are dependent on three variables:

- whether the mine is an underground or open-pit operation

- the type of plant required to extract the gold from the ore
- the location of the mine

The building of the mine itself can be quick and inexpensive or it can be a long, drawn-out and very expensive proposition. The contrast is most vivid between Australian open-pit mines that have come into production in the past few years and the new South African underground mines. The Australian mines are small, open-pit operations located near existing roads, power lines and towns. They're close to the surface with little ground to remove before production can begin. In this case, the costs of building the mine consist only of unskilled labour and dirt-moving equipment, and even that can be rented if the mine has only a short life. On the other hand, in South Africa the new mines are deep beneath the earth at a depth of 5,000 to 8,000 feet. Just sinking the shaft can take years. Anglo American will spend $1 billion (U.S.) developing a mine which will not produce an ounce of gold for another five years. While the shaft is being sunk, you cannot reach the ore deposit and nothing else can happen. Even after the shaft is in, the tons of waste that are produced while developing the mine cannot be stored underground. This waste has to be moved up through the shaft and prevents actual mining. All this work has to be done in sequence and is not only time-consuming but very expensive.

Underground versus open-pit

Usually, the decision to mine a deposit by a particular method is dictated by the ore body itself, but in a few cases the mining company does have a choice. It is easy to understand that the large, low-grade ore bodies that are near the surface, such as the Nevada Carlin Trend, are better mined from open pits. The narrow, high-grade, deep-vein deposits such as Campbell Red Lake in Ontario and Homestake in South Dakota can only be mined as underground operations. The nature of the gold deposit also dictates the milling method and the ultimate recovery factor.

Processing methods

Gold can be found in three different forms: free coarse gold, oxide and sulfide ore. In mines, gold can occur in one form or in all three. In the Canadian Shield, most mines will have free coarse gold in the sulfide ore while most southwest U.S. mines will have both oxide and sulfide materials. Free coarse gold, gold that can be seen in the

The Cost of Building a Gold Mine* ($U.S.)

Type of operation	Project	Location	Operator	Orig. est. ounces in reserve	Planned annual ounces	Annual tons of ore (mm)	Budgeted cap. cost ($mm)	Capital cost per— oz. in reserve	annual oz.	annual ton of ore
Underground mine and mill										
	Porgera	PNG	Placer Pacific	12,600,000	800,000	3.000	800	63	1,000	267
	Hope Brook	Newfoundland	BP Canada	1,371,000	126,000	3.300	151	110	1,198	46
	Bousquet #2	Quebec	Lac Minerals	1,740,000	230,000	1.050	125	72	543	119
	Golden Pond	Quebec	TVX Gold	1,200,000	120,000	0.462	90	75	750	195
	Holt McDermott	Ontario	Am. Barrick	611,000	80,000	0.525	62	101	775	118
	LaRonde	Quebec	Agnico Eagle	737,000	100,000	0.735	62	84	620	84
	Kettle River	Washington	Echo Bay	833,000	60,000	0.380	55	66	917	145
	Cheni	British Columbia	Cheni Gold	580,000	50,000	0.193	37	64	740	192
	Dona Lake	Ontario	Placer Dome	378,900	40,000	0.193	36	95	900	187
	Magnacon	Ontario	Muscocho	340,000	60,000	0.210	26	76	433	124
	Kremzar	Ontario	Canamax	165,243	30,000	0.150	22	133	733	147
	Ketza	Yukon	Canamax/PTX	257,000	50,000	0.123	18	70	360	146
	Jolu	Saskatchewan	Int. Corona	240,000	50,000	0.140	16	67	320	114
	Average							**83**	**715**	**145**
Open-pit mine and mill										
	Betze-Post	Nevada	Am. Barrick	12,000,000	900,000	4.400	395	33	439	90
	Misima	PNG	Placer Pacific	2,500,000	220,000	5.775	220	88	1,000	38
	Colomac	NWT	Northgate	1,560,000	200,000	3.200	130	83	650	41
	Bullfrog	Nevada	Bond Gold	1,800,000	200,000	2.700	110	61	550	41

TABLE XIV

The Cost of Building a Gold Mine (continued) ($U.S.)

Type of operation	Project	Location	Operator	Orig. est. ounces in reserve	Planned annual ounces	Annual tons of ore (mm)	Budgeted cap. cost (mm)	Capital cost per— oz. in reserve	Annual oz.	Annual ton of ore
	Getchell	Nevada	FirstMiss	1,272,000	140,000	1.050	90	71	643	86
	Ridgeway	S.Carolina	Kennecott	1,792,000	135,000	5.475	80	45	593	15
	Granny Smith	Australia	Placer Pacific	1,150,000	235,000	3.300	77	67	328	23
	Premier	British Columbia	Westmin	800,000	89,000	0.777	75	94	843	97
	Nickel Plate	British Columbia	Int. Corona	1,250,000	110,000	1.000	63	50	573	63
	Marigold	Nevada	Rayrock	658,000	60,000	1.168	37	56	617	32
	Rabbitt Creek	Nevada	Santa Fe Pacific	3,600,000	200,000	1.100	137	38	685	125
	Kelian	Indonesia	CRA	3,400,000	260,000	6.500	232	68	892	36
	Average							**63**	**651**	**57**
Open-pit mine and leach										
	Mesquite	California	Gold Fields	2,150,000	150,000	4.500	70	33	467	16
	Castle Mountain	California	Viceroy/MK	1,770,000	100,000	2.800	50	28	500	18
	Colosseum	California	Bond Gold	653,400	72,000	1.212	30	46	417	25
	Golden Reward	S. Dakota	United Coin	882,000	65,000	2.400	28	32	431	12
	Gilt Edge	S. Dakota	Minven	283,000	45,000	1.400	18	64	400	13
	Santa Fe	Nevada	Int. Corona	314,500	50,000	2.000	11	35	220	6
	Lone Tree	Nevada	Santa Fe Pacific	921,000	100,000	1.000	53	58	530	53
	Average							**42**	**423**	**20**

*Based on feasibility studies expectations. Actual costs and outputs were often significantly different from expectations.

TABLE XIV continued

ore, is easily recovered by gravity separation. After the ore is crushed down to less than 0.25 inches in diameter and before the actual milling operation, the ore is passed over a special table where the gold falls to the bottom and is recovered. Placer mines use this principle with the sluice box. Some California quartz vein mines use only the dry gravity separation method of shaking tables to recover 70 per cent to 90 per cent of the gold.

Oxide deposits are former sulfitic ore bodies that have been oxidized through contact with air over tens of thousands of years. The oxidation breaks the bond between the gold and the host rock and makes it easier for today's miner to recover. Oxide ore can be heap-leached and 60 per cent to 75 per cent of the gold recovered. Ore can be milled and tank-leached with a strong cyanide solution in a few hours with recoveries in the 80 per cent to 95 per cent range. The cost of the mill and recovery complex will be determined by the size of the plant and retention time.

Sulfide ore, which is the most common form of gold ore, can be treated in a variety of ways. The method chosen will depend on the host rock itself and the degree of recovery one wants to achieve within acceptable costs. In Canada, most sulfide ore is simple to treat, requiring only grinding and cyanidation to recover 90 per cent to 95 per cent of the gold. If the gold is encapsulated, which means it is locked in the sulfides, the ore has to be ground as finely as possible and put through a flotation stage where most of the gold is floated into a concentrate. The flotation concentrate can be treated with cyanide or shipped directly to a smelter, depending on the economics of recoveries of the two methods.

As the sulfide reserve gets more complicated so do the treatment methods and costs. Refractory gold ore, like that at the McLaughlin and Getchell mines, is especially difficult to treat because the gold particles are tightly woven into the matrix of the rock itself and cannot be treated by conventional methods. To liberate the gold, the rock matrix itself must be destroyed through either a roasting process, autoclaving or a chlorination process. All these processes demand a heavy investment in plant and equipment. They are plausible only for large, high-grade deposits.

The choice of process is a function of the ore itself. Freeport Gold, at its Bull Run mine in Nevada, has chosen to use a roasting facility whereby the gold ore is roasted in a large kiln to liberate the gold. However, roasting produces sulphuric gases which must be removed from the plant's waste with a scrubbing system to prevent acid rain. Chlorination is a chemical process that achieves the same results as roasting but is very costly and extremely hazardous. Autoclaving plants, such as the one at American Barrick's Goldstrike mine, resemble a complicated chemical complex more than a milling operation as they try to imitate nature by oxidizing the sulfide ore with oxygen under high pressure and temperature. A process that would take thousands of years in nature is achieved in a few hours.

In looking at the money spent or committed over the past five years to build gold mines, it is clear that the winners are the large open-pit mines of Nevada such as American Barrick's Goldstrike and Newmont's Gold Quarry. Both companies have depreciated capital costs of less than $40 (U.S.) an ounce. At the other end of the scale, the high-cost underground mines with limited reserves have depreciated costs that exceed $100 (U.S.) an ounce. The average for North America in 1995 was about $59 (U.S.).

At a $380 (U.S.) gold price and a cost of $280 (U.S.), the pretax profit margin for the mining company is slightly over 25 per cent. If you look only at the cash costs of $220 (U.S.), the profit margin is 42 per cent. This is actually quite remarkable. Gold companies do not need to carry any inventory, which means they don't suffer from the "shrinkage" or theft that other industries experience. Selling costs are no more than a few dollars an ounce and, because the producer can always sell his entire production at any time, he never has to sell his gold at a discount to clear inventory.

Sustaining capital

Few promoters of junior exploration companies know the meaning of the term "sustaining capital." But ask the mine managers of this world and the term is very real — it represents an additional expense. Once a new mine is brought into production, it will run efficiently for a few years. But the plant then starts to age rapidly and more money is needed to keep it operating efficiently. Mining equipment has a life expectancy of only five to seven years before it has to be rebuilt or replaced. Shaft deepening, new crushing stations, new overburden stripping, the extension of tailings ponds, raising of dams, mill improvements and increasing capacity are all parts of the continuing capital requirements of a mine. To satisfy these demands for capital, it is necessary to make provisions to reinvest some of the mine's cash flow. That money, the sustaining capital, will not be available to shareholders if a mine is to be kept operating at top efficiency.

A mine's need for sustaining capital will depend partly on the capital invested in the first place — just as a Mercedes-Benz needs less maintenance than a Lada — and on the particular circumstances. An open-pit mine in the southwestern U.S., for instance, will require less maintenance than an underground mine in northwestern Quebec. As a rule of thumb, the mine will need a yearly influx of capital amounting to between three per cent and five per cent of the original capital costs. Typically, a $100 million (U.S.) mine will require $3 million (U.S.) to $5 million (U.S.) a year just to keep going. As an investor, it's important that you identify these expenditures in the funds flow statement if they are not spelled out in the management analysis that follows the financial reporting in the annual report. They may tip you off to problems faced by a mine. You should also deduct these expenses when evaluating the company's worth because, while they sustain the company, they don't add value.

Forward-selling

Not only can gold producers sell everything they produce at any time, but, with the development of the futures markets over the past 10 years they can increase their revenues by capturing the forward premium that is built into the futures markets. These are two unique features of gold that are not shared by other commodities such as oil, copper or orange juice.

If you open your newspaper to the financial pages and seek out details on futures contracts for gold, you will notice the price that gold can fetch rises for contracts coming due in months that are progressively further in the future. This difference between the current, or "spot," price and the future price is known as the "contango." The contango represents the costs of financing, insuring and storing the bullion for that period of time. If the current spot price is $380 (U.S.) an ounce and the price a year away is $390 (U.S.) an ounce, the contango is $10 (U.S.) an ounce — an imputed interest rate of 2.6 per cent. If the price of gold is stable or falling, the gold-producing company can benefit. Indeed, by continuously selling forward in a stable gold price environment, the mining company will realize a 2.6 per cent higher rate of return, if the contango is 2.6 per cent, than if it sells its gold on the spot market.

Another characteristic of the gold financial market is the availability of options. Options, combined with the futures market, can give the gold operator tremendous flexibility in managing gold revenues. For example, Barrick Gold spent $440 million (U.S.) over a period of four years to bring its Goldstrike mine into production. This is a very large amount of money for any company to risk. To assure itself of a decent return on its investment under virtually any gold price scenario, the company used the options and futures market to hedge its risks. It bought "put" options, giving it the right to sell 75 per cent of the gold it will produce over the next three years at a minimum price of $418 (U.S.) an ounce. To cover the costs of purchasing the put options, Barrick sold "call" options. These gave the buyers of the options the right to purchase 25 per cent of Barrick Gold's gold, if the gold price is between $421 (U.S.) and $507 (U.S.) and 64 per cent of the production if the gold price is above $507 (U.S.). The effect of this transaction, which didn't cost Barrick anything, is to protect its profit margin. If the price of gold drops over the next three years, Barrick has calculated that it will earn at least 33 per cent on its investment; should the price of gold rise, Barrick's profit margin could reach 45 per cent.

Another technique using options and futures is the "gold averaging price." Let's assume the spot price of gold is $400 (U.S.), but a two-year futures contract is selling for $484 (U.S.) and a four-year contract for $585 (U.S.). Assuming the premium is 10 per cent, the company buys calls for the first two years and sells puts for the following two years. It would then receive an average price of $475 (U.S.) an ounce over the four years of the contracts. For a mine that has marginal profitability, perhaps with cash costs in excess of $300 an ounce, this strategy can be a winning combination if gold prices are weak.

The most unusual financial instrument a gold company can use is the "gold loan." Because gold is riskless money, you can actually borrow gold at an effective rate of 1.5 per cent to 3.0 per cent a year depending on the size and the risk associated with the company. Of course, there is always a risk that the mine's production could fall short or cease entirely and the borrower will never see his gold. Therefore, all gold loans are backed by collateral, not only by the gold in the ground but also, in most cases, by the assets or credit of the company.

From the producer's standpoint, the beauty of the gold loan is the extremely favourable financing terms. By using the main asset of the company, its gold reserves, the company can obtain part if not most of its financing needs at a cost of only 1.5 per cent to 3 per cent. Again, in an environment of stable or falling gold prices, this strategy works doubly well because it not only gives the company cheap financing but also protects part of its production at a fixed price.

Let's say a company has borrowed 100,000 ounces of gold which it then sold at $425 (U.S.) to realize $42.5 million (U.S.) to develop its mine. When it repays the gold loan, perhaps a year later, if gold happens to be $400 (U.S.) an ounce the company realizes a profit of $25 (U.S.) an ounce or $2.5 million (U.S.). However, if the gold price actually rose to $450 (U.S.) by the time the company repays its loan, then the net cost of the loan is not only the gold loan interest rate of 2 per cent ($850,000 [U.S.]) but also the amount that the company could have earned if it had not sold the gold at $425 (U.S.). This incremental cost amounts to $2.5 million (U.S.); added to the $850,000 (U.S.) it brings the effective interest rate to 7.88 per cent over a one-year period. While still much better than a bank loan at today's interest rates, it's not as attractive as initially envisaged. Despite this danger, it is clear that no other commercial enterprise can avail itself of such incredibly attractive financing costs.

Overview

You can see that the gold business is unique. Look at all the elements:

- The discovery or replacement cost of $25 (U.S.) an ounce can generate a robust growth rate.
- Cash costs of $233 (U.S.) an ounce in North America give mining companies an operating profit margin of 39 per cent at $380 (U.S.) gold.
- Capital costs add only another $59 (U.S.) an ounce for a total cost of $292 (U.S.).
- The selling structure can give producers full price protection for as long as five years.

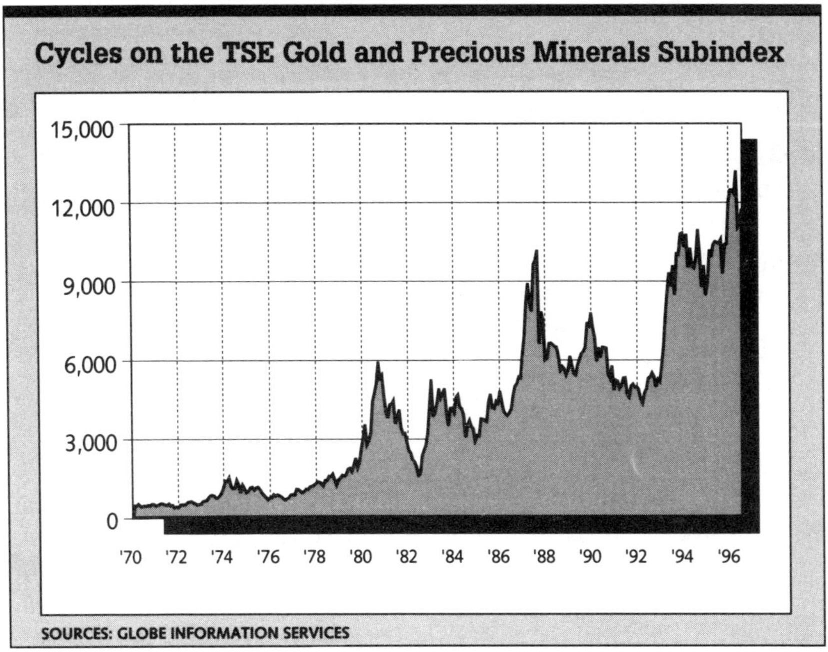

CHART VIII

- Financing costs can be as low as 1.5 per cent for gold loans which use the main asset of the company, its gold reserves, as collateral.

Blended together, these elements have given gold stocks a financial appeal that explains why players in equity markets have been willing to pay a premium for these stocks over the years. All of these factors, combined with a relatively high gold price throughout the past 20 years, have led to explosive growth of the moribund North American gold industry.

For a hint of the magnitude of this growth, consider the performance of the Toronto Stock Exchange gold subindex from 1972 to 1996. The first bull market on the TSE began just after the First World War as a flurry of discoveries spurred by the jump in the gold price to $35 (U.S.) in 1934. The market peaked at over 700 in 1937, plummeting to a low of 200 in 1958. By 1970, it had doubled to 400. Since then there have been five distinct cycles.

From Chart VIII, you can see the similarities among the cycles. Since 1958, the index has risen in four successive waves, reaching a peak of over 10,000 in the fall of 1987. However, the 20-year-old pattern of successively higher lows was decisively broken in 1991 as the index plunged to 4200, a level not seen since the mid-1980s. This is a significant breakdown in the index that will require some time to repair; too many investors lost money while promoters pocketed hefty profits. The index found solid support at the 4200 level and, after languishing there for two years, bounced back to the old highs of 10,000 in the fall of 1993 — a gain of more than 100 per cent in that year. Through 1994 and most of 1995, the index has been treading water as it has consolidated those gains. Early 1996 looked like the beginning of the long-awaited breakout, but by summer the momentum faded. The big question now: Is the stage set for a renewed breakout or breakdown?

This crystal-ball gazing is very appealing due to our bullish nature, but be careful not to put too much reliance on it. You cannot ignore fundamental analysis or technical trends. Still, there are two reasons why the index could reach the level mentioned above. First, as I discussed earlier, North American gold production will continue to grow for another two to three years, bringing with it growth in profits. The industry is likely to be producing more gold than ever before, with most of the exploration and development expenses behind it, at the same time as the gold price could stage a recovery. This double whammy could produce spectacular earnings for the major producers and keep the cycle alive longer than expected. However, as production starts to stabilize by the mid-1990s, the gold index will be dependent more than ever on the performance of the gold price itself.

CHAPTER 8

The Life Cycle of a Mining Share

MOST PEOPLE WHO INVEST IN the stock market end up at some time dabbling in gold shares. The lure of gold, the rags-to-riches stories, the excitement and the frenzy generated by new gold discoveries are too much for the average investor to ignore. Unfortunately, too many investors fail to distinguish hype from reality and lose their money. Gold companies are riskier and more volatile than most other kinds of stocks — but there are guidelines that will help you understand the risk structure of gold equities and recognize good value or bad value within each segment of the industry. The key word here is "guidelines"; there aren't any absolute rules in any market, let alone the gold equity market.

Gold company tiers

In the early 1980s, the explosive growth in the gold industry made it extremely difficult for analysts or investors to sort out the investment merits of different companies. Exploration companies were founded, existing base metal companies began producing gold and well-established gold companies became the blue-chip stocks of the industry. For investors, there's little point comparing an exploration company with a firm producing a million ounces of gold a year. To make it easier to compare apples with apples, it became necessary to segregate gold stocks by size into three tiers.

The Tier I stocks are those largest established gold producers with capitalizations near or in excess of $1 billion (U.S.) that produce at least 500,000 ounces of gold every year. They also are most likely to be companies with more than one mine and multimillion-ounce reserves. The Tier II stocks are all the smaller gold-producing companies. Often they have only one mine, producing anywhere from 20,000 ounces of gold a year up to 500,000 ounces a year. The Tier III gold stocks are the development companies or ones that

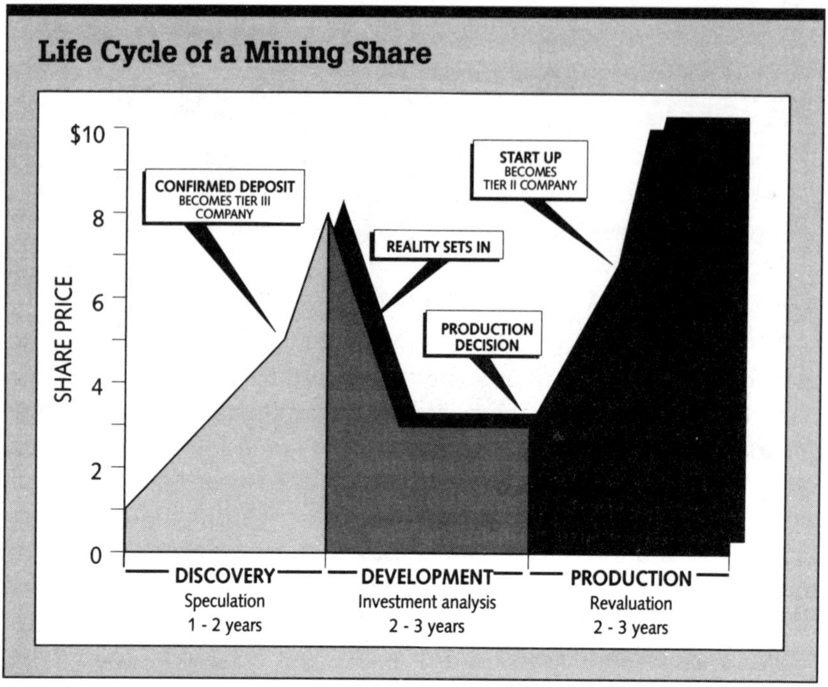

CHART IX

have been operating for too short a time to present a production track record. The "pure" exploration companies — the "drill-hole bets" — are the most volatile of all stocks. The fortunes of most of these companies usually depend on the results of a few drill holes.

The exploration companies

The birth of most mining companies can be traced back to one major event — the discovery of a major new ore body. In 1917, Edmund Horne, a Nova Scotian living in Ontario, organized the Tremoy Lake prospecting syndicate, which identified gold and copper at Noranda, Que. But it wasn't until 1922, when the syndicate linked up with two wealthy Americans, that it had enough money to start developing what was to become Noranda Mines, one of the world's great mining companies.

Bostonian Thayer Lindsley was the driving force and promoter behind a company incorporated in 1928 as Ventures Ltd. Through this company, Lindsley became one of the most prolific mine finders and developers of the century. Falconbridge, Sherritt-Gordon, Beattie, Canadian Malartic and Giant Yellowknife are only a few of the mines he founded. Lindsley once inscribed a book with the advice: "Remember, Jim, always listen carefully to a prospector. He will tell you what's good about a property. You can always hire an engineer or geologist to tell you what's wrong with it."

It's a good piece of advice. More than 50 per cent of all new discoveries are made by individual prospectors working for themselves, grubstaking for a small group of people or working for small, junior exploration companies. Without these people we would be much the poorer in the development of our natural resources.

In Canada, junior companies can get their start directly on the Toronto Stock Exchange or Montreal Exchange, but the great majority are created, nurtured and promoted on the Vancouver Stock Exchange. The VSE prides itself as the largest venture capital market in the world and, despite the occasional scandal, so it is. In the United States, most of the speculative exchanges that provided the capital that fuelled the exploration booms of the 1800s and the early years of this century have been dying under the weight of regulations imposed on them over the years. The last one to pass away was the Spokane Exchange in July, 1991. As a result, the rate of new discoveries in the U.S. made by small American companies is a fraction of what is seen in Canada.

Peter Lynch said in his book *One Up on Wall Street*, "An investment is simply a gamble in which you've managed to tilt the odds in your favor." The stock market, he says, is very much like a stud poker game where you can see only four of the seven cards everyone else is holding. If there ever was a poker game worth playing, it's the one that is played in Vancouver; but before you start playing find out who the other players are and learn the rules of the game.

Rule 1:
Never bet more than you can afford to lose

In a game played with 52 cards, you have 16 face cards. So each time you're given a card, you have a one in four chance of getting a face card. In the world of mineral exploration, the discovery of a new mineral occurrence is a significant event. It is estimated that less than one in every 100 junior companies finds gold, while no more than one in 500 find gold worth mining.

To be absolutely sure of winning in this game, you would have to hold hundreds of stocks in your portfolio. This is impractical and most investors end up with 10 to 15 stocks, making their odds of

North American Gold Tiers

(sorted by market capitalization as at Aug. 19,1996)

	Stock symbol	Price (8/19/96)	Shares (mm)	Market cap ($US mm)	Est. 1996 prod. (000 oz.)
TIER I SENIOR PRODUCERS					
Barrick Gold Corp.	ABX	$C36.55	357.2	9,531	3,190
Freeport Copper & Gold	FCX-N	$US29.30	198.9	5,828	1,546
Placer Dome	PDG	$C32.65	239.4	5,706	1,989
Newmont Mining	NEM-N	$US52.70	99.4	5,238	2,091
Homestake Mining	HM-N	$US17.00	147.7	2,511	1,697
Ashanti Goldfields	AGL	$US22.00	102.0	2,244	1,014
Santa Fe Pacific Gold	GLD-N	$US12.70	131.4	1,669	955
Battle Mountain	BMG	$C8.40	244.5	1,499	681
TVX Gold	TVX	$C10.60	160.0	1,238	507
Echo Bay Mines	ECO	$C13.60	112.5	1,117	1,051
Kinross Gold	K	$C10.00	118.0	861	522
Cambior	CBJ	$C18.90	60.1	829	511
TIER II* JUNIOR PRODUCERS					
Bema Gold	BGO	$C12.10	85.3	753	119
Greenstone Resources	GRE	$C18.55	52.1	706	71
Prime Resources	PRU	$C10.65	80.1	623	547
Amax Gold	AU(AXG)	$C7.25	81.3	589	230
Agnico-Eagle	AGE	$C20.50	36.8	551	164
Goldcorp	G.A	$C11.95	62.7	547	120
Royal Oak Mines	RYO	$C5.05	140.1	516	425
Pegasus Gold	PGU	$C15.65	40.9	467	531
Dayton Mining	DAY	$C10.10	42.1	310	138
Eldorado Gold	ELD	$C8.00	47.0	274	109
Miramar Mining	MAE	$C7.25	49.2	260	156
Viceroy Resources	VOY	$C7.20	48.7	256	157
TIER III START UP/DEVELOPMENT					
Rea Gold	REO	$C2.30	91.5	154	37
William Resources	WIM	$C1.68	118.0	145	30
Caledonia Mining	CAL	$C6.45	28.8	136	86
Dakota Mining	DKT	$US2.50	26.5	66	60
High River Gold	HRG	$C4.15	20.7	63	50
Triton Mining	TIM	$C3.00	24.0	53	44
Canyon Resources	CAU	$C2.30	25.7	43	49

* cut off at market capitalization of less than $200 million

TABLE XV

winning one in 50. It's better than a lottery but worse than a good poker game. If you win, the speculation surrounding a new discovery can push your stock to incredible prices and you could make 10, 20, even 50 times your money. Just don't forget that the odds are not good.

A 1979 government-sponsored study entitled "Public Financing of Junior Resource Securities in British Columbia" revealed that at the time only 51 per cent of the money raised by junior companies was actually received by these companies; the rest of it went into the pockets of brokers, promoters and property vendors. After overhead expenses and other incidentals, no more than 20 per cent of the money raised was actually spent in the ground. New regulations have since been put in place and the record is certainly much improved. But even now, the North American Securities Administrators Association estimates that penny stock buyers lose some or all of their investment in 70 per cent of legitimate offerings. When fraudulent schemes are included, the proportion reaches 90 per cent.

Before you invest in a penny stock, remember the definition of a good promotion: "In the beginning, the promoter has the vision and the public has the money. In the end, the promoter has the money, the public has the vision." It's irreverent but it does cover two key questions every investor should ask: Who is the promoter and what is the vision?

Rule 2:
Know what you are buying

If you are interested in a stock, read the company's latest annual report, its latest information circular and, if it's an American company, the 10-K or 10-Q, the statements that must be filed quarterly and annually with the Securities and Exchange Commission. To get these, simply telephone the company and have them sent to you by mail. If the company is being recommended by your broker, ask him to provide you with the information. While you're at it, ask for corporate profiles of the top people as well as other corporate material. In most cases, you will be surprised at how much information you will receive.

Rule 3:
Know the people behind the promotion

Promoters are a unique breed of people who have a common ability to create and share a vision. Some of them can do it with an almost evangelical fervour. In the 1980s, the undisputed star in Vancouver was Murray Pezim, affectionately known as "the Pez." Pezim has been around for decades in the promotion of junior mining companies, but his most spectacular success was Corona Corp. which discovered the giant Hemlo gold field in Ontario. Although he subsequently lost control of Corona, Pezim retained control of Prime Equities, his flagship company.

Pezim swings from being Howe Street's darling to abruptly falling from grace. In the fall of 1989, Prime Resources made a promising gold discovery in the Eskay Creek area of northern British Columbia. The VSE was humming — at the same time, Pezim and his associates were selling some stock. Only a few months after being chosen promoter of the year, Pezim was facing lawsuits over the transactions. Pezim is active in about 50 companies on the VSE, but he doesn't confine his affairs to gold. He's ploughed money into everything from ice cream and greeting cards to football and boxing fights. Unhappily, poor health is now slowing his activity. He will be missed.

Robert Friedland is the quintessential promoter. Dubbed both a "genius" and a "space cadet" by his peers, Friedland's career was launched when he floated Galactic Resources Ltd. on the VSE for 50 cents a share in 1982. Galactic did not have any of the essential ingredients for a successful mining company. It lacked property, capital and proven management, but Friedland was able to create a gold producer. Raising over $250 million for Galactic, mostly from European institutions, he went on an acquisition spree and the share price soared to $18 in 1987. Unfortunately, few of Galactic's ventures proved to be economic and in 1992 the company went bankrupt over the mounting environmental cleanup cost at Summitville, its original gold mine in Colorado.

Friedland has an unusual background for someone in this industry. Born into a prominent Boston family, he graduated from a small college in Oregon, where he was friends with Steve Jobs, founder of the Apple Computer empire. Friedland spent seven years in India, immersed in Eastern philosophy. He traded commodities in Switzerland before he went on to deal in timber tracts in Oregon in the early 1980s. After arriving in Vancouver in 1981 without a cent in his pocket, Friedland spent a year watching the market and promoters before he launched Galactic. He then bought a mountain at Summitville, Colo., and a 49 per cent interest in a mine in South Carolina. He has purchased properties in Nevada and signed agreements with both the Philippines and China to explore and develop deposits. In 1992, Freidland entered the South American gold scene by purchasing land in the Venezuela Kilometre 88 gold district for a large sum of money, and transferring it to Vengold, his new public company. The stock went from 50 cents to more than $16 on promotion alone before collapsing to $2.50 when little gold was found in the first phase of exploration. But all of this has to be forgotten in light of Friedland's most recent achievement. A diamond exploration company that he launched during his Vengold activities discovered one of the world's richest nickel-cobalt deposits in Labrador. From late 1994, Diamond Fields Resources Inc. has gone from just another exploration story to one of the most exciting base metal development plays with a market capitalization of over $4 billion. It proves that you can never write off anyone in this business.

As an investor, you should ignore the eccentricities of the individual promoter and look for honesty. Avoid anyone involved in bankruptcy proceedings, justice department filings, fraud charges, tax evasions or any other legal problem. Look carefully at the promoter's track record. Success attracts success, especially in the mining industry, and any prospector who finds something interesting will go immediately to the most successful promoter he can. Indeed, the best plays are often in companies where a combination of strong promotional and excellent technical skills is at the helm.

Once you have all the information you can find on the promoter, find out about his vision. Try to distinguish between reality and fantasy. Ask what the promoter intends to do with your money. You want to see it spent in the ground and not on corporate offices, salaries, perks, excessive brokerage commissions or the promoter's past mistakes and debts. The people behind the promotion should take their chances along with the investors and reap their returns from appreciation of the shares.

You don't have to be a geologist to evaluate the play. Ore bodies are flukes of nature and there is no way to tell where and when someone will discover one. Remember the old mining cliché: The best place to look for an ore body is right beside an existing one. The geological conditions that produced one ore body are likely to be favourable to the formation of others. Think of the Carlin Trend in Nevada. Thirty years ago, only one deposit was known, 10 years later, there were four known deposits, today there are more than 21 known deposits with gold reserves of over 70 million ounces. The cliché doesn't hold true at Hemlo, so far. It is still early in the history of gold mining in the area and even though millions of dollars have been spent on exploration in the surrounding area, Hemlo still doesn't have a cousin-mine.

Rule 4:
Don't overpay

When it comes to paying for your stock, don't pay any more than double what the promoter paid if it's a new promotion. To find out how much his stock cost, go back to the information circular or the prospectus. Add the escrowed stock — the stock the exchanges allow the promoter to take for creating the company — to the stock he may have purchased and average the cost of his shares. If the promoter's average cost for each share is 35 cents, don't pay more than 70 cents. Once the stock hits $1, he'll start selling his stock and at $1.50 he'll be gone.

A second guideline is to pay no more than twice the cash value or working capital per share. If a company has $1 million in cash and four million shares outstanding, the cash per share is 25 cents and you can comfortably pay 50 cents a share. Usually, that's a pretty good deal.

Rule 5:
Don't be greedy

Investors in junior exploration companies should try to get their money back as soon as possible and let their profits ride intelligently. Once a stock has doubled in price without any support from the results of exploration or drill holes, don't be fooled — sell half of your shares and get your money back. Then let the rest of the money ride. Speculating on penny stocks is risky, but if you always get your ante back you can keep playing. If you see in the insider trading reports issued by the stock exchanges that the promoter is bailing out, follow him.

Another effective valuation technique is to compare the total market capitalization of the "star-du-jour" with that of a known, established company of a size that the new company might ultimately become. Sell as soon as the valuations are equal. The reason is simple: The younger company may have the same size ore body, but it will have to raise hundreds of millions of dollars to erect the mine and mill complex to develop its discovery. It could take two or three years to build these facilities before investors will begin to see any returns.

There might come a time when one of the stocks you own becomes outrageously overpriced. But no matter how good the story, sell before reality reasserts itself. Look at the stock market performance of the better-known gold companies such as Viceroy Resources, Prime Resources and Golden Knight. The rocket that moves a company into the second stage of a mine's life cycle never fires immediately after the initial discovery.

Rule 6:
Don't hang on to your losers

The great majority of investors tend to hang on to stocks they bought at lofty prices, even though those stocks have slipped to only pennies a share. Get rid of them; casting off your losers early will "make" you more money than you might care to admit. The only reason many speculative juniors drift in the market at 15 or 20 cents a share is because of thousands of investors hanging on in vain hope. Don't fall in love with your stocks. Try to spot your mistakes early and be ruthless. Put a mental stop-loss on your stock. For example, if the price drops down to half of your purchase price, then sell immediately. You may miss a rebound but you'll never end up holding bundles of worthless certificates.

The development stage

The transition from a pure exploration company to a junior mining company is usually marked by an announcement that the company has ordered a feasibility study. Most people see this as a good sign and believe the stock price will go even higher. To me, it means the stock is about to lose its sizzle and you should sell. The feasibility study will put all the factual information about the mine in black and white, and this is usually a more sober vision than the promoter's. A feasibility study will spell out the minable reserves, which are always smaller than the geological reserves, the possible production rate and the capital and operating costs, the most sobering piece of information. If it's an economically viable mine, the promoter is faced with a task he is seldom prepared for — becoming an operator.

It can take six months to a year to complete the feasibility study and during that time the stock is likely to drift down if there is a vacuum of information. The longer the study takes, the more suspicious the market will become. On the other hand, if all the mining and milling parameters seem to be confirmed one by one, the stock price may remain firm but it will not likely rise. The market is aware that there could be a dilution of the stock as the company moves into the market to raise money to develop the project.

The concept of a feasibility study has too often been abused by promoters and has left investors confused by the true significance of such a document. Just as an artist's painting begins with a rough sketch that is enhanced by a pencil drawing, then the colouring and finally the finish, a feasibility study has several stages. There is a prefeasibility study, which sets out the general parameters of a proposed mining venture with an accuracy of plus or minus 20 per cent; in other words, the actual cost of producing gold could be 20 per cent higher or lower than the estimates in these studies. A second study defines the project more closely, within 10 per cent of actual costs. There will then be a third and final "bankable" study, which can be used to convince international banks to lend money. Some companies will try to deliberately confuse investors by talking about final feasibility studies when studies have never been conducted to determine whether a project is viable.

Most large mining companies have their own engineering staffs to analyze projects and develop prefeasibility studies. Only after a project has progressed past this stage do they turn to outside engineering consultants to prepare the final feasibility study. The consultants act as a check on work done internally. A junior company, however, does not have the staff to do any of this work and must rely entirely on consultants. Sometimes this puts the engineering consultants in a conflicting dual role; there is pressure to come up with good news that will keep the stock price up and bring in money to pay the bills.

If the final feasibility study recommends putting the deposit into production, a company's board of directors will meet and probably recommend that the company fulfill the recommendation. The key question the investor must ask is: How will the company raise the money to proceed to production? Basically there are three ways:

- The company can issue new shares. This is often possible only in a strong gold equity market. If this can't be done, it may be nearly impossible for the company to raise money at a reasonable price without excessively diluting the equity of existing shareholders.
- A joint venture partner can fund the cost of the entire project for a right to earn a certain interest, perhaps 50 per cent, in the property. The company loses half its ore body but it shelters itself

Some Major Gold Deposits Outside South Africa

Name of deposit	Ownership	Total resource (millions of oz.)
Carlin Trend (Nevada)	Barrick Gold/Newmont Gold	75.0
Ertsberg/Grasberg (Indonesia)	Freeport Copper & Gold	52.1*
Busang (Indonesia)	Bre-X/PT Askatindo	46.9†
Sukhoi Log (Siberia)	Lena Gold	43.4†
Lihir Island (PNG)	RTZ/Battle Mountain/VenGold	42.0†
Zarafshan (Uzbekistan)	Uzbekistan/Newmont Mining	21.1
Obuasi (Ghana)	Ashanti Goldfields/Lonrho/Gov't	21.0
Kalgoorlie (Australia)	GMK/Homestake	16.0
Bajo de la Alumbrera (Argentina)	MIM/North/Rio Algom	15.7†
Batu Hijou (Indonesia)	Newmont/P.T. Tanjung	14.6†
Kumtor (Kyrgystan)	Kyrgystan/Cameco	13.2
Porgera (PNG)	Placer Pacific/Highland/Renison	12.7
Tarkwa (Ghana)	Gold Fields S.A.	13.0
Hemlo Camp (Ontario)	Teck/Homestake/Battle Mountain	13.0
Twin Creeks (Nevada)	Sante Fe Pacific Gold	10.0
Leninogorsk (Kazakhstan)	Bakyrchik Gold/Gov't	10.0†
El Indio/Tambo/Pascua (Chile)	Barrick Gold	9.5
Teberebie (Ghana)	Pioneer	9.2
Amantaytau (Uzbekistan)	Gov't/Lonhro	9.0
Bougainville (PNG)	Bougainville Copper/RTZ	8.7†
Las Cristinas (Venezuela)	Placer Dome/CVG	8.6†
Refugio (Chile)	Bema Gold/Amax Gold	8.6†
Cadia Hill (New South Wales)	Newcrest Mining	8.3†
Yanacocha (Peru)	Newmont/Buenaventura/BRGM	8.2
Pueblo Viejo (D.R.)	Central Bank	8.0†
Bingham Canyon (Utah)	Kennecott Corp.	7.9*
Round Mountain (Nevada)	Echo Bay/Homestake/Case	7.8
Vasilkovskoye (Kazakhstan)	Gov't	7.7†
Metates (Mexico)	Cambior/Luismin	7.7†
Pipeline + South (Nevada)	Placer Dome/Kennecott Corp.	7.6†
Zeravshan (Tajikistan)	Nelson Gold/Gov't	6.7†
Baley-Taseevskoe (Siberia)	Armada Gold/Balgold	6.0†
Campbell Red Lake (Ontario)	Placer Dome	5.3
Kingking (Philippines)	Echo Bay/TVI Pacific	5.1†
Sadiola Hill (Mali)	Anglo American/IAMGOLD	4.5†
Iduapriem (Ghana)	Golden Shamrock	4.3

† not in operation or pending development
* gold is a byproduct or co-product to other metals

TABLE XVI

from having to raise money and acquires a partner who might have operating experience.

• The company might be able to arrange debt financing — perhaps gold loans, convertible debentures or straight bank debt. This depends on the size of the company and richness of the ore body, but it never covers the entire capital costs. Even if the company can arrange debt financing it will have to either issue shares or find a partner.

While a company ponders how it will finance the development and construction of a mine, the market will wait to see how much the company has to give up and how it will pay for the project. This brings us to the next critical point — the production decision.

This is when the troubles begin, even though it's not always apparent at first. Between the raising of funds, the engineering, procurement and construction schedule, the mine development and the vagaries of the metal markets you can count on some bad news. It is very rare to go through all these steps without problems. For this reason, the transition period from Tier III to Tier II creates a classic buying opportunity. In terms of risk, it is the most favourable entry point, but there are still a few rules you should follow.

Rule 1:
Buy a forgiving ore body

Whether the company is an experienced operator or a novice, there is every likelihood of problems in the first year of production. If the ore body is rich enough, it will accommodate those mistakes and let the company survive. As an investor, you want a mine that will have low operating costs compared to those for the rest of the industry. Remember, the average cash cost of producing gold from a Canadian or American mine is around $240 (U.S.) an ounce. Your risks will be lower if you invest in a company with a cash cost below $200 (U.S.) an ounce. Mines with a high cost of operating and a short mine life could mean disaster. These marginal mines are the ones that experience the most dramatic price increases if the price of gold rises, but when the price turns down the price of these stocks will also plummet.

In a recent three-year period, at least 24 mines which had begun production in the previous two years in North America shut down because they could not be operated economically. The common characteristics of all of these disappointments were first and foremost lower grade than expected followed by unexpectedly high mining and operating costs.

Rule 2:
Choose a good operator

Tread carefully if the company that has discovered the gold decides that it is also capable of financing and putting the mine into production. Not only will it probably make every possible mistake, it won't have the deep pockets of the large mining companies. Too many trips to the equity market can depress the stock price. A good operator, on the other hand, will have people who will anticipate most of the problems and be able to adhere to the feasibility study schedule. They can usually bring the mine into production within 5 per cent to 10 per cent of the budgeted capital costs and within a reasonable amount of time.

Rule 3:
Buy 12 to 18 months before production is scheduled to begin

The ideal time to buy mining stock is usually a few months after the production decision has been reached. The financing is in place for the entire capital cost and the company has actually broken ground and has started erection of the mine-mill complex. From here to opening day, not much can happen to the ore body itself, as there will be no production. The expectations surrounding the mine and the company will mount as time passes. And as the public's confidence builds, the stock is likely to rise.

Rule 4:
Sell some stock and get a bit of your money back close to the day production begins

This rule does not apply to all the stocks you have purchased 12 to 18 months before opening day, but be aware that three out of 10 mines that actually start production will prove to be uneconomic and shut down within two years. Any signs of trouble during the preproduction period — such as a grade that is lower than originally forecast, a lower production target than predicted or higher operating costs — are sure signs that there could be more trouble ahead. Any mines that have a predicted operating cash cost higher than $275 (U.S.) an ounce are particularly susceptible to problems and should be watched closely. If within three to six months after the mine opens the stock price loses more than 30 per cent of its value, there are likely some serious problems at the mine. Consider

Some North American Gold Mining Failures (1)

Location	Mine	Ownership	Invested cap. $US (mm)(2)	Subsequent valuation and status (3)	
Canada					
Ontario	Bell Creek	Canamax Resources	$25	3	mothballed
Ontario	Kerr	Golden Shield	40	5	custom mill
Ontario	Magnacon	Flanagan McAdam	59	0	mothballed
Ontario	Magino	McNellan Resources	25	1	shut down
Ontario	Golden Rose	Noramco	20	0	closed
Ontario	Kremzar	Canamax Resources	24	1	mothballed/sold
Quebec	Astoria	Yorbeau	20	0	mothballed
Quebec	Beauchastel	Augmitto	18	0	bankrupt
Quebec	Beacon	D'Or Val	10	0	closed/restructured
Quebec	Estrades	Breakwater	10	2	mothballed
B.C.	Johnny Mtn.	Skyline Gold	43	3	mothballed
B.C.	Erickson	Total Erickson	15	0	closed
B.C.	Nickel Plate	Homestake Mining	138	36	operating
B.C.	Golden Bear	Homestake Mining	69	0	operating
B.C.	Premier	Westmin Resources	75	0	alternate mill feed
Sask.	Seebee	Claude Resources	29	0	bankrupt
Manitoba	Puffy Lake	Pioneer Metals	28	0	closed
Manitoba	Tartan Lake	Granges/Abermin	30	1	mothballed
Manitoba	MacLellan	Lynngold	44	0	closed/bankrupt
Nfld.	Hope Brook	BP Canada	151	10	new owner
N.S.	Seabright	Western Mining	80	0	closed/lawsuit
NWT	Colomac	Northgate/ABM	113	7	reactivated
Yukon	Mt. Skukum	AGIP/Total Erickson	15	1	closed/acquired
Yukon	Ketza River	Canamax/PTX	25	1	closed/bankrupt
United States					
Calif.	Colosseum	Bond Gold	60	12	closed
Calif.	Hayden Hill	Amax Gold	169	100	mill on standby
Calif.	Carson Hill	Grandview	15	0	closed
Calif.	Jamestown	Sonora Gold/ABM	100	10	closed
Nevada	McCoy/Cove	Echo Bay	383	110	operating
Nevada	Kingston	Nevada Goldfields	10	1	closed/acquired
S. Dakota	Gilt Edge	MinVen Gold	42	5	operating
S. Dakota	Golden Rwd.	United Coin/Minven	28	5	restructuring
Montana	Montana Tun.	Pegasus Gold	82	45	operating
Montana	Basin Creek	Pegasus Gold	34	0	closed
Montana	Spotted Horse	Chelsea Resources	15	0	closed
Colorado	Sunnyside	Echo Bay/Alta Bay	31	0	operating
Colorado	Summitville	Galactic Resources	56	0	closed
Idaho	GrouseCreek	Hecla/Great Lakes	130	0	operating
Arizona	McCabe	Stan-West Mining	25	1	new owner
Michigan	Ropes	Callahan Mining	16	1	mothballed

(1) A mining failure is a project that appears unlikely to recover its original capital cost at current gold prices. (2) Reported carrying values including acquisition costs or capitalized exploration but not including operating losses and prewritedowns. (3) Per the accounting writedown or the implied valuation in the company's market capitalization plus repayable debt or by a sales transaction or estimated realizable.

TABLE XVII

selling the stock and waiting until all the bad news is out before you consider repurchasing shares.

In 1983, I was asked by a group of shareholders who were funding Breakwater Resources to represent them on the company's board of directors. The company and Asamera Minerals, its operating partner, had just made a significant discovery near Wenatchee in Washington State. Initial capital costs were estimated at less than $30 million (U.S.) by the operator, the reserves were high grade and the mine appeared to have a life of at least six years. Breakwater raised its share of the capital cost and waited expectantly for the official opening. At the time, it had no personnel or staff, so it relied entirely on the operating partner to carry out construction and development. In fact, it had no choice, since the joint venture contract specifically prohibited Breakwater from getting involved in the mine's operation.

It was an expensive mistake. Asamera's people didn't have any expertise in building a 2,000-ton-a-day gold mine in an environmentally sensitive state like Washington. Less than one year later, Asamera came up with a revised capital cost estimate of $55 million (U.S.), almost double the original estimate. By that time the market knew there was trouble because of the lack of news, so the stock dipped from $11 (U.S.) a share to less than $5 (U.S.). Breakwater found more financing, the construction schedule was straightened out and a few heads rolled. By the time the mine was officially opened, the capital costs exceeded $62 million (U.S.) and the operating costs were running substantially higher than the feasibility study had indicated. Little by little the problems were resolved, the mill recovery improved and costs dropped. After two years of operation, the mine performed better than originally expected. If it hadn't been for the high grade of the ore body — more than 0.30 ounces of gold per ton of ore — and the fact that all the money had been arranged through equity and not debt, Breakwater could have ended dead-in-the-water.

Finding information on junior gold stocks

The most useful newspaper for the mining investor is *The Northern Miner*. It has a staff of competent reporters across Canada and also covers the United States in a thorough and professional manner. Reporters carefully screen the information given to them to distill facts from the fiction and add depth to their stories through interviews, mine visits and a few carefully selected brokers' reports. The paper has a weekly listing of stock quotes from all the Canadian exchanges, as well as exchanges in the U.S., South Africa and Britain.

Two publications, the *George Cross News Letter* and *The Vancouver Stock Watch*, simply report the news sent to them by the mining companies. *The Vancouver Stock Watch* is probably easier to read but it's costlier than the older *George Cross News Letter*. If you want all the news on every company you'll need one of these.

The next level of information comes from the several independent newsletters published mainly in the U.S. I prefer the *Gold Mining Stock Report* by Robert Bishop. Bishop is an independent thinker who does his own research and analysis. He goes out to the mines — I've bumped into him a few times out in the field — and writes an interesting letter. Gerry Pogue of National Securities Corp. in Seattle, Wash., has been writing a newsletter on gold, the *North American Mining and Energy Report*, for a decade. He's also conscientious and tries hard to screen the dross from the gold. Adrian Day's *Investment Analyst* is another good letter, but not as focused on gold as Bishop's or Pogue's.

Finally, there are the general newsletters. My favourite is the *Dow Theory Letters* by Richard Russell. Having been around for so long he always has something interesting to say, particularly about gold. *Deliberations: The Ian McAvity Market Letter* is mainly a technical analysis; it contains excellent charts. If you were to subscribe to all of these you wouldn't have any money left to invest. Get *The Northern Miner* and try the newsletters one at a time before deciding which ones suit your needs and style. You don't want to receive more than three publications a week or you will suffer from information overload.

If you want to follow a company closely without risking too much money, you might consider buying 10 or 100 shares of the company and have them registered in your name, not the name of your broker. You will automatically receive all the shareholder information put out by the company, including annual and quarterly reports, and information packages.

Tier II companies — the producer

Once a company has a producing mine, it joins a select club of fewer than 150 publicly traded companies in North America, and about 300 worldwide, that derive all or most of their revenues from gold mining.

When you look at the universe of Tier II stocks, your prime consideration as a buyer should be the potential for future growth. Over a three- to five-year period, the money in this industry is made by companies that will see their gold reserves and production expand due to new discoveries or acquisitions. As production, reserves and cash flow expand, the total capitalization of the company will increase at a faster pace than production. It seldom happens overnight, but if you have patience and have chosen the right company, your money can increase by 10 to 20 times.

At Beutel Goodman, we first purchased the shares of Pancana Resources in 1986 for $2.37 per share when it was a little-known company with a land position in the Carlin Trend. A year later, it was acquired by American Barrick (now called Barrick Gold) for stock in a deal that saw Barrick take full ownership of the Goldstrike property. At that time there were only 600,000 ounces of gold in reserves at Goldstrike and company-wide reserves were less than two million ounces. The stock at that time was $1.75 (U.S.) (adjusting for splits) and we increased our position. Over the past five years, Barrick has had a tremendous success at Goldstrike, increasing reserves to 30 million ounces of gold and production from 35,000 ounces of gold per year to probably over two million ounces in 1995. The stock has reflected that growth, surging to over $30 (U.S.).

There are two ways a company can grow. It can grow by acquisition, like Echo Bay, or it can make discoveries on its land, like Newmont Gold and Barrick Gold. Newmont controls a 400-square-mile area along the Carlin Trend in Nevada. Over the past 20 years Newmont has made no less than 20 discoveries on its ground and has increased its reserves and resources from two million ounces to over 40 million ounces of gold in the ground by the end of 1995. And it's still making discoveries.

The Tier II gold stocks able to generate free cash flow are likely to be the big winners in the long run. It comes back to the cash cost of production: The lower it is and the higher the gold price, the more money the company has to acquire or explore.

Evaluating producing gold mines

Chapter 7 examined some of the more unusual characteristics of gold mining companies and the significant differences between gold stocks and those of other companies. But gold stocks are not immune from the laws of economics. Despite their unique characteristics, gold mining companies can go broke. In the long run, they must not only be profitable, they must be able to grow and pay dividends to reward shareholders.

In the meantime, as an investor about to put money into a gold mining stock, you need to be able to determine whether the company represents good value at the trading price. This can be a confusing task. A recent report by a major Canadian brokerage firm outlined no less than 12 methods for evaluating a company.

The formula for evaluating stocks that I propose is a simple five-step method that incorporates in one formula several of the valuation methods that are standard in financial circles. Since the fundamental value of the company is its gold reserves, the fundamental value of its shares is really just its gold reserves multiplied by the company's profitability. The first step is to calculate the after-tax profit margin per ounce of gold — the price of gold minus the company's costs. The formula would be: net profit margin = price of gold — (cash costs + depreciation costs + exploration and administration costs + taxes). The net profit margin is then multiplied by the company's gold reserves to arrive at the total amount of money the company would pocket if it sold all of its gold at once. However, this value of the company has to be adjusted to reflect the company's working capital, long-term liabilities including gold loans and the capital expenditures required to bring its mine into production. This final figure is divided by the number of outstanding shares to give you a value per share.

While the procedure is actually quite simple, selecting the valid numbers that go into it is critical.

Reserves

The main assets of a gold mining company are its gold reserves. Physical assets such as the mill, plant, tailings pond, shaft, galleries and pits which usually make up most of the book value of a company are only valuable as long as the mine is operating. Indeed, the value of these, whether the mine operates for one month or 10 years, is very little because the shaft or tailings pond cannot be moved and the cost of dismantling, transporting and reassembling the mill is too high to be worthwhile. As an investor, look at the physical installations strictly as one of the costs of getting the gold out of the ground.

Mining companies publish their gold reserves annually. There are two broad categories of reserves: the geological reserves and the minable ore reserves. These are further divided into three classes: proven, probable and possible reserves. The geological reserves are calculated by giving all gold intercepts a tonnage and grade factor and adding it all up, regardless of the cost of mining those reserves. Minable reserves are those that can be mined economically. There can be, and usually is, quite a difference between geological resources and minable reserves. For example, Newmont Gold's geological resources at the end of 1994 were over 56 million ounces of gold, while its minable reserves were 26 million ounces. These are the reserves for which Newmont has a mining plan, and a metallurgical recovery plant that make it possible to extract gold at a profit with gold at $375 (U.S.) per ounce.

At the same time, Newmont will continue to drill, test and improve its knowledge of its geological reserves to bring them into the minable category. Reserve figures are one of the most important considerations when evaluating a stock. If the grade doesn't stand up, the reserves may be sharply reduced. This could result in a contraction of the valuation and the stock price. On the other hand, if the company keeps finding more gold, the price of its stock will increase over time to reflect the improved prospects of the company. Therefore, it is critical that you form a judgment of the quality of the reported numbers and the potential for an increase or decrease in reserves.

At least 50 per cent of the mines that reach full production end up extracting at least as much gold as their initial geological reserves. The better mines can produce several times their initial reserves. The Homestake mine in South Dakota, for example, has approximately 4.5 million ounces of gold reserves. That number has not changed for 50 years, even though the company has been in production for 114 years and has produced 36 million ounces of gold. The Hemlo camp started with 18 million ounces of gold in reserves in 1985, but the reserves have already expanded by at least 30 per cent.

COMPARISON OF TIER I GOLD SHARES ($U.S.)

SORTED BY MARKET CAPITALIZATION

	Stock symbol	Share price 09/09/96	Shares (mm)	Market cap ($U.S. mm)	Adj. cap (1) ($U.S. mm)	Rec. reserve (mm oz.) (2)	1996 Prod. (mm oz.)	Cash cost (U.S. $/oz.)
Barrick Gold	ABX	$26.50	357.2	$9,466	$11,305	51.7	3.100	$183
Freeport Copper & Gold	FCX	30.00	198.9	5,967	7,428	47.0	1.550	75
Newmont Mining	NEM	51.60	110.0	5,676	6,969	40.0	2.050	212
Placer Dome	PDG	23.36	239.4	5,592	7,323	37.4	1.900	238
Homestake Mining	HM	16.00	147.7	2,363	3,225	24.4	1.750	260
Santa Fe Pacific Gold	GLD	12.60	131.4	1,656	2,613	20.0	0.900	223
Battle Mountain/Hemlo	BMG	6.06	229.0	1,388	1,842	11.5	1.000	190
Echo Bay	ECO	9.53	130.0	1,239	1,989	7.7	0.650	245
TVX Gold	TVX	7.63	160.0	1,221	1,988	13.5	0.450	231
Cambior	CBJ	14.13	60.1	849	549	6.0	0.480	260
AVERAGE								$212

(1) Adjusts market capitalization for working capital, debt and capex differences.
(2) In-situ reserves times expected recovery rate.

TABLE XVIII

COMPARISON OF TIER I GOLD SHARES (continued)

	Stock symbol	Adjusted market capitalization per ounce of Production	Recoverable reserve	Adjusted capital/ gross margin (3)
Barrick Gold	ABX	$3,647	$219	1.01
Freeport Copper & Gold	FCX	4,792	158	0.49
Newmont Mining	NEM	3,400	174	0.93
Placer Dome	PDG	3,854	196	1.21
Homestake Mining	HM	1,843	132	0.94
Santa Fe Pacific Gold	GLD	2,930	131	0.74
Battle Mountain/Hemlo	HEM	1,842	160	0.76
Echo Bay	ECO	3,060	258	1.67
TVX Gold	TVX	4,418	147	0.87
Cambior	CBJ	1,144	92	0.65
AVERAGE		$3,090	$167	0.93

(3) Adjusted market capitalization divided by the company's gross margin (recoverable reserves x ($400 gold-cash cost/oz.). The lower the ratio, the better the relative value.

TABLE XVIII (continued)

Look back at the recent mining failures; those should not be forgotten, especially if you are thinking of investing in a marginal gold producer whose reserve quality might be in doubt. The reserve number that counts is the one that will be closest to the amount of gold that will ultimately be mined. In the case of Newmont, for example, since it will likely end up mining all of its reserves, the geological reserve number should be used.

Total operating costs

The cost of producing an ounce of gold is made up of three components: the cash cost, depreciation and the general exploration and overhead costs. As explained in Chapter 7, you can find these costs outlined in the profit and loss statement in an annual report. Obviously, the lower the cost of extracting an ounce of gold, the higher the fundamental value of the company extracting the gold. This can readily be seen by comparing the market capitalization per recoverable ounce of gold in reserves at $292 (U.S.) for Barrick Gold, with its total operating cost of $170 (U.S.) per ounce of gold, and the $124 (U.S.) market capitalization per ounce for Homestake Mining, which spends $240 (U.S.) to mine an ounce of gold.

The gold price

Choosing a gold price with which you can calculate the value of reserves is another important decision you will have to make. Indeed, the gold equity market seems to be always trying to predict the future by discounting high gold prices in an optimistic environment and low gold prices in a pessimistic environment. In this kind of market you may choose to be a contrarian, that is, adopt an opinion contrary to that of the majority. The problem with always being a contrarian is that occasionally the crowd is bound to be right and you're bound to be wrong. If you don't want to take a stand on the future movement of the price of gold, use the current price. That way, if you unearth an undervalued stock and the gold price rises, you'll enjoy a double whammy.

Balance sheet adjustments

Before you are able to compare various companies you have to make one last adjustment. You must take into consideration the debt that the company has on its balance sheet. This is done by adding up any cash or positive working capital and deducting long-term loans, including gold loans, or a negative working capital position. If the company has to raise money for capital expenditures, you should deduct these amounts from the total valuation. The result is the adjusted market capitalization for the company. One can then compare this adjusted market capitalization to the theoretical value of the company's reserves in the ground (i.e., total recoverable ounces times the margin that might be obtained for each ounce considering the cash cost to produce each ounce). Table XVIII gives you sample valuations of 10 Tier I North American companies at a gold price of $400 (U.S.) an ounce.

In late 1996, at an assumed gold price of $400 (U.S.) an ounce, you can see that the ratio of the average, actual value of the 10 stocks to their average, theoretical market capitalization was 0.93 or 93 per cent. The market seems to be very efficient at adjusting stock prices to the current gold price. By spotting stocks that are relatively undervalued, an investor stands to make a healthy profit. Santa Fe Pacific Gold, for example, is trading at 74 per cent of its theoretical value while Freeport Copper and Gold at only 49 per cent seems an incredible bargain. Why? Perhaps investors are too pessimistic about the future of these companies; just as they may be too optimistic about the future of Placer Dome, which was trading at a 121 per cent premium to its theoretical value. By doing your homework, you can spot such anomalies and capitalize on them to your benefit.

This model does not consider the time value of money; it calculates the value of the company as if the entire reserves are being processed and sold on the same day. That is obviously impossible, yet the valuation still makes sense. It can be argued that since bullion does not yield any interest, and since gold mining stocks are proxies for gold bullion, theoretically one can use a zero discount rate. Furthermore, it can also be argued that the lack of the time value of money is offset by potential discoveries and acquisitions and the probable expansion of ore reserves at the existing location. Finally, it can also be argued that if bullion sells at about a 10 per cent premium a year and you use a discount rate of 10 per cent or less, the value of bullion in the future would be higher than today, making it nonsensical to discount in the first place.

As far as I'm concerned, the biggest drawback of the zero discount is the fact that it doesn't take into consideration the mining risk associated with each gold mine. The investor who buys a bullion coin and puts it away in his safe doesn't incur any other risk than a fall in the gold price. On the other hand, the investor in equities is subject not only to the ups and downs of the stock market, but also to changes in the gold price and the fortunes of the mining company. It would, therefore, seem appropriate to compensate the investor for taking a mining risk that is commensurate with the size, location and political environment affecting a particular gold mine or company.

In 1996, gold bullion loans were around 2.5 per cent a year. This is the risk-free rate at which large, sophisticated bullion lenders are willing to do business. If you were to add a mining risk of 5.5 per cent, the annual premium would be up to 8 per cent, which is double the current rate of the forward market on gold bullion. As for inflation, gold is a perfect hedge, so it should not concern you. Therefore, if you add 3.5 per cent to the gold price and discount it by 7 per cent for the time value of money you will, in fact, discount at 3.5 per cent your theoretical zero value. This factor does vary, however, depending on the gold loan rate and mining risk. Indeed, the risk-free rate has been as high as 3.5 per cent and as low as 1 per cent. The mining risk can be as low as 5 per cent for a world-class gold mine in Ontario or Nevada. On the other hand, if the project is located in an unfriendly Third World country where there is a great deal of political and financial risk, the premium required by the investor could soar to above 15 per cent. In these circumstances, you would have to adjust the theoretical market capitalization of the formula down to account for the higher risks.

As an investor, you want an emerging gold equity with reserves that are rapidly expanding at the same time the mine is coming into production. Expanding reserves from this valuation formula means expanding market capitalization and a rising equity price. Of course, the company can cut costs, reduce exploration and lower expenditures to increase its valuation — but it can only do so for a certain period of time.

Financial ratios

Over the past 20 years, gold stocks have usually sold at twice the price to earnings ratio, or P/E, of the general market. The P/E is a stock's current market price divided by its annual earnings per share. Between 1970 and 1990, the average P/E of the TSE gold subindex has been 22 to one, although in mid-1995 it was well above 30 to one. This would seem to indicate that the market is expecting a strong rally in the gold price or, conversely, that stocks are significantly overvalued. It is also interesting that the P/E ratios of Tier I stocks are around 50 per cent higher than those of Tier II stocks. This is due to the fact that the market places higher value on the companies with large reserves and low costs than the one-mine companies that make up most of Tier II.

Dividends and yields have never been major factors in the values of North American gold equities. Prior to 1980, most Canadian and American gold companies that were still in existence were operating near the break-even point while during the past decade they have been using every bit of cash flow available to explore and to increase and develop their reserves. However, in the 1990s the number of new opportunities could diminish and spending will concentrate on known deposits. Mining companies should have significant cash surpluses, which they might pass on to shareholders in the form of dividends. While the average yield on North American gold stocks has been barely 0.5 per cent in the past five years, I expect dividend yields to climb to the risk-free gold lending rate of 1.5 per cent to 2.5 per cent by the late 1990s. It will be worthwhile for the investor to watch the use of cash flow by the gold companies, as well as their dividend policies. The company that pays a low dividend could be at a significant disadvantage in the gold industry, and this stinginess could be reflected in a lower share price.

Conclusion

Some investors might remain convinced that picking a winning gold stock ranks next to picking a winning lottery number. In some ways this is true, since the most successful companies will be those that increase their gold reserves the fastest — and it's impossible to predict with certainty which those will be. However, good management is likely to prove itself, and that's where investors should place most of their bets.

Once you have decided on the percentage of your portfolio that should be in gold equities, you should earmark at least 50 per cent of that money for gold stocks in Tier I. Prepare a valuation table similar to the one explained in this chapter and pick the stocks that represent the most value for your money at the time. The next 30 to 40 per cent of your gold stock portfolio should be invested in Tier II gold stocks that have good reserves with at least 10 years of life, a low cost of production and good management. Then put 10 to 20 per cent of your portfolio in Tier III or exploration companies — preferably companies that have already outlined a deposit or are in the process of developing one and whose prospects look good.

CHAPTER 9

What's Hot, What's Not: The Scams

GOLD SCAMS HAVE BEEN around for centuries, and modern-day alchemists have descended from a long tradition of charlatans trying to deceive a naive public. Alchemy actually started in the sixth century BC in Greece, when astrologers of the time believed that they could turn lead into gold. They paved the way for today's con artists by devising symbolic names and rituals in an effort to elevate and preserve the esoteric nature of their acts. The alchemists of the 15th and 16th centuries bilked only the rich and aristocrats but today's con man preys on all levels of society. In its May, 1988, bulletin, the Northwest Mining Association based in Spokane, Wash., mentioned that in 1987 alone, thousands of Americans and Canadians had lost an estimated $250 million (U.S.) to gold scams. The prime target of today's con artist is the retired, well-to-do North American couple who own their own home and have substantial savings and a generous pension. Being retired, they are likely to be at home when the telephone rings and they're susceptible to the tales of the swindler at the other end of the line. Gold mine con artists have also been known to clip the savings of lawyers, doctors and accountants. Gold scams today are international, with known swindlers operating in Europe, the Far East and North and South America.

Scams prey on one element of human character — greed. The attraction of getting rich quickly prompts many people to ignore some basic advice: If it sounds too good to be true, stay away from it. Before you even think of investing in a gold mine or a hotly promoted gold stock, make sure you're not being talked into buying a ton of worthless desert dirt.

The dirt-pile swindle

In 1987, there were eight cases of "dirt-pile swindles" under investigation in the United States; in 1988, there were 52. Although none are under investigation in Canada, there is no doubt the dirt-pile swindle is the most prevalent and most costly gold scam in North America. After the stock market disaster of 1987, many investors shifted from the stock market, which they considered too volatile, to something more tangible. This shift happened at a most inopportune time for state and federal securities regulators in the U.S.; two recent court rulings have held that aggregate ore promotions — dirt-pile swindles — do not involve securities and are therefore not subject to laws governing such transactions. The swindlers have seen the door open in all Nevada, Hawaii, Arizona, Washington, Oregon, Idaho, Montana, Alaska and California. Investors will have to be extremely cautious in appraising any gold mine investments because many con artists can operate legally in these states by skirting the fringes of fraud.

The making of a fool's gold mine

The preparation that goes into a successful dirt-pile swindle is not only intricate but detailed and expensive. To compensate himself for his trouble, the swindler will expect hefty returns; in the few cases that have been prosecuted, the average take is $2.25 million. Most con artists follow the same series of steps, from the creation of a fictitious mine to its marketing and the inevitable disappearance of victims' money.

Step 1: The swindler acquires a legitimate mining claim

The con artist's first move is to stake legitimate mining claims or to purchase them from an existing landowner. Both methods have their advantages and disadvantages. The staking of a lode mining claim in the U.S. is still based on 1872 mining law. Although each state's law varies somewhat in the actual staking procedure, all claims are staked by establishing with four corner posts a rectangular area with a maximum dimension of 600 feet wide and 1,500 feet in length. The next step is to record the claims with the county where the claims are located within 60 days of being placed. The next step is to register your claim with the federal Bureau of Land Management by filing a claim-staking form or registration and paying a fee of $200 (U.S.) for each claim. All that is required to keep those claims in good standing is payment of a fee of $100 (U.S.) for each claim every year. This gives you ownership of the mineral rights under these claims. This does not, however, give you an operating licence or any sign of approval by the BLM or any U.S. government agency.

For the swindler, the disadvantage of this method is that he has to explain to the potential investor how he was able to discover gold that had been missed by geologists from large mining companies who are continually looking for gold deposits. Unless the prospective investor is gullible, he isn't going to believe it. It may be easier for the swindler to purchase the claims from an accomplice who will swear that the claims have been in his family for generations and that there has been a long history of profitable mining.

In either case, the deal will be given an aura of respectability if the claims can be backed up by an official document or agency. For example, if the claim is located in or near Ord Mountain in California, the swindler can use the California division of mines and geology report on the geology and mineral deposits of the Ord Mountain District. To make his claim more credible, the swindler will choose a piece of ground that is within or close to an old mining district so he can claim that deposits have been mined in the area in the past and his ground was overlooked. In some cases, the swindlers are so brazen they don't bother with all of this and they don't even own the dirt they intend to sell to the public.

Step 2: The packaging of the scam

The next step entails the preparation of a glossy sales document. This booklet or information document, sometimes vaguely dubbed a prospectus, is designed to lend legitimacy to the scheme. The raison d'être of the document is to create a fictitious gold mine and surround it with so much smoke and mirrors that only a discerning investor or mining professional can separate fiction from the truth. This prospectus is usually divided into several parts that are meant to address any questions the investor might have on the legitimacy of the deal.

I. The geological report

The sales document usually kicks off with a geological report about the area where the so-called mine is located. The report could have been written by a respectable geologist but quoted out of context; it may even be an official report of the United States Geological Survey, or occasionally the Geological Survey of Canada if the claim is in Canada, which would lend a more formal air of authenticity. The description of the geological feature has nothing to do with the piece of moose pasture or desert dirt that is being promoted. For example, the swindler might use a description of the geology of the Carlin Trend, which could be hundreds of miles away. The professional will realize this is irrelevant, but to the novice it will sound good.

Just for good measure, the special geological report of the promoter will give the names of successful mines anywhere within 50 miles of the claims. Again, this is irrelevant. Furthermore, most of the mines mentioned will probably be lode or large open-pit mines, even though the swindler's claim is usually a placer deposit.

Geology, like computer science, has its own language. The sights and sounds of the scientific terms used by geologists can easily overwhelm the novice investor. The con man's esoteric language can be as befuddling as the incantations of alchemists in the Middle Ages. Sometimes the modern alchemist won't even understand the incantations of geology; he just wants to overwhelm the poor investor. Be wary. The more incantations, the more likely it is that the speaker is a swindler.

II. The assays

Once the con artist has bought or staked a valid claim and has described the setting of the claims in the most advanced geological terms, he now moves on to the next step. He's ready to reveal the "unbelievable" wealth on his property. Every document contains copies of an official-looking laboratory assay that reveals the piece of ground you're about to be sold contains fabulous amounts of precious metals. Aside from the fact that nine times out of 10 the assays are fictitious, there are a number of things you have to watch out for. First, the assays are usually produced on an official-looking piece of paper that appears to legitimize the assay. In one scam, the assays had been done at MHS Laboratory, which was supposedly run by specialists in platinum and palladium assaying. After some checking, it was found that MHS stood for Mullan High School, where few students had even seen a chunk of precious metal.

It's important to keep in mind that neither the assaying laboratories nor the technical people actually gather the field samples which they are asked to assay or test. This is done by a geologist who knows what should be sampled and what he is looking for. The assayer merely analyzes what he has been given.

Therefore, the con artist has two choices: He can "salt" the sample by putting gold in a worthless piece of dirt and using a reputable assaying firm; or he can hire a crooked assayer who can produce whatever values the con artist asks for. This is easily done because there are few rules and regulations governing assayers and assay labs in either Canada or the U.S.

One of the most obvious warnings that something is amiss is the promoter's claim that his mine can produce equal quantities of platinum, palladium and silver and gold. Any assayer that can find all four of these metals in the same proportion is doing something that nature itself could not replicate. Gold and silver are generally found in different geological environments from platinum and palladium. In North America, the only known mines producing platinum and palladium are the nickel ores of Sudbury and the Stillwater complex in Montana. Stillwater does not produce gold. There are a few known occurrences of platinum group metals in North America such as the Good News Bay deposit in Alaska, the Ungava trough in northern Quebec, Lac des Iles and Marathon in Ontario and Wellgreen in the Yukon. None of these deposits contain a significant amount of gold. So far, the only major deposit, other than Sudbury, where both gold and platinum are known to occur together is the Skaergaard intrusion in Eastern Greenland.

Another tipoff is the incredible richness of the deposit usually reported by the con artist. In one case, an American company reported a gigantic discovery in New Mexico that supposedly contained so much gold and platinum that it would have been the richest ore body on earth. There is no known platinum in New Mexico and very little gold. The investors lost $25 million.

III. The mine potential

The swindler takes the official reports and the doctored assays and interprets the "results" to predict the potential of the property. The prospectus may claim that hundreds of thousands of dollars have been spent to establish the potential of the mine, even though there has been no systematic drilling or sampling. The swindler carves a block of land from the so-called mining area and arbitrarily estimates that it contains hundreds of ounces of gold which he is willing to sell to you at a discount. Should you ask why no one found this gold before, the promoter will probably say he has found a new way to assay the ore and a new technique to extract it.

The most extravagant claims of mine potential came from a U.S. company that said it was mining beach sand in Costa Rica. The gold, the company claimed, was a renewable resource since it was brought in by the tides! The tremendous opportunity to become unimaginably wealthy was only available to U.S. investors willing to part with $5,000 to $10,000. Needless to say, the investors' money came and went with the tide.

IV. The black box

It is the "black box" — the "new" technology — in the prospectus that is most intriguing to me. If the language of the geologist forms the basis of the incantations of the modern alchemist, the black box is the equivalent of the secret ingredient of the ancient alchemist. The huge multinational mining companies spend millions of dollars on research and development to improve the recovery of gold in their mining and milling operations and pay professionals to always be on top of developments in the field. Yet every year a con artist and his imaginative flunkies convince naive investors that they have discovered a unique way to recover gold.

One swindler claimed he could recover gold by running water over the mined ore; another said he could trap the gold with a specially designed material. One claim I found particularly interesting was that "several fractional factorial experiments were run to develop new recovery procedures." It sounds very impressive, but I do not know what fractional factorial experiments are.

There aren't any gold recovery techniques that are exclusively known by only one company. There is an extensive body of literature on gold recovery and there are countless seminars and courses where everything about gold recovery can be learned and applied. If you see a black box appearing in a document, you can be sure it's bogus.

V. Mine development plan

If gold scams have one common denominator, it is that they all propose building a small mill with the promise of a much larger plant once the viability of the mine has been demonstrated. In one case the prospectus stated that "although we may have to demonstrate that we also have a way to extract the platinum group metal, we may be able to demonstrate this by building a tiny one-tenth-of-a-ton per day mill." This company also stated that it had reserves of more than 30 million ounces in the ground. This doesn't make sense. A company with proven reserves would never build a smaller mill than required to efficiently mine its ore.

In another case, a firm stated that "the cost of mining may appear immoderate to the uninitiated. It is a reflection of the complex chemistry of the ore body itself and the special cold recovery system developed by the company." Most swindlers are peddling placer deposits, the easiest gold to recover. Remember, gold in placer deposits has accumulated over millions of years at the bottom of crevices and rivers. It is recovered in nuggets or small flakes by panning. The gold is already 70 per cent to 80 per cent pure, amalgamated with a bit of silver or other metal. There aren't any special recovery mechanisms, systems or chemistry involved in placer gold mining.

In any case, before anyone can build a mine or mill in North America, an operating permit must be obtained. This means assembling a comprehensive set of data covering the mine's reserves, planned operations and a complete environmental impact study. This study alone can take two to three years to complete, especially in states such as California. Getting permits covering emissions into the air, water intake and discharge and full operation will take months. These permits are handed out by the county, state or province in which the mine will be located. You can find out if the company has even applied for permits by contacting the regulatory authorities in the area in which the mine is to be located. If none has been applied for, you know the deal is bogus.

VI. The résumé

The con artist always tries to prove that the people behind the discovery and management of the mine have a great deal of expertise in the mining business. Usually, the people behind the scheme haven't any relevant experience, but on paper they sound good. In one case, a day labourer who had worked in a couple of mines was cited as an expert in recovery techniques. In another, the operator of a bulldozer on road construction was referred to as an expert on trenching, drilling, stripping, sampling and mine planning. An art school graduate was said to have operated mines and mills of all types. Where are the geologists, mining engineers and lawyers?

VII. The name and the pictures
The glossy brochure is not complete until there are photographs and an impressive name for the company and the mine. What's in a name? Everything. A well-known name can lend an enormous amount of credibility and respectability. It is not unusual, nor surprising, to see the name of the largest and most successful mining companies being used. Often the words Noranda, Homestake or Goldfield are combined with the magic words platinum or gold to give the enterprise the ultimate sign of legitimacy.

Of course, seeing is believing. This is why most brochures contain photographs and sketches of the so-called mine and its equipment. The swindler is fully aware that few people will ever take a trip to the property, so he makes a point of inviting prospective purchasers to inspect the claim. The photographs are seldom of a real mine — but if you've never seen a mine you'll never know the difference. Most brochures have photographs of a strip of desert or pasture which supposedly show the mine. The so-called mining equipment is often dirt-moving equipment used in road construction.

The selling of the scam

With all the pieces in place, the swindler has to recruit a person or a firm to sell the project to investors. This key individual is sometimes referred to as the "master broker" and he'll share up to half the take with the con artist. His task is to set up the telephone sales operations, known as the "boiler room." The boiler room is not usually in the state or province where the "mine" is located. To confuse the authorities and to stay out of the public eye, the people involved in the scam are usually scattered across several states — the promoter will be in one, the master broker in another, the mine in another, and the boiler rooms in several other states.

The term "boiler room" captures the pressure put on the salespeople working for the master broker and the pressure exerted on investors to come up with money. Typically, the boiler room is in a low-rent office divided by sound-reducing partitions into cubicles. Each cubicle has a telephone and the salespeople are given a number of scripts to read in making their sales pitches. The salespeople work strictly on commissions, so their motivation is money.

A boiler room salesperson will usually try to put the prospective investor at ease by talking about gold and its performance before he introduces the idea of an investment that could be the opportunity of a lifetime. Skirting anything that might worry the prospective investor, the salesperson will make the most of the wildest claims about the potential of the mine. He'll promise the investor that he cannot possibly lose money because the company guarantees everything. He'll pressure the investor to make an immediate decision.

Most boiler room operations use a "sucker's list" that has been compiled over the years by con artists and sold to other boiler room operations. These lists are of individuals who have in the past invested in questionable deals or who are known to respond to cold calls from high-pressure salespeople. If you have succumbed to a telephone offer, you're probably on one of these lists.

Con artists prefer the telephone, but they've also been known to strut their stuff at gold shows and trade shows, particularly if unsophisticated but eager gold investors are likely to be there. The presence of scam artists in booths at gold shows is deplorable, especially since many of the people at the show erroneously believe that the sponsors of the show have screened the advertisers. Scam artists have also been known to advertise in well-known publications such as *Barron's* as well as trade journals.

The investment pitch

The investor, or "sucker," is usually offered a patch of dirt called gold-bearing ore, aggregate ore, bank-run ore or placer gravel which the salesperson will claim contains a certain amount of gold. He will be asked to put up $5,000 or $10,000; the incentive will be the opportunity to buy into the operation at a fraction of the value of the gold in the ground. The purchaser is offered an unqualified guarantee that the dirt will contain the amount of gold described in the prospectus. If you ask why you are being offered such an incredible opportunity, you will be told that you are providing the seed capital, or patient money, to start the mining operation. The con artist may try to keep you on the hook by telling you that it will take months before any gold is delivered because the company processing the ore has to set up its operation and the "black box" requires a great deal of fine-tuning and time to digest the gold.

In 12 to 18 months, if the scam hasn't bilked the public of enough money, the promoter will be back with stories of problems with the delivery of heavy equipment, permit snags, labour problems, in-clement weather or bureaucratic bungling. He'll also want more money. Eventually, the promoter vanishes.

Penny-stock fraud

While the dirt-pile swindle is a very lucrative way for scam artists to take your money, it pales in comparison with the money being made by white-collar criminals who defraud the public through the penny stock market. The size of the fraud is uncertain, but it is estimated that unscrupulous broker-dealers using high-pressure telephone sales tactics defraud the public of over $200 million a year in North America alone. What can you do to protect yourself?

Rule 1: Be informed

Don't buy stocks from brokers whom you don't know or trust. Understand the fundamentals of the company itself and of the market for the stock. Many penny stocks, particularly in the U.S., are traded by a single brokerage firm which controls the market. Whenever a broker has a monopoly, there is always a higher risk of market manipulation or price-fixing.

And remember, broker-dealers who deal in penny stocks earn their living from the commissions they charge on their sales. Some firms and dishonest salespeople might mark up the price of the stocks they're peddling by as much as 100 per cent, which is illegal. Furthermore, because most of these penny stocks do not trade on an exchange, it will be difficult for you to monitor your investment without relying on the broker-dealer who sold it to you. Finally, many of these companies do not issue quarterly or annual financial reports, making it impossible for the investor to evaluate the true value of the investment.

Rule 2: Stay cool under pressure

Most penny-stock frauds are committed by broker-dealers using "boiler room" sales tactics. The sales call could come from a broker you do not know; in fact, he will probably be calling from another city. He'll represent a firm unknown to you. He'll offer you an investment opportunity that he will aggressively insist is your chance to become rich.

You should never be pressured into making a quick investment decision, especially over the telephone. Don't let this stranger make you feel guilty, silly or stupid for taking the time to think and investigate before buying a penny stock. Be skeptical when the salesperson tells you that the opportunity may slip past if you don't act immediately. Under "boiler room" tactics, this salesperson won't let go easily; if he won't stop, then hang up.

Rule 3: Watch for misleading information

The most common misinformation is the assurance that the proposed investment has little risk while the probable gains are high. In the real world, investment returns are commensurate with their risks. Low risk and high returns never go hand in hand.

Sometimes the salesperson will tell you that he has "inside" information about an event or situation that will affect the price of the stock within weeks. Beware that trading on inside information is illegal and the penalties which you and the broker could suffer include a possible jail sentence. More often than not, however, the broker doesn't have any special information. It's just another lie.

How can you protect yourself? One way is to ask for written information on the proposed investment. Don't accept any of the common excuses — the company is new, the developments have been so rapid or that you haven't time to receive the information before the opportunity is lost. If the broker doesn't provide the information, you can be sure the opportunity is bogus.

In January, 1990, the U.S. Securities and Exchange Commission issued Rule 15 C2-6, a document called Penny Stock Cold Calling. This new rule was designed to protect the public against high-pressure telephone sales tactics by requiring a broker-dealer to have you sign a suitability agreement before he can sell you a penny stock. In other words, the salesperson is required to evaluate your personal financial situation and investment experience as well as explain in writing the appropriateness of high-risk penny stocks for you. Finally, he must obtain your signature to prove that you have read and agree with his statements.

Furthermore, the rule requires that for your first three purchases you must sign a written agreement spelling out the name and the number of shares that you have agreed to buy. Even if you agree verbally to buy the stock you are not obligated to do so if you do not return the signed agreement. For a copy of the rule, contact the Securities and Exchange Commission, Publications, Mail Stop C-11, Washington, D.C. 20549.

In Ontario, if you have second thoughts about your "can't-fail" investment, you have the right to cancel your purchase of a new issue offered by prospectus within two days after your receipt of the prospectus. Under all other circumstances, you have no recourse.

If you've been cheated, do something about it. Report it to the authorities immediately and help put the thieves out of business. Your prompt complaint could prevent other people from losing money. Help protect your own legal rights and assist the security regulators in putting a stop to a type of fraud that siphons hundreds of millions of dollars from honest investors.

CHAPTER 10

Silver: The Poor Man's Gold

"THE COMMON MAN'S GOLD" might be a better term for silver. From Alexander the Great through Roman times, the Middle Ages and the Renaissance, silver was the currency of choice for most nations. Just like gold, it was portable and divisible, making it a convenient medium of exchange. But its availability was far greater than that of gold. Its value lay between that of gold, which was too precious for ordinary transactions, and that of copper or bronze, which were the metals used for the smaller currencies. The Roman denarium was made of silver and widely circulated throughout the known world from as far north as Norway and Sweden to as far east as India. The denarium, the backbone of Roman coinage, was much abused by the Roman emperors who tampered with its value. From a coin of pure silver during Augustan times at the time of Christ's birth, the denarium was at times as much as 50 per cent zinc or lead. By the middle of the third century, it was worth less than one-fiftieth of the value of the Augustan coins. This was in sharp contrast to the gold coins which, even though they too had been lightened a few times, maintained their high quality.

When Christopher Columbus began his expedition to find a shorter route to India and the Orient, he could hardly have imagined that in the following 50 years his discoveries would increase the world's stock of gold and silver by 50 per cent. In his contract with Queen Isabella of Spain, Columbus was to retain 10 per cent of all revenues, specifically that of gold and silver, derived from the expedition.

With the opening of the great silver mines of Cerro de Potosi in Bolivia in 1545, silver prices temporarily dropped. These mines were officially producing more than 22 tons of silver a year but in reality were probably producing four to five times that amount. The new supply of silver, as well as gold, became so great in relation to existing stocks that it sparked a round of inflation that was felt in all of Europe.

From 1550, when mining in the New World became firmly organized by the Spanish Crown, until 1650, when Spain's hegemony over the New World started to fade, as much as 2,000 tons of gold and 50,000 to 60,000 tons of silver were sent to Europe by the Spanish colonies. Despite the riches pouring into its coffers, Spain did not last as a powerhouse on the European continent. As succeeding Spanish monarchs fought wars against England and France while expanding their empire in the New World, they not only used every bit of gold and silver sent to them by the colonies but fell deeply into debt. The pressure to meet payments on the royal debt increased steadily, making the need for more gold and silver from the New World more pressing with each passing year. As mine output started to decrease in the latter part of the 16th century, the monarchy could not support the mountain of debt that had accumulated: In the years between 1557 and 1680, the Spanish crown defaulted no less than seven times on its debt. As the 17th century wore on, it became clear that the real beneficiary of Spain's wealth was not Spain itself. Instead, the winners were the northern manufacturing countries, especially England, which had little gold of its own but produced the goods that the newly rich Spaniards wanted.

The demonetization of silver

Up until the mid-19th century, the world had had a bimetallic standard of silver and gold backing its currencies. However, the enormous amount of new gold that came to market in the late part of the century was enough to displace silver in its monetary role, and gold became the sole reserve currency. By the 1870s, all of Europe was on a gold standard, leaving only the United States and the Asian countries demanding silver. Because silver was no longer supported by monetary demand, its price started to fall. At the same time, the establishment of the gold standard created a dramatic increase in the demand for gold. The result was a shortage of gold and persistent inflation which lasted from 1865 to 1895.

By 1880, the price of silver had fallen to as low as 65 cents an ounce and the silver mines of the western United States were having difficulty surviving. The Sherman Silver Purchase Act was passed requiring the U.S. treasury to buy 4.5 million ounces of silver each month, practically the entire output of the U.S. mines. De-

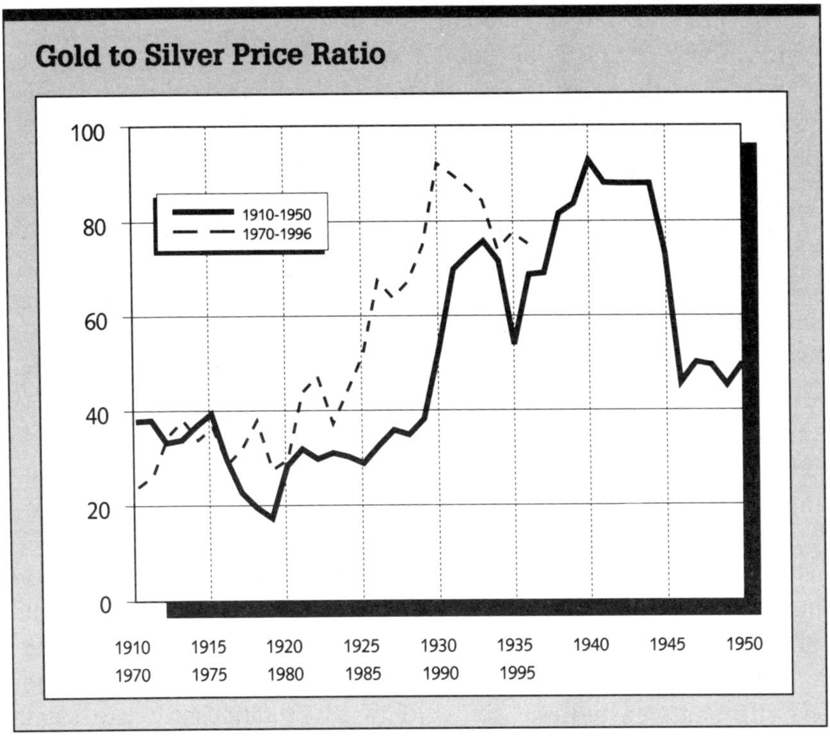

CHART X

spite the act, the price of silver continued to fall for the following six years, reaching 50 cents an ounce by 1896.

Many western politicians, in particular those from the silver-producing states, continued to push for the reestablishment of a bi-metallic currency. This movement culminated in the famous "cross of gold" speech of William Jennings Bryan of Nebraska who became the Democratic Party candidate for president that year. Bryan gave an impassioned speech, telling the crowd: "We will answer their demand for a gold standard by saying to them, 'You should not press down upon the brow of labor this crown of thorns, you shall not crucify mankind upon a cross of gold.' " Bryan lost to William McKinley and the movement to restore silver as currency was effectively dead. As mining of pure silver in the United States became unprofitable, most of the mines shut down and much of the production became a byproduct of the mining of base metals such as lead, zinc and copper.

The price of silver gradually declined until 1915, when only China and a handful of smaller countries remained on a silver standard. As the inflationary pressure of the First World War started to build, the price of silver rose sharply to $1.085 (U.S.) by September, 1917. Two years later, it reached a peak of $1.375 (U.S.). This is not all that surprising since the increase in silver price simply mirrored the increase in the wholesale commodity price index which had risen by 127 per cent in the same time. As the war came to an end and inflation began to abate, the price of silver fell by 75 per cent from 1920 to 1932, yet the commodity price index fell by only 53 per cent. These sharp price movements in silver reflected its position as strictly a commodity with some speculative appeal in times of inflation. Gold on the other hand was still the ultimate hard money. The gold to silver ratio became an indicator of inflationary or deflationary pressures.

At the turn of the century when inflationary pressure was nonexistent and gold was fixed at $20.67 (U.S.), the gold to silver ratio hovered around 40 to 1. By 1919, as the inflationary pressures of the First World War drove the price of silver up, the ratio began to fall, reaching a low of 18 to 1 by 1919. Throughout the 1920s, inflationary pressures abated and the gold to silver ratio started to climb back. As the Great Depression took hold, the ratio kept climbing to reach a peak of 95:1 in 1940. This was the highest ratio the price of gold to silver has ever reached.

Is there a lesson in this for silver investors today? In the 1960s when gold was still fixed at $35 (U.S.) an ounce, the inflationary pressures of the Vietnam War were reflected by the drop in the gold to silver price ratio to a low of 19:1 in 1968. In the early 1970s when the gold price was set free, the ratio climbed back up but quickly fell again in the latter part of the 1970s when the extreme inflationary pressure brought about by the OPEC oil crisis in 1980 pushed the gold to silver ratio to a low of 18:1. Since 1980, the ratio has been gradually climbing as the continuing deflationary pressure brought about by the tightening of the money supply produces high real rates of interest and creates tremendous competitive pressures in the global economy. The gold to silver ratio reached a high of 90:1 in 1990. If deflationary pressures continue to exert themselves, we could well see a repeat of the 95:1 ratio reached in 1940.

In fact, with the silver supply rapidly expanding because of increased base metal mines production where silver is a co-product,

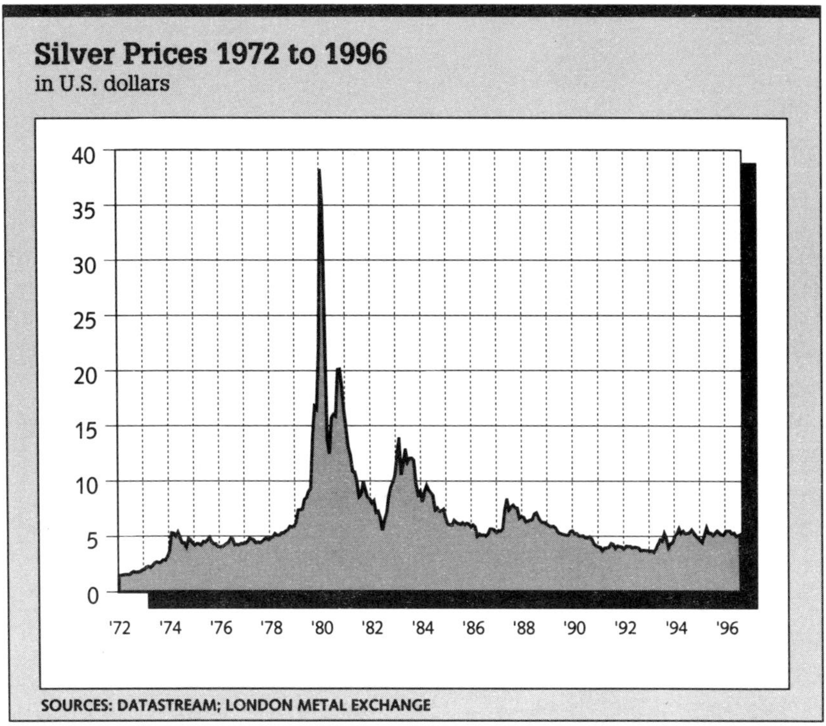

CHART XI

the gold to silver price ratio could even surpass its old high of 95:1, perhaps breaking the barrier of 100:1. This could imply a silver price of $3.50 (U.S.) an ounce and gold at $350 (U.S.) an ounce. If history repeats itself, silver prices would then be at their historic lows and could start the long climb back. In fact, gold and silver briefly touched these prices in 1990 and silver has been picking up ever since. The gold to silver ratio has plummeted in the past four years from 90:1 to 73:1. Should the world experience another inflationary cycle and the gold to silver ratio return to its more traditional value of 18:1, silver could turn out to be a great investment for those who are patient.

Silver supply and demand

The price of silver in real or deflated terms is near a 20-year low, and mine production, after reaching a high of 514 million ounces in 1990, has declined by less than 14 per cent over the last five years to 444 million ounces in 1994. This high level of production has occurred despite problems during the period in Peru, the world's second-largest silver producer, which has seen its silver output fall by about 10 per cent in the last five years. A strong new president with a free market orientation is bringing a new stability to Peru. But it could take years before Peru remobilizes the capital and labour necessary to regain its former levels of silver production.

Mexico remains the foremost silver-producing country in the world, a position it has enjoyed for more than 400 years. In 1994, it produced 75 million ounces of silver or 20 per cent of the total Western world new-mine production. Most of the silver production is controlled by Mexican-owned companies of which Industrias Penoles SAdeCV ranks as the world's largest individual refined-silver producer with production of approximately 50 million ounces a year.

As a result of large-scale gold exploration over the past 10 years as well as the development of several new base metal mines, the United States finds itself as the fourth-largest silver-producing country. Much of the U.S. silver production increase is a byproduct of new gold or base metal mines. Only 14 per cent of silver production is from primary silver mines. The rest was a byproduct of gold, copper and lead/zinc operations.

The same phenomenon is taking place in Australia, which is the fifth-largest producer. Much of today's silver production is price inelastic, meaning that the silver will be produced no matter what the price. This seemingly peculiar situation arises from the fact that over 87 per cent of today's silver production is mined as a byproduct of lead, zinc, copper or gold mining. Most of Arizona's copper mines, for example, contain silver which is recovered along with copper.

To keep their accounting simple, mining companies attribute all costs to the main product of the mine. Once they've sold the silver, they credit the revenue to the cost of producing the principal metal. In some cases, revenues from the byproduct may surpass revenues from the main product if the byproduct price has increased rapidly. El Indio in Chile, for example, is a primary gold producer with copper as a byproduct. In 1989, as copper prices rose to over $1.50 (U.S.) a pound, the cost of producing an ounce of gold at Indio fell dramatically from $200 (U.S.) to $120 (U.S.) an ounce because of the increased byproduct credit from copper. Mining companies in general prefer polymetallic ore bodies, deposits containing more

World Silver Supply and Demand

IN MILLIONS OF OUNCES

SUPPLY	1991	1992	1993	1994	1995
Mine production	504.6	499.4	468.4	444.2	468.8
Official sector sales	11.5	8.1	13.8	32.4	26.2
Old silver scrap	120.6	124.7	128.6	132.5	140.8
Hedging	22.9	-	23.6	-	5.5
Implied disinvestment	21.7	82.0	126.7	150.2	123.1
Total supply	681.2	714.2	761.1	759.3	764.4
DEMAND					
Fabrication					
Industrial / decorative	270.8	268.8	263.7	279.4	291.2
Photography	213.7	212.6	212.9	219.3	222.1
Jewelry/silverware	168.1	197.8	244.7	208.3	228.2
Official coins	28.1	33.3	39.5	42.9	22.9
Total fabrication	681.2	712.5	761.1	749.3	764.4
Hedging	-	1.7	-	9.9	-
Implied investment	-	-	-	-	-
Total demand	681.2	714.2	761.1	759.3	764.4
Silver price (US$/oz.)	$4.06	$3.95	$4.31	$5.29	$5.20

SOURCE: THE SILVER INSTITUTE WORLD SILVER SURVEY 1996

TABLE XIX

than one kind of ore, because their revenues are often more stable than single commodity deposits.

In 1993, the largest silver producers were the Mount Isa lead and zinc mine in Australia with 18.6 million ounces, the La Coipa gold mine in Chile which produced 13.3 million ounces, the McCoy/Cove gold mine in Nevada with 12.5 million ounces and the Brunswick lead and zinc mine with 6.7 million ounces. In 1995, the Eskay gold mine in Canada began producing over nine million ounces of silver a year, making it the fourth-largest silver mine in the world and vaulting Canada from the world's ninth-largest silver producing country to fifth. Note that all of the largest silver-producing mines produce silver as a byproduct. These giant multimetallic

The Top 10 Silver Producers in the World
MILLION OUNCES

	1995 rank	1995 production
Mexico	1	74.7
Peru	2	61.4
United States	3	49.8
CIS	4	45.2
Canada	5	38.8
Chile	6	33.5
Poland	7	31.6
Australia	8	29.6
China	9	27.0
Bolivia	10	11.9

SOURCE: THE SILVER INSTITUTE WORLD SILVER SURVEY 1996

TABLE XX

ore bodies now account for 77 per cent of total world silver production, while primary silver mines only produce 23 per cent.

The five largest silver-producing countries in the world are Mexico, Peru, the United States, the CIS and Canada. These countries produce almost 58 per cent of the world's silver. Their position is unlikely to be challenged; Africa, Asia and Europe have been hard-pressed to keep up their production over the past five years. None of these areas are expected to show any significant silver production increase in the coming decade.

Secondary supply

In any one year, the secondary silver market supplies almost 40 per cent of total silver available to consumers. It is, therefore, a very important component of the overall supply and demand balance of the silver market. While secondary silver supply can be broken down into several major components such as central bank buying or selling, South Asian dishoarding or silver trading by the Eastern Bloc, the biggest component of secondary supply is old scrap.

Over the past decade, old scrap has represented 75 to 95 per cent of total available secondary supply. Photographic materials such as film and silver-coated paper make up close to 50 per cent of overall scrap supplies in a typical year. The rest is made up of industrial components, including silver contacts from electrical and electronic equipment such as telephone switching systems, computers and telephones. When silver prices are high, as in 1980, scrap supplies

Sources of Silver Production

MILLION OUNCES

	1991	1992	1993	1994
Primary silver	73.27	54.88	50.76	53.39
Gold	47.80	64.78	61.21	55.28
Copper	130.32	132.52	128.98	124.21
Lead and zinc	191.18	189.04	172.10	154.25
Total sources	442.58	441.22	413.06	387.13
% of world total	87.7	88.3	88.2	87.1

SOURCE: THE SILVER INSTITUTE WORLD SILVER SURVEY 1995

TABLE XXI

increase sharply as the public sells small bars, coins and silver tableware. High silver prices also make it worthwhile for mining companies to extract silver from much lower-grade material that would be considered waste at other times.

Demand for silver had been heavily curtailed in the early 1980s by extraordinarily high prices that inhibited demand for silver in the fabrication and photography industries. Falling silver prices decreased secondary supply from 153 million ounces in 1985 to 141 million ounces in 1993. Industrial users found ways to reduce silver consumption, not only because it was expensive but because it was volatile in price. After a five- to six-year period, most of the economies of scale sought by industries have been realized and consumption began to grow in earnest in 1985. Industry is now the foremost user of silver, only just recently edging ahead of photographic and siverware and jewelry demand. The increasingly diverse uses of silver in industrial applications and in fast-growing special areas like water purification should maintain this leading position.

Silver's next main use is in the photography industry. Every year, almost 50 per cent of the world's silver production goes into the billions of feet of film used by photographers around the world and the films used in X-ray machines, which represents more than a third of the silver demand in the photography industry. The photography industry was also shocked by the rapid rise in the price of silver of the early 1980s and went through a readjustment process whereby it decreased the amount of silver in film. This process was essentially complete by the mid-1980s and silver use in photography increased by more than 5 per cent a year from 1985 to 1990. Since 1990, photographic silver consumption has remained essentially flat at about 219 million ounces.

Looking forward, the greatest threat that silver faces comes precisely from the photography industry. The development by the Japanese of alternative technologies, specifically that of electronic imaging, is likely to have a negative impact on silver consumption in the coming decade. Electronic imaging is unlikely to replace silver completely in amateur or professional photography but in some specialized applications, such as X-rays, it might be more convenient to use digitized images that are directly connected to a computer which may have diagnostic capabilities.

The third-largest component of silver demand is for jewelry, sterling ware and silver plate, which consume approximately 208 million ounces of silver a year. Demand had been very soft in the early 1980s due to the high prices. The decline had been acutely felt in Europe where fabrication of silver, which stood at around 58 million ounces by the end of the 1970s, dropped sharply to a low of 25 million ounces in 1984. However, low prices and improving economic activity have stimulated jewelry demand throughout the world causing silver consumption in jewelry to more than quadruple between 1985 and 1994.

Silver bullion and coins

Investors in the precious metals sector have a choice of purchasing silver bullion in one-, five-, 10-, 50- and 100-ounce bars or the standard one-kilogram bar. The volatility of silver prices and the fact that a one-kilogram silver bar is worth approximately $165 compared with $12,000 (U.S.) for a one-kilogram gold bar have combined to make silver an investor's favourite and the poor man's gold.

However, before putting serious money into silver, you should think about where you can safely store all these bars. For the same $12,000 (U.S.) that you would spend on one gold kilo-bar, you could end up with 73 silver kilo-bars. You can purchase silver from the same dealers who sell gold and, just as with gold, you must be sure you deal only with reputable firms. Make sure that you purchase a silver bar with a fineness of 0.99 purity and that it comes from an internationally recognized refiner. You should also shop around and compare the premiums charged by different dealers.

Your goal is to purchase a good quality silver bar at the lowest premium possible. Remember, the smaller your purchase, the higher the premium is likely to be. Typically, the premium on the one-kilogram bar will range between 8 to 10 per cent; premiums on smaller bars could reach 20 per cent to 30 per cent of the price of the bar. To recoup your investment, silver would have to increase by that much before you would break even. As far as taxes are concerned, in most cases the state or provincial tax legislation in effect for gold bullion also applies to silver bullion.

Not one of the major silver-producing countries has a silver bullion coin program. In part, the high cost of producing a bullion coin would make it unprofitable in a one-ounce or smaller denomination. Also, coins would command a far greater premium than the standard bullion bar and would, therefore, not be attractive to investors. Also, there are already thousands of tons of silver dollars and quarters in circulation that were minted over the past 100 years in the United States and Canada and are still in circulation. Up until 1966, Canadian quarters were 90 per cent silver, the year in which the silver content of the coin was reduced to 75 per cent. In 1968, all silver in coins was replaced by copper and zinc.

To facilitate trading, these old silver coins can be bought in bags. These bags contain silver quarters with a real face value of $1,000 (U.S.). The coins are real money but the trading of these bags is done strictly on the silver content. Again, when you purchase these bags be careful of the premium you pay and, if you harbour any doubts, you're better off purchasing silver bars. A 100-ounce bar is likely to carry a lower overall premium and better liquidity than a bag of coins.

Trading in silver futures

Should you have a more speculative bend, silver futures contracts are offered in New York, Chicago and Tokyo. By far the largest of the exchanges for silver contracts is the New York Comex. It accounts for 90 per cent of the trades in silver futures. But remember, over 90 per cent of the silver futures market is made up of speculators betting against each other in a zero-sum game. The heavy commissions charged on futures trading mean the brokers are the only people who are consistently making money.

Commodity trading is a broker's dream. As an active trader, you can easily pay commissions that will equal the full value of your account. Your portfolio could earn 80 per cent in a year, yet you could end up with exactly the same capital that you started with. The lure of the futures market is in its leverage — you only have to put up 5 to 10 per cent of the capital riding on a contract. However, the commission is always calculated on the total amount of the contract. Therefore, assuming a 4 per cent commission rate for every $1,000 contract, you will pay $40 in commission even though you have put out only $100 to join the game. This amounts to a commission of 40 per cent of your capital. It is not unusual for a futures trader to make 20 trades a year, making it imperative that he hit it big at least once in a while to be a winner.

Investing in silver equities

As I pointed out earlier, there are few pure silver mines in North America. Since some of these mines are owned by several companies, there are even fewer public companies that are pure silver plays. In Canada, pure silver plays such as Equity Silver or United Keno Hill Mines are no longer operating. In the United States, Coeur d'Alene Mines and Sunshine Mining would be the only two silver plays, and the latter is more of a silver refiner. All other silver producers derive more of their revenues from other metals, such as gold and copper, than silver. Nevertheless, companies such as Anvil Range, Prime Resources, TVX Gold and Hecla Mining do derive a meaningful part of their revenues from silver production. You can measure your exposure to the silver market in buying a share of these companies by dividing their total silver production by the number of shares outstanding. A silver investor will want to purchase as many ounces of silver per share as possible for the lowest possible price. Another way is to buy a company that has no silver production but a number of silver deposits that could be developed, especially with higher silver prices. Probably the best example of this strategy is Pan American Silver Corp., currently being assembled by Ross Beatty.

As an investor in silver equities, look for the same characteristics you would look for in gold equities: low production costs, long mine life, potential for growth and solid management. Like gold stocks, silver stocks tend to trade at a premium to the rest of the market even though silver is strictly a commodity and not money.

The outlook for silver

The last decade of the 20th century may turn out to be a difficult one for silver. There has been a relentless increase in production as a spin-off from the increase in gold and base metal mining, yet demand is likely to plateau. This will continue to put pressure on prices that are already at a 50-year low in real terms. At the same time, the high level of stocks on Comex and the London Mercantile Exchange will likely prevent a repeat performance of the great price movement of the early 1980s. However, as an investor, you should not lose sight of the fact that silver is still the poor man's gold and at the eleventh hour of a gold bull market, silver will likely perform that role once more. In an inflationary environment, silver has always proven to be more volatile than gold and a 50 per cent increase in the price of gold could easily translate into a 100 per cent increase in the price of silver, as we saw in the 1980s. However, in a deflationary environment, silver is not likely to perform well and holding silver in your portfolio would not be recommended. Your decision to invest a small component of your precious metals portfolio in silver will depend on your outlook for inflation over the next two to three years.

CHAPTER 11

Platinum and Palladium

PLATINUM WAS UNKNOWN TO the Europeans until the Spanish Conquistadors found it in the mid-16th century in South America. They called the new metal "platina del pinto" or "little silver" because of its resemblance to silver. The Ecuadorian metalsmiths mixed platinum with gold but its very high melting point (1773°C) made it extremely difficult for the jewellers of that time to work. It wasn't until the early part of the 19th century that a second source of the metal was found in the Ural Mountains of Russia, and uses were found for it in industry and science.

It was at that time that two new metals, palladium and rhodium, were discovered by Dr. William Hyde Woolaston. Palladium is similar to platinum in colour and has many of the same characteristics, but it has a lower melting point of 1652°C and a specific gravity of little over half that of platinum. The remaining members of the platinum subgroup, so-called because of the member-metals' resemblance to platinum, are iridium and rhodium, both discovered in 1803; osmium, discovered in 1804, and ruthenium, discovered in 1845.

Until the beginning of the 20th century, more than 90 per cent of the world's platinum group metals came from alluvial deposits. The discovery of the nickel-copper-platinum group metal deposits of Sudbury in Ontario in the 1890s was followed in 1924 by the discovery of the major hard-rock deposit in the Bushveldt igneous complex of South Africa. These discoveries marked the turning point in the production and usage of these metals as the mining of the platinum group metals on a large scale finally became possible.

Supply of platinum and palladium

In 1994, the global platinum supply from mine production amounted to 4.5 million ounces while the global supply of palladium was 5.3 million ounces. As you can see, it is approximately one-sixteenth of the available 74 million ounces of gold supply in the same year. South Africa continues to dominate the world supply of the platinum group metals as it accounts for almost 70 per cent of the total supply of these metals. Russian production, or at least what they sell to the West increased dramatically from 300,000 ounces in 1989 to over one million ounces in 1991 and again in 1994. From my visit to Siberia in 1991, I believe that these sales levels are unsustainable and will level out about 40 per cent lower by the mid-1990s. In Canada, the Sudbury Basin in Ontario accounted for 4 per cent of total supply. The Stillwater mine in Montana, the only primary platinum group metal mine outside of South Africa, accounts for approximately 2 per cent of supply.

Anyone worried about the availability of gold should South Africa's problems worsen should be doubly worried about the availability of platinum and palladium. These metals are not only important to all industry; they are the key components of our electronic and electrochemical industries. For example, we simply would not have emission control catalysts for our automobiles without platinum and palladium. Without them, our modern refineries could not produce the petroleum products that our society requires.

The need for new supply has been increasing; in the past five years, platinum's demand growth rate has been 3.7 per cent, while palladium's demand has been growing even faster at 7.1 per cent. The pre-eminence of South African platinum group production is unlikely to be challenged for the next decade. In fact, the three existing mining groups that control production in South Africa are steadily expanding the size of their operations. Historically, there has always been a $50 (U.S.) to $100 (U.S.) difference in the price of gold and platinum, but throughout the 1970s platinum traded consistently at a discount to gold; the price of platinum went to a premium to gold in the mid-1980s until the U.S. recession of 1991, when the price weakened below that of gold.

Intensive exploration efforts in North America over the past 20 years have led to the discovery and building of only one significant platinum/palladium mine — the mine at Stillwater, Mont. By South African standards, Stillwater is a puny operation, producing 210,000 ounces of palladium and 63,000 ounces of platinum a year, but a significant expansion is in the works. There are two mines in South Africa, Rustenburg and Impala, that each produce over one million ounces of platinum every year. In Canada, concentrated ex-

Platinum Supply and Demand

IN THOUSANDS OF OUNCES

	1985	1991	1992	1993	1994	1995
Supply						
South Africa	2,340	2,770	2,750	3,360	3,160	3,370
North America	150	220	200	220	220	230
Others	40	70	120	130	140	100
Russia	230	1,100	750	680	1,010	1,280
Total supply	2,760	4,160	3,820	4,390	4,530	4,980
Demand by application						
Autocatalyst	910	1,350	1,305	1,410	1,560	1,515
Chemical	225	240	215	180	190	210
Electrical	200	175	165	165	185	383
Glass	140	120	80	80	145	220
Investment	430	415	255	305	395	345
Jewelry	810	1,470	1,510	1,615	1,740	1,810
Petroleum	15	150	120	105	90	119
Other	130	140	150	165	190	138
Total demand	2,860	4,060	3,800	4,025	4,560	4,790
Surplus (shortage)	(100)	100	20	365	(30)	190

SOURCE: JOHNSON MATTHEY PLATINUM 1996

TABLE XXII

ploration efforts in Northern Quebec, Ontario and the Northwest Territories have resulted in only the very small Lac des Iles mine in Ontario, which started production very late in 1993. The same can be said of efforts in Greenland, Australia and New Zealand, as well as in Zimbabwe, where platinum group metals have been found but their commercial potential has yet to be determined. For the next decade at least, the world will continue to rely heavily on stability in South Africa for continued availability of both platinum and palladium. Any signs of trouble, especially at the mines, could send prices of these two metals sharply higher. While I believe that the probability of such events is small, it would be easier to shut down the entire South African platinum group metal production than its much larger gold mining operations. Therefore, there could be some merit to holding a small percentage of your bullion portfolio in the

Palladium Supply and Demand
IN THOUSANDS OF OUNCES

	1985	1991	1992	1993	1994	1995
Supply						
South Africa	1,010	1,270	1,260	1,395	1,500	1,600
North America	190	420	450	395	410	470
Others	90	70	70	70	70	70
Russia	1,440	2,150	2,100	2,400	3,300	4,200
Total supply	2,730	3,910	3,880	4,260	5,280	6,340
Demand by application						
Autocatalyst net	290	270	395	605	870	1,615
Dental	870	1,165	1,195	1,210	1,265	1,300
Electrical	1,100	1,855	1,830	2,015	2,230	2,650
Jewelry	210	210	205	210	205	205
Other	270	290	265	225	300	330
Total demand	2,740	3,790	3,890	4,265	4,870	6,100
Surplus (shortage)	(10)	120	(10)	(5)	410	240

SOURCE: JOHNSON MATTHEY PLATINUM 1996

TABLE XXIII

form of platinum or palladium. This would be especially true if the price of platinum dipped to a discount from the gold price, which does happen from time to time.

Platinum and palladium demand

The demand for platinum for fabrication is heavily concentrated in two sectors, in jewelry and the auto industry, where it is used in car emission control catalysts or autocatalysts. Together, these two industries account for more than two-thirds of worldwide platinum consumption. Demand for platinum jewelry is dominated by Japan, which has accounted for 90 per cent of demand, excluding Russia, over the past 10 years. There are two reasons that could explain the Japanese affinity for platinum jewelry. Platinum's subdued appearance — along with its high quality and investment value — appeals to the Japanese sense of modesty and sobriety. Also, platinum was brought to Japan after the Meiji Restoration in 1868, which ended the isolation of Japan under the Tokugawa Shogunate. The exten-

Projected Platinum Supply

IN THOUSANDS OF OUNCES

	1995a	1996	1997	1998	1999	2000
Rusplats	1,477	1,560	1,596	1,624	1,624	1,624
Implats	977	1,013	1,042	1,055	1,055	1,055
Lonrho	570	585	643	696	696	696
PP Rust	137	157	198	239	255	255
Northam	129	176	198	204	207	207
Lebowa	80	89	102	115	120	120
Total South African	3,370	3,580	3,779	3,932	3,956	3,956
Russia	1,280	1,092	1,077	997	1,130	1,372
North America	230	250	275	325	325	325
Others	100	130	150	150	150	150
Zimbabwe	0	16	82	211	280	280
Total supply	4,980	5,068	5,362	5,615	5,840	6,083
Growth (%)	9.9	1.8	5.8	4.7	4.0	4.1

SOURCE: Fleming Martin, May, 1996

TABLE XXIV

sive use of platinum by the nobility gave the metal a special position in the mind of the Japanese people that remains virtually unchanged to this day.

Second, the price of platinum in Japanese terms has been steadily falling as the yen appreciates against the U.S. dollar. The Japanese investor can purchase an ounce of platinum today at the same yen price as in the early 1980s. Since the price of other hard assets, particularly of land, has risen rapidly over most of the past 10 years, platinum is relatively cheaper than it was 10 years ago. It is, therefore, not surprising that jewelry demand has reached record levels in Japan. At the same time, sales of large bars to investment buyers in Japan hit new highs in the latter part of the 1980s and small investors are scurrying to buy new platinum and medallion coins. Future platinum demand for jewelry, however, will be affected by economic conditions and could weaken if Japan experienced slower growth or a recession.

Globally, the demand for platinum for jewelry has been surpassed by its use in emission control catalysts. This trend is likely to continue as the European community tightens its car emission requirements. While Europe is finally catching on to the need for pollution control, California, birthplace of the environment movement, is set to tighten even further its car emission limits. The new requirements are likely to increase the demand for platinum as the industry works to reduce emission levels and increase the durability of auto catalysts from the existing 50,000-mile requirement to over 100,000 miles.

The only threat to platinum is the possibility of lower-price palladium acting as a substitute. While autocatalyst demand has increased for platinum, in 1995 it exploded for palladium. Auto makers are very sensitive to material costs and have recently been very successful in finding ways of using palladium in the place of platinum.

Palladium fabrication demand is also dominated by the electrical/electronic sector, which takes over 40 per cent of the palladium used each year. The strong growth in demand for palladium in this sector throughout the 1980s is likely to continue in the current decade as the demand for palladium pastes, multilayer ceramic capacitors and hybrid integrated circuits and ceramic capacitors continues to grow along with the growth in demand for products such as laptop personal computers, facsimile machines, televisions, videocassette recorders and automobile electronic systems. The dental sector, which accounts for 20 per cent of palladium demand, is also growing as the number of palladium materials suitable for dental work increases, replacing the more traditional, and expensive, gold. The palladium-based materials are not only lighter and cheaper, but increase the hardness and corrosion resistance of standard dental ceramics.

The "green" metals of the 1990s

Looking into the future is always very risky but closing your eyes ensures that you will never detect a trend in time. While mankind has been working with platinum for centuries, it is only in the past few decades that we have learned to adapt the platinum group metals for the benefit of society. This trend seems to be accelerating as we discover that platinum and palladium could play a significant role in cleaning up our environment. The first such application was the car emission control catalyst, where platinum plays a key role in reducing the emission of carbon monoxide, oxides of nitrogen and unburned hydrocarbons. As the lagging European auto industry finally catches up with North America and Japan, which are both tightening their standards, total platinum consumption should continue to increase over the next decade.

Fuel cell development is another indication of platinum's environment-friendly nature. In a fuel cell, hydrogen and oxygen are combined by using electrodes made of platinum to produce water and generate an electric current. Initially developed for the U.S. space missions, fuel cell technology was adapted by the electric utilities to be used in the production of electricity for peak consumption. While costs are still far in excess of conventional power-production methods, this technology is becoming increasingly attractive, particularly to the Japanese who are erecting an 11-megawatt plant outside of Tokyo. The fact that fuel cell waste is water and not carbon dioxide — the waste generated by conventional fossil fuel plants — renders the fuel cell increasingly attractive to the people who are concerned with the greenhouse effect. Within 20 years, fuel cell technology could be consuming as much as 100,000 ounces of platinum each year.

In March, 1989, two scientists from the University of Utah made the dramatic announcement that they had been able to achieve nuclear fusion at room temperatures using a platinum/palladium apparatus. Almost three years have passed since then. The physics principles behind the results are still not fully understood but repetitions of the experiment have produced large numbers of neutrons and tritium which give evidence that fusion has taken place. There is a great deal of skepticism, but there are a few scientists who remain hopeful that cold fusion can be made to work predictably. If they prove to be right, it will have tremendous implications for platinum and palladium; they are the key elements of this potentially incredible source of new power. By its very nature, cold fusion would provide the world with a cheap and limitless supply of energy, yet would be environmentally friendly since it does not produce any residues. The only problem would be finding the necessary platinum and palladium metals required to build these plants. Current supply could easily be overwhelmed and lead to a price boom reminiscent of the boom in uranium in the 1950s and 1970s when the price of uranium jumped from less than $5 (U.S.) a pound to $56 (U.S.) a pound. The price of platinum could jump from its current $390 (U.S.) an ounce range to over $2,000 (U.S.) an ounce, while palladium could go from $130 (U.S.) an ounce to $800 (U.S.) an ounce. It could take years, if not decades, before commercial application of this technology is feasible, yet these two metals could very well be an interesting speculation on what might be mankind's only hope for clean energy.

Another area where platinum has a high profile is in biomedical use such as in the anti-cancer drugs cis-platin and carbo-platin as well as in components for body implants. Cis-platin, approved in 1978 in the United States, has been shown to be 90 to 95 per cent effective in the treatment of testicular and ovarian cancer. Carboplatin, the newer drug, received U.S. approval in late 1988. These drugs are based on research started over 20 years ago whereby platinum electrodes are used to pass a current through bacteria which then produce anti-cancer cells. The prospects for further pharmaceutical applications are exceptionally good, although at this time they do not involve a great deal of metal demand.

Investing in platinum and palladium

Neither platinum nor palladium can be seen as a substitute for gold as money. Even though both metals are portable and divisible, they are so rare that it would be impractical to use them as currency. In addition, there isn't a central bank that owns either metal as reserve currency. However, they can provide the investor in precious metals with a lucrative means of diversifying his precious metals portfolio.

The platinum market is more liquid than palladium at the bullion level. As with gold, you have the choice between bullion and equities. You can purchase platinum bars and coins or you can purchase stocks in the South African companies that produce the metals. For the speculators there is also the New York COMEX platinum futures or the Tokyo futures market.

For wealthy investors, large bars are available from nearly all of the major gold trading firms. These firms usually carry one-, two-, five- and 10-kilogram bars and their sale and storage are subject to the same charges and taxes as gold. However, with platinum at $390 (U.S.), a one kilogram bar is worth $12,500 (U.S.). On a more practical level, there are small bars and platinum coins such as the Canadian Maple Leaf and the Australian Koala series. Both come in one-, 1/2-, 1/4- and 1/10-ounce coins. They are legal tender, just like gold coins, and are struck from 99.95 per cent pure platinum. So far, the

Koala has been a better seller than the Maple Leaf, particularly in North America where its sales are almost double that of the domestic coin. The only other available platinum legal tender coin is the Nobel, first issued in 1983 by the Isle of Man. Just as you would when buying a gold coin, check the premium being charged by different venders by shopping around. Also compare premiums between the Koala and Maple Leaf, since one may be cheaper than the other, depending on availability or demand.

As for palladium, Russia launched the world's first palladium coin in 1990. Depicting a ballerina, the one-ounce coin is available at your regular bullion dealer. Because of the expected limited availability, watch the premium on these coins.

The high level of Japanese investment demand in platinum is evident in the activity on the TOKOM where both platinum and gold futures are traded. In a typical year, there are more platinum contracts traded than gold contracts. In 1988, two million one-kilogram contracts of gold traded versus 4.4 million 500-gram platinum contracts. Turnover on the TOKOM is primarily related to higher volatility in the price of the metal which encourages speculation. The return of a bull market in gold could have a spillover effect on the platinum market, and prices could be driven sharply higher if it was coincidental with higher fabrication demand from the industry. Overall, investment demand could continue to increase strongly in the 1990s, but continuing growth in fabrication demand will provide the foundation for a price that will likely stay around the $400 (U.S.) range.

The platinum group metal equities

Notwithstanding the futures market and bullion coins, an investor's best strategy may be to buy shares in one or two of the platinum group metal producers. In doing so, you immediately increase your exposure to the entire gamut of platinum group metals since they are produced collectively. The only problem with this strategy is that, apart from Stillwater Mining which is mostly a small palladium producer, you will have to buy a South African stock and your choice is rather restricted. Rustenburg Platinum Holdings, the largest platinum producer in the world, with 1.5 million ounces produced in 1995 or 30 per cent of world mine supply, is part of the Anglo American group. Impala Platinum Mines is the second-largest South African producer with production of almost one million ounces in 1995. A recent arrival is Potgietersrust Platinum, which along with Rustenberg and Lebowa Platinum, is part of the Anglo American and JCI conglomerates.

Western Platinum is part of the Lonrho group. Recently, a potential merger of Lonrho's Western Platinum interests with those of Gencor's Impala interest has been announced. Northern Platinum Mines, part of Gold Fields of South Africa, is the black sheep of South African platinum mines, suffering from severe mining engineering problems.

Other platinum production is as a byproduct from nickel mining such as by Inco or Falconbridge. However, platinum group revenues are not significant relative to those companies' other operations.

CHAPTER 12

The Death of the Golden Bear

AS WE LOOK BACK OVER 22 years of free-floating gold prices, we can see two distinct periods. In the first decade, the price of gold rose from $35 (U.S.) an ounce in 1970 to $850 (U.S.) an ounce on Jan. 21, 1980. The gold companies kicking around at that time were the survivors of the 1950s and 1960s: tired old mines whose deaths were postponed by rising gold prices. In fact, worldwide gold production kept falling right through the 1970s to reach a 30-year low by 1980.

In contrast, the decade of the 1980s saw gold prices fluctuate between $300 (U.S.) and $500 (U.S.) an ounce. By the end of the decade the price was $350 (U.S.) an ounce, even though we had mild but continuous inflation right through the 10 years, making the gold price even lower in real value. Yet immense new discoveries were made during the decade and a plethora of companies was created. Of the 10 top gold mining companies in America, only three existed prior to 1980. Mining companies and the public in general, particularly in Canada where a tax incentive known as flowthrough shares encouraged people to invest in mining ventures, poured billions of dollars into gold exploration. Every geological or geochemical anomaly that was known has been tested; every prospect has been assayed and every square inch of promising ground has been staked. In Canada, this culminated in the discoveries of the Hemlo and Holt/McDermott gold camps in Ontario; Casa Berardi in Quebec; and Eskay Creek and Iskut River in British Columbia. Elsewhere came the incredibly rich Carlin Gold Trend and the Battle Mountain Trend in Nevada; the Rim of Fire in the Pacific, including Porgera, Misima and Lihir Islands.

All this activity has been reflected in the growth of the Toronto gold and silver subindex. In 1982, the subindex represented less than 1 per cent of the Toronto Stock Exchange 300 composite index.

This representation climbed to more than 10 per cent in 1987, where it has been hovering since. This growth required immense amounts of capital from the public, the banking system and cash flow from existing mines.

What, then, can be expected for the balance of the 1990s?

As the law of diminishing returns takes hold, you can expect the rate of increase in discoveries and production to slow down considerably. Much of the gold that has been found in the past 10 years has been in a form that our predecessors in the 1920s and 1930s could not see or did not have the technical capability to mine or mill at a profit. In the past 20 years, the mining industry has developed the heap-leaching process to recover gold from very low- grade material; it has developed the autoclaving system to crack the toughest ore where gold is encapsulated in sulfide material; and it has perfected the roasting system to protect the environment.

Mining equipment — even shovels and trucks — is much bigger, making open-pit mining more efficient. Automation has increased the size and capacity of underground equipment and remote control operation has made it safer. Impressive strides have been taken, but we are reaching the limit of these technical innovations. The same is true of the exploration methods that we are using. From raw prospecting, the industry has gone into the sky with remote sensing to find deposits; the industry has developed sophisticated geophysical and geochemical techniques that were not available even five or 10 years ago. Again, we are getting closer and closer to the limit of current technology where the knowledge curve starts to flatten out and the law of diminishing returns starts to apply.

In North America, the rate of new discoveries started to flatten in the early 1990s as mining companies reduced their U.S. exploration budgets due to negative environmental and taxation initiatives by the U.S. Democratic Party. A spate of exciting new discoveries in Nevada is just now helping to undo some of that damage.

In Australia, the small, close-to-the-surface deposits that have already been discovered have been mined quickly. The underground sulfide deposits will require more advanced technology and more capital to develop. However, a surge in the Australian gold equity market in recent years could provide the money for Australia to stay on a plateau until the turn of the century.

Papua New Guinea and Indonesia are underexplored and are extremely fertile for large gold deposits. The rate of discovery in this region could continue to increase through the 1990s and the world-class discovery at Busang in Indonesia looks likely to dominate the news for another year. The main question, however, will be the extent to which these discoveries will actually come into production. Capital costs will be exceedingly high because the gold deposits are in remote areas where no modern infrastructure of any kind exists. There is also risk of political instability. Ultimately, the extensive gold reserves of these countries will be mined since their development will be beneficial to the countries themselves. However, there will be delays.

In South America, Brazil's production peaked in 1988 at 3.5 million ounces and 1996 production will be down to 2.2 million ounces. Its large placer deposits are fast being depleted by the garimpeiros and there are few rivers or known deposits left untouched. The country now has to make the transition to hard-rock mining. A new mining code and steps to privatize government-held mineral concessions are all positive signs. The international exploration fraternity is beginning to have a second look at Brazil. In Chile, the so-called Switzerland of South America, gold production is on the increase as dozens of multinational gold companies provide money and people because both the investment climate and the geology of the country are favourable. Chile will probably see more discoveries such as Barrick's recent announcement of the Pascua deposit, and, barring a change in government and economic policies, it should continue to increase gold production at a modest pace. Two other countries in South America that are likely to increase production are Peru and Venezuela, where sizable new discoveries have been made. Overall, production in South America declined dramatically in the early 1990s, but in the last two years, it has started to grow again at a modest rate and should do better in the longer-term future.

Most of Africa has been bypassed by the 1980s boom in gold exploration as companies have avoided war-torn countries like Mozambique and Namibia and the Communist-led or dictatorial regimes in Zaire, Zambia, Ghana and Nigeria. Slowly but surely, Africa is realizing that it has been sinking deeper into poverty by closing its door on private investment and democracy. We are seeing the tide turn and countries that have a rich history in gold mining, such as Ghana, are now looking to foreign investors to help them regain some of the past glories. Africa is rich in mineral wealth, and gold in particular. Given the recent trend toward democratization and a return to capitalism, improvements throughout the 1990s in production in Africa can be expected.

In Eastern Europe and Russia, the recent freedom and moves toward democracy bode well for trade between the East and the West. Eastern European governments will probably make gold mining a priority because of the hard currency gold can bring into the country. Russia, in particular, which is lagging in the application of new gold-mining technology and sadly in need of capital, could easily boost production over the next 10 years. The only question is whether there will be opportunities for North American gold-mining companies to participate in the development of these reserves.

Finally, there is South Africa. Production in this gold-rich country has been falling for over 10 years reaching a new low in 1995. The South African gold-mining industry will have to improve its productivity through the 1990s to maintain its share of global production in the face of stiff competition from the lower-cost open-pit mines of North America and the Pacific Rim. It is unlikely, however, that South Africa will ever regain its position as the country of the lowest production cost.

Overall, we can look at the early 1990s as a time of historically high gold production. As these record levels of production are achieved, it will become more and more apparent that it will be difficult to replace reserves. If history repeats itself, worldwide production will stabilize at these record levels for a few years, falling back by the end of the decade or earlier if prices don't improve from the 1995 level of $380 an ounce.

For gold-mining companies, the trend described above means two things. First, as the rate of new discoveries tapers off, companies will find fewer opportunities to spend wisely on exploration and development. Second, as known deposits are brought into production, the demand for capital will lessen — which, in turn, will provide companies with increasing cash flow. Of course, not all companies will benefit to the same degree. Companies that have made major capital expenditures to bring their mines into production will enjoy a much faster cash flow than those that will require reinvestment into the early to mid-1990s.

As the industry matures, companies will have several alternatives to deal with the cash accumulation and growing free cash flow that their reserve bases should provide. For investors, the way a company deals with its finances will provide investment opportunities and pitfalls. As always, there will be winners and losers in the 1990s; the sooner you recognize where you should place your bet, the better off you'll be at the end of the race.

Dividends

With rising cash flows, reduced demand for capital expenditures and fewer exploration opportunities, many gold-mining companies will be in a position to increase returns to shareholders in the form of dividends. Through the 1980s, the rate of dividend payment — less than 1 per cent in North America, for instance — has been dismal. This is understandable. Companies were in a vigorous growth period that required tremendous amounts of capital to sustain the growth rate. But in the 1990s, the companies that have free cash flow should be able to provide investors with handsome returns, perhaps raising their dividends to the risk-free gold loan rate of 1.5 per cent to 3 per cent. The best way for the investor to spot companies that could be generous payers of dividends is to examine the funds flow and determine the free cash flow of a company. It is not enough to look only at the cash costs; if the sustaining capital or the development costs have not been included in the cash costs, the dividend potential will be obscured. Look at the funds flow statement and watch for the repayment of gold loans. These loans could have a significant impact on companies that relied heavily on this form of financing.

Over the coming decade, it will become important for management to decide on a dividend payout policy and to ensure that the policy has been clearly stated to shareholders. Medium-sized companies with successful records of exploration that have ample free cash flow, pay a generous dividend and continue to reinvest their surplus funds in the things they know best are likely to be at the top of the winners' list by the end of the decade.

Mergers and acquisitions

If cash-rich gold-mining companies find themselves unable to spend their hard-earned money on exploration or development projects they just might go shopping. Small, junior companies will probably still be struggling for capital and could become the targets of takeovers from the majors. The gold mining industry is in the throes of a major shakeout comparable to the rationalization in base metals mining in the 1970s and 1980s. This trend started with Lac Minerals taking over Bond Gold and Homestake Mining taking over North American Metals and International Corona. In 1994, the blockbuster acquisition was Lac Minerals itself being taken over by Barrick Gold.

In this scenario, an opportunity exists for investors to look for undervalued juniors that could be takeover candidates; the large companies are likely to bid up the share price of these juniors in an acquisition race. The best example in 1996 was Barrick Gold's nearly $1 billion bid for Arequipa Resources, based on the results of only nine promising drill holes on a mountain side in Peru. On the other hand, an investor wants to make sure he is not holding the stock of a company on the buying end of a bidding war; it might end up overpaying for the junior, reducing the net value of the stock that he owns. So far, Homestake Mining has twice overpaid for mining properties and stocks. First, it bought North American Metals, whose Golden Bear mine in British Columbia ended up costing twice the projected capital costs. Second, it purchased shares of Galactic at over $10; two years later, they were trading for less than 50 cents before Galactic finally went bankrupt in 1993. However their latest acquisition, International Corona, could have been the best move they've made in a long time.

Diversification

Instead of paying dividends, some companies will try to increase their shareholders' value by diversifying beyond gold into other businesses. Investors should remember author Peter Lynch's remark in *One Up on Wall Street*: "The dedicated diversifier seeks out merchandise that is (1) overpriced, and (2) completely beyond his or her realm of understanding. This ensures that losses will be maximized." Just like some individuals, some companies just can't stand prosperity.

Remember the oil companies in the late 1970s and early 1980s? Money was rolling into their coffers, opportunities in the oil patch were getting slimmer, competition was ferocious and every drill rig on earth was drilling somewhere. Money was burning a hole in their pockets so they started buying metals companies, computer makers and retail firms which eventually shut down or sold at fire sales. As an investor, you want to stay away from this.

Investors should also take note of companies that start moving offshore into areas such as the Pacific Basin or South America. As capital and assets shift from North America to more unstable countries, the risk-reward characteristic of that company will definitely change. Unless the money is invested in highly profitable ventures, shareholders will be at risk. A case in point is Battle Mountain Gold, which in 1988 drew all of its gold production and cash flow from one mine in Nevada and another in Australia. However, in the past two years it has invested heavily in a Bolivian project and has taken a share of the giant Lihir Island project in Papua New Guinea through a 50 per cent ownership of Niugini Mining. As the reserve life of its North American assets decreases, the impact of a negative turn of events in Bolivia or Papua New Guinea would be significant.

Some gold companies have their roots in gold but over the years have shifted to base metals and back to gold. Newmont, Placer and Teck are all good examples. These companies were born out of gold discoveries and all were exclusively in base metals at one time. In the 1970s, they started moving back to gold, which now forms the core of each company. I would not be surprised to see these firms and other pure gold companies moving back into base metals by the turn of the century. As an investor, you have to watch the trend carefully. The attributes of base metals are not nearly as appealing to an investor as gold and the companies mining them have to be valued accordingly.

Investors should also watch the debt loads of the companies in which they invest. Companies that are highly leveraged may find it tough in the 1990s. Investors are going to be expecting generous dividends and the companies will need clean balance sheets to weather the ups and downs of the gold market. Finally, as an investor, you should be wary of companies that dilute their stock at every opportunity. During the 1980s, companies required tremendous amounts of new capital to support their growth rate and much of that had to be raised through the sale of equities. As this phase comes to an end, the companies should generate sufficient cash from their mines to be able to make ends meet without having to continually raise money by issuing new shares.

Gold bullion

As we move through the last decade of the 20th century, the one banking tradition that will not fade is gold's role as the cornerstone of central bank reserves. In July, 1993, Michel Camdessus, managing director of the International Monetary Fund, confirmed this belief in gold as a safeguard against uncertainty when he said: "The gold of the IMF fund is the strength of the institution, and we have to think twice before diverting it to other purposes. Who can tell us what the situation will be at the beginning of the next century when the world will need a still stronger fund?" As we have seen earlier, gold currently accounts for approximately 29 per cent of total central bank reserves. That figure has fluctuated between 29 per cent and 59 per cent in this century. The central banks that are low in gold — such as Japan, Korea and Taiwan — are likely to be net buyers of gold while the large central banks of Europe and the U.S. will probably just hold on to current reserves.

However, it is becoming more apparent that central bankers increasingly see their gold reserves as another currency and are becoming active in the management of their gold reserves. Central banks have an important part of their reserves in gold and they have a great deal of interest in keeping the gold price above a floor level: They are likely to be buyers of gold at $350 (U.S.) to $375 (U.S.) and sellers of gold when its price hits $500 (U.S.). The effect of this new-found active policy would be to keep the gold price in a price band.

From the fabrication standpoint, particularly for jewelry, demand is at an all-time record level and with widespread prosperity it is likely to continue through the 1990s. The opening of Eastern Europe, the rapid development of the Pacific Rim countries and the resurgence of India and the Far East should sustain the growth in demand for gold jewelry and coins through the 1990s. However, jewelry demand is also very sensitive to prices and will shrink if prices skyrocket. This sensitivity creates a ceiling on the gold price.

From everything that we have seen so far, it will come as no surprise that I believe that $380 (U.S.) an ounce in 1996 dollars is equivalent to the old $35 (U.S.) an ounce of 60 years ago. It's a price that supports healthy jewelry demand and yet provides a decent profit margin for producers. In real terms, the price will probably remain at or near this level for some time. However, as with any commodity, there will be cycles.

Gold will continue to reflect, at least in part, the monetary policies of the countries that make up the Group of Seven. Also, its tie to the fortunes of the U.S. dollar will remain for as long as the dollar is the world reserve currency. Recently, there have been discussions among the chairmen of the central banks about achieving zero inflation in the 1990s. While this is a commendable goal, it remains to be seen whether the elected officials who appoint the central bankers can tolerate the political heat that would be generated by the pains and miseries that such a policy would produce. Both Canada and the U.S. have accumulated incredible debts and are continuing to incur annual budget deficits. Should governments try to deflate the economy, the crushing burden of debt would make the economic pain unbearable and ensure a quick exit for the existing governments in favour of less painful but more inflationary policies and governments.

On the other hand, if they try to inflate the economic problems away, the gold market will pick up the scent in a hurry. Even if inflation were to hover at only 4 per cent a year for the next 10 years, to match this rate of inflation the gold price would be 50 per cent higher than it is today — $550 (U.S.) an ounce by the turn of the century. The average annual rate of inflation over the past 20 years was 4 per cent but in the 1950s and 1960s it was barely 1.5 per cent. At that rate, gold would be only $430 (U.S.) by the end of the decade. Of course, in the 1960s the United States was the undisputed world power; it had balanced budgets, individuals and corporations were not burdened with debt, long-term interest rates were low and governments were half the size. And the world was on a gold standard.

One of the most interesting indicators of movements in the gold price has been the U.S. foreign-held debt in relation to the ounces of gold held by the U.S. treasury. This relationship embodies several of the gold price determinants that we looked at earlier; the money supply and issuance of credit, currency appreciation or depreciation vis-à-vis our creditors, the inflation or perceived inflation rate to be sustained by the U.S. dollar and, finally, the creditworthiness of America as a whole.

The price of gold today does not cover even half of the U.S. foreign debt. If all the foreigners who own U.S. debt were to present themselves at the Federal Reserve window and ask for gold in place of their paper, the price of gold would have to be at least $1,600 (U.S.) an ounce to cover the redemption.

That fact is not meaningful in itself; more important are the following points.

- The U.S. foreign-held debt per ounce of gold in the treasury has consistently peaked 18 months or so ahead of the peak in the gold price in the past three economic cycles.
- After a quantum jump in 1970-71, the U.S. foreign-held debt per ounce of gold has been growing at a steady rate for almost 20 years.
- The gold price has followed the upward trend by moving up in a channel throughout that time frame. By the end of 1991, gold was at the low end of its long-term trend. It bottomed in late 1992 and has since surged upward.

The fact that the gold price is close to the long-term support trend line means one of two things: Either the relationship will not hold any more for some unknown reason and the gold price will move lower, or the gold price is excellent value and is likely to move up.

The countries of the Far East, particularly Japan, Taiwan and China have been large purchasers of gold. A widespread comment in the press is that this is an aberration and that when they terminate their purchases, the gold price will collapse. For a better idea of the reasons behind these large purchases, let's look at the deflated gold price in Japanese yen.

There are three important observations to be made from Chart XII. The first is that the gold price was in a bull market from 1971 to 1980 before it reached an all-time high in yen. Second, from 1980 through to the end of 1992 the gold price in yen has been in a bear market. Third, and probably most important, at today's price and current exchange rate the gold price in deflated yen terms is as low as it was between 1976 and 1978 or in 1973, when you could buy an ounce of gold in the United States for $100 (U.S.). If you could buy an ounce of gold today for $100 an ounce, what would you do? The same as the Japanese — you'd buy a ton of it. In fact, in 1988 they bought over 600 tons — 17.45 million ounces.

The gold price in yen is good value and the Japanese who have little gold are likely to be substantial purchasers for years to come. The same can be said of the Taiwanese, the South Koreans and most of the so-called tiger nations of the Pacific Rim. The Taiwanese, for example, are simply replacing part of their $80 billion (U.S.) currency reserves, which are mainly made up of U.S. dollars, with gold. After seeing their reserves devalued by more than 50 per cent in the past four years as their own currency appreciated against the

The Price of Gold in U.S. Dollars and Yen

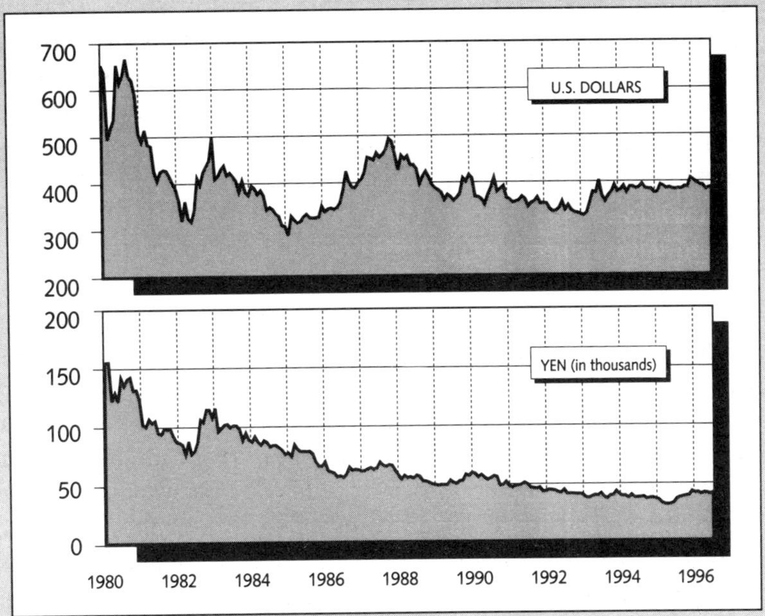

SOURCES: DATASTREAM; LONDON AFTERNOON GOLD FIX

CHART XII

dollar, it is only reasonable that they diversify themselves out of the U.S. dollar into something more stable.

As an individual investor, you have to look at the different possibilities for the future and arrange your portfolio to protect yourself no matter what the future brings — even in a stable political and economic environment.

What about the next 10 years?

My intention is not to predict. What I see happening is simply the result of economic or demographic forces already in place. Of course, the interplay and development of these forces can be altered by significant outside events over which you or I have little or no control. The only way you can protect yourself is to hold a variety of assets — in other words, a diversified portfolio. Only then can you prevent anyone from destroying your financial well-being.

Land or real estate remains, within reason, a cornerstone of the average North American family. And throughout history, it has proven to be one of the best investments one can make. But there are a few drawbacks to real estate. First, it is not always liquid, and in times of recession or depression you may not be able to sell your real estate holdings at all. Second, it's not portable. You can't roll it up, pack it up or truck it out. The value of real estate is driven by outside events which can seldom be predicted. If you are to protect yourself, you can't afford to have all your wealth in one asset.

Once they've bought a home, people usually begin building their wealth through savings. Whether it's Canada Savings Bonds, or a simple savings account, most people like the feeling of having readily available cash on hand in case of emergency. Sometimes people build a pool of cash as a nest egg for retirement or to give them the flexibility to invest when opportunity knocks. In times of severe economic stress, such as a recession or depression, cash is king. However, during inflation cash depreciates rapidly as the after-tax cost of holding cash is almost always less than inflation itself.

Once an individual has a home and a bit of cash, most begin using their surplus wealth to build a portfolio. Investors begin eyeing the stock and bond markets, art and gold. You can buy insurance on your house, your silverware or your art collection to protect you against fire, theft, earthquakes and tornadoes. But what do you buy to protect yourself from economic instability? Gold.

We have seen economic cycles come and go. The problem for investors is predicting those cycles, especially when they seem to be picking up speed. While you can't predict what will happen, you should be prepared to respond quickly. In 1980, gold at $850 (U.S.) an ounce reflected the fear that not only was double-digit inflation here to stay but that it would get worse. It didn't. The subsequent worldwide recession took care of inflation, at least for a while, and it has been subdued through the last 13 years.

What's next?

Inflation has been part of human history for as long as there has been money. While it is not a necessary part of the human condition, it has been a recurring phenomenon that is likely to happen again and again. The problem is rather simple: "Money" is an elusive device, difficult to pin down or to fix in the desired quantity for the economy.

Every time the various central banks try to stabilize or regulate some quantity of money, the market creates new forms of money. In recent years, we've seen the emergence of the Eurodollar, Euro-yen, commodity-backed bonds, junk bonds and, in more recent years, derivatives, instruments that are only regulated by the market itself.

Gold, too, will fluctuate above and below its fundamental value as investors' objectives and emotions swing from optimism to pessimism. Gold is both money and a commodity; at any time, its value is predicated on a balance between two, sometimes contrary, forces. During deflationary periods, such as between 1930 and 1934, commodity prices will fall but gold will take on the role of the money of last resort and can rise in value. In periods of high inflation, gold becomes another hard asset that will protect your personal wealth against the ravages of inflation and, again, it may rise in value, as it did in early 1980.

At $350 (U.S.) to $400 (U.S.) an ounce, the strong jewelry market tells us that gold is fairly valued from a fundamental commodity standpoint. The world is simply too prosperous for gold to be cheap. At this time, the future direction of the gold price is firmly in the hands of the politicians and central bankers. In almost all currencies, gold has already reached or is close to its bottom and the strength and direction of the next move will be determined by what they do or don't do.

Warren Buffett, chairman of Berkshire Hathaway Inc. in Omaha, Neb., and one of the most successful investors of the 20th century, said in his company's 1989 annual report, "We have not lost our aversion to long-term bonds. We will become enthused about such securities only when we become enthused about prospects for long-term stability in the purchasing power of money. And that kind of stability isn't in the cards; both society and elected officials simply have too many higher-ranking priorities that conflict with purchasing power stability."

For the record, I believe he's right. And protecting your purchasing power does *not* seem to be a priority of society or elected officials. Therefore, you must do so yourself with the one commodity used by mankind to protect itself against inflation and economic or political upheaval for centuries — gold.

Index